Management of Government
Information Resources
in Libraries

Management of Government Information Resources in Libraries

Edited by
Diane H. Smith

1993
LIBRARIES UNLIMITED, INC.
Englewood, Colorado

Copyright © 1993 Libraries Unlimited, Inc.
All Rights Reserved
Printed in the United States of America

No part of this publication may be reproduced, stored in a retrieval system, or transmitted, in any form or by any means, electronic, mechanical, photocopying, recording, or otherwise, without the prior written permission of the publisher.

LIBRARIES UNLIMITED, INC.
P.O. Box 6633
Englewood, CO 80155-6633

Library of Congress Cataloging-in-Publication Data

Smith, Diane H.
  Management of government information resources in libraries / edited by Diane H. Smith.
    xiv, 260 p. 17x25 cm.
  Includes index.
  ISBN 1-56308-051-6
  1. Documents libraries--United States.
Z675.D63S63 1993
025.17'34'0973--dc20   93-2055
                                                                           CIP

Contents

Acknowledgments xi

Introduction xiii

1—Government Documents in Libraries and Society
(Barbara Kile) 1
What Is A Document? 1
Types of Documents 3
Types of Depository Collections 4
    U.S. Federal Depository Program 4
    State Programs 5
    Municipal Programs 5
    Intergovernmental Programs 5
    Foreign Programs 6
Integrated Versus Separate Documents Collections 6
"Fee Versus Free" Documents 7
Notes 7

2—Collection Development *(Bruce Morton)* 9
The Literature 9
Concepts of Genre and Package 10
Paradigms Lost and Regained 11
Implications of Automation for Collection Development 12
GPO Collection Development Tools 14
Government Information in the Marketplace 15
Classification and Collection Development 17
Articulation of Policy 18
Application of Paradigmatic Thought 19
Access to What is Not Held Locally 21
Integration of Collections 21
Accounting and Accountability 22
Conclusions 23
Notes 24
Appendix 2.1 28

vi □ Contents

3—Acquisition of Government Information Resources (*Carolyn C. Sherayko* and *Diane H. Smith*)..............................31
   United States Documents...................................31
      Acquisition of GPO Depository Publications.....................32
      Non-Depository Publications.............................35
      Fugitive and Quasi-Governmental Publications...................36
   United Nations Documents.................................36
      Acquiring U.N. Depository Publications......................36
      Receiving U.N. Documents in the Library.....................37
      Acquisition of U.N. Publications by Non-Depository Libraries.......................................37
   International Governmental Organization (IGO) Documents..............38
   Canadian Federal Documents...............................38
   Other Foreign Documents.................................39
   State Government Documents..............................40
   Local Documents......................................40
   Conclusion 41
   Notes 41

4—Bibliographic Control and Access (*Carolyn C. Sherayko*)...............43
   Choice of Means of Bibliographic Access to Documents.................43
      Separate Access...................................43
      Integrated Access..................................44
      Computerized Access................................45
   Choice of Classification Schemes............................46
      Superintendent of Documents Classification System................47
      United Nations Series Symbol...........................50
      Department of Supply and Service Catalogue Numbers (Canada).......................................51
      Library of Congress and Dewey Decimal Classifications.............53
      CODOC 54
      Locally Developed Classification Schemes.....................54
   Notes 56

5—Bibliographic Processing (*Carolyn C. Sherayko*).......................60
   Processing Routines....................................60
      Ownership Stamps.................................60
      Labeling.......................................61
      Preparation for Circulation.............................62
      Statistics 62
   Cataloging...63
      MARC-Speak....................................63
      Monographs and Serials..............................68
      Bibliographic Record Acquisition—One-by-One..................69
      Bibliographic Record Acquisition—Tape Loads...................70
      Retrospective Conversion.............................71
   Classification 72
      Locally Assigned SuDoc Numbers.........................72
      Class Corrections..................................73
      Reclassification 73

Special Issues..75
  Series Control...75
  Serials Within Series..76
  Electronic Formats...76
Notes..77

6—Collection Maintenance (*Sandra K. Peterson*)................80
Organization...80
  Closed Stacks..81
  Open Stacks..81
  Aids for Stack Maintenance...................................81
  Space Planning...82
Special Patterns of Publishing...................................82
  Cumulations..83
  Superseded Editions..83
  Transmittals, Errata, and Supplements........................83
Special Handling Required..84
  Microfiche...85
  Maps...85
  Posters..86
  Nonprint Materials...86
Preservation...87
  Vacuuming and Cleaning.......................................87
  Repairs..87
  Binding..88
  Government Documents as Rare Documents.......................89
Weeding..90
  When Can You Weed?...90
  How to Weed..91
  Disposal of Materials..91
Automation of Collection Maintenance Records.....................92
Notes..92
Appendix 6.1...95
Appendix 6.2...96
Appendix 6.3..105
Appendix 6.4..110

7—Technology in Document Collections (*Debora Cheney*)........111
Microformats in Government Document Collections.................112
  Providing Access to Microformats: A Primer..................113
Electronic Formats in Government Document Collections...........116
  The Realities of Electronic Resource Distribution...........117
  The Pilot Projects..119
  The Technology Tea..119
  Providing Access to Electronic Formats: A Primer............120
Conclusion..124
Notes...124

viii □ Contents

8—Circulation (*Susan Tulis*)...129
  To Circulate or Not to Circulate...129
    If You Decide to Circulate ... Questions to Consider...............131
    Circulation Management Data...132
  Notes..133

9—Staff Training and Development (*Jack Sulzer*)...........................134
  The Nature of Training and the Environment...................................134
  Selecting Employees..135
    Job Descriptions...136
    Interviews...136
  Stages of a Training Program..139
    Contents of a Training Manual...140
  Initial Training Procedures...142
  Training for the Public Service Desk: The Fundamentals.....................142
    Core of Knowledge..143
    Technical Knowledge of Departmental Routines...............................143
    Service Priorities...143
    Desk Etiquette...145
    Dealing with Patrons...145
  Reference Training: Beyond the Fundamentals................................145
  Ongoing Staff Development and Training......................................148
  Evaluating Performance..148
  Notes..150
  Appendix 9.1..151
  Appendix 9.2..154

10—Providing Reference Service to Document Collections
    (*Diane Garner*)..157
  Nature of Documents Reference...157
    The Library Context..158
    Networking..159
  A Taxonomy of Documents Reference...160
    Local Government...161
    Regional Organizations...161
    State Government...161
    U.S. Federal Government..162
    Non-U.S. National Documents..162
    International Documents..163
  Managing a Documents Reference Desk..163
    Staffing the Documents Desk..164
    Statistics: To Keep or Not to Keep..165
    Nonbook Media at the Reference Desk...166
    Frequently Asked Questions...166
    The Desk Reference Collection..167
  Access Tools for the Documents Collection...................................168
  Some Practical Aids..169
  Appendix 10.1..171

Contents □ ix

11—Outreach, Promotion, and Bibliographic Instruction
    (*Susan Anthes*)..173
  Outreach Programs...173
    Promotion and Outreach...................................174
  Bibliographic Instruction....................................178
    Research Strategy...179
  New Technologies...181
  Conclusions...182
  Notes...182

12—The Politics of Documents Librarianship (*Ridley Kessler* and
    Jack Sulzer)...183
  The Government Printing Office..............................184
  The Superintendent of Documents............................185
    Sales Service..185
    The Library Programs Service..............................186
  Congressional Oversight of the GPO...........................190
  Role of Federal Agencies in Information Distribution..........192
  Regional Libraries...192
  Depository Library Council...................................194
  Awareness of the Information Issues..........................194
    Information Policy Development and Reform.................195
    Electronic Publishing and Information Handling.............197
    Access to and Dissemination of Government Information.....198
    High-Performance Computing and High-Capacity
        Telecommunications Networking....................199
    Future of the GPO and the Depository Library Program.......200
  Conclusion..202
  Notes...203
  Appendix 12.1...205

13—Costs and Benefits of Running a Documents Collection
    (*Carol Turner*)...213
  Who Needs Cost Information and Why?........................213
  Cost Definitions...214
  Identifying and Gathering Costs..............................215
    Personnel, Salaried and Hourly............................216
    Books and Other Library Materials.........................216
    Equipment..217
    Expendable Supplies and Services..........................218
    Automation...218
    Facilities...218
    Non-Dollar Costs...219
  Cost Analysis...219
  Benefits..220
  Cost Recovery..221
  Conclusion..221
  Notes...221

14—Government Documents: Assets or Liabilities? A Management
        Perspective *(Nancy M. Cline)* 222
    Costs and Benefits of Government Documents Collections 222
    Future of Government Information in Libraries 226

Selected Bibliography 229

Notes About Contributors 243

Index 247

Acknowledgments

The undertaking of this text, incorporating as it does the work of colleagues throughout the United States, was indeed an interesting and a learning experience. A debt of gratitude is due all chapter authors who willingly agreed to take up the task of writing practical and useful advice for those dealing with government information. This sharing of their years of experience, perspective, and knowledge through publication is indicative of the level of professional commitment that they all have to government information librarianship. I am also indebted to Nancy Struble and Peggy Myers of The Pennsylvania State University Libraries for their excellent secretarial support throughout the project. Finally, I owe special thanks to my husband, Steve, who supported me through many edits, kept our children occupied when deadlines were approaching, and tolerated paper everywhere.

Introduction

In librarianship, rapid changes in information technology and economics have created an environment in which success depends on the ability to respond positively and quickly to change. For years government documents collections processed publications and provided access to materials with methods that were reliable and paper-dependent, but antiquated and, at times, unlike any of the systems that were being developed for the remainder of the library's collections. In the last few years, however, technology has finally come to government information collections, at a speed far outstripping its development in cataloging. Simultaneously, the challenge of providing reference service to a myriad of paper, microfiche, and electronic resources that cover bibliographic, numeric, graphic, and textual data has launched these collections into the world of electronic reference at a speed much faster than traditional reference departments have experienced. Even the name itself, *government information*, implies a change in attitude among those working with government document collections. Today one is not dealing solely with paper resources, but rather a variety of sources. In this book, the terms *government documents, documents, government publications,* and *government information* are used interchangeably—and intentionally—to emphasize the shifts that have occurred and the breadth of materials that fall within these collections. These changes and the costs involved in mainstreaming documents into all library services make the administration of government information collections a growing concern within librarianship.

This publication is designed as a textbook for those learning about government information resources and the management of such collections. It is targeted at those who are in library schools, enrolled in standard government document courses, and those who suddenly find themselves as managers of government information collections. It may even be of interest to those who have many years of experience with government documents and now need to manage rapid change. It attempts to update earlier standard sources on the administration of government documents, while covering management topics that have not traditionally been included in document texts. It also discusses collections other than those from the U.S. government, although there is a natural inclination to emphasize U.S. federal resources because these tend to be the largest and most frequently encountered collections. This text provides a realistic view of the problems encountered in working with government documents, emphasizes issues of current importance to the profession, and provides background information that is essential to understanding the management of document collections. Finally, it gathers into one source the best of the current literature, both serial and monographic, on the issues and questions involved in managing such collections.

Reflecting the traditional view that government information collections are a "library within a library," the text is divided into functional areas. Each chapter covers a specific topic and was written by an expert in the field of government information. The authors are all individuals who have a love for documents librarianship and have made a difference to the profession through their scholarship and professional service. Collectively the authors represent over 220 years of experience with government information.

Chapter 1 provides a brief overview of government publications, definitional problems, and the types of depository collections encountered. The second chapter discusses the history of collection development in government information collections and encourages new techniques and approaches for the future. Chapter 3 covers the acquisition of publications from issuing agencies, once one has identified specific titles of interest. The fourth and fifth chapters then follow the processing procedures, both in cataloging and classification, that are necessary to provide bibliographic access to an item. Chapter 6 provides a detailed overview of the collection management issues that must be faced when dealing with document collections. The seventh chapter is a history of the use of technology in government information dissemination and also suggests questions that must be addressed for the varying formats of government information. Chapter 8 reviews questions that must be considered when automating a documents collection. Chapter 9 discusses the elements and development of a staff training program that will create a staff sufficiently flexible and knowledgeable to deal with the increasing demands placed on document collections. Chapter 10 covers issues involved in documents public service and suggests strategies for providing quality reference service to government information resources in libraries. Chapter 11 further elaborates on the idea of public service in its discussion of methods to promote the use of documents collections, either through advertising, the development of specific programs or seminars, or bibliographic instruction. The twelfth chapter is unique in document literature in that it discusses the actual politics and political climate in which documents librarians now find themselves embroiled. Chapter 13 raises the cost and benefit questions that government information specialists must be ready to address in a changing economic environment. Finally, chapter 14 offers challenges for library administrators to consider as they view the future of government information resources within their libraries.

1

Government Documents in Libraries and Society

Barbara Kile
*Director, Department of Government Publications
and Special Resources
Rice University*

In the study of governments, one criterion used to decide whether a government has validated itself is if it has left a record of its proceedings and activities. Throughout the centuries, governments of all types have published accounts of their debates, decisions, and laws, perhaps in an attempt to meet this definition. As societies have developed, flourished, and changed, so too has the appearance of a *government document* changed, working its way from clay tablet to vellum to paper to computer tape. Today, in libraries throughout the world, there are large collections of government documents comprised of printed materials, microforms, maps, computerized data, and audiovisual materials. These fascinating collections have become the living record of government proceedings and offer researchers first-hand experience with primary materials.

WHAT IS A DOCUMENT?

Before beginning any discussion on the management of government documents collections, it is necessary to establish a common definition of what is a *government document*. However, this is not easy, because of the complexity of government publishing practices and dissemination policies.

In the United States, the first statutory definition was approved in 1847. It stated:

> Such publications or books as have been or may be published, procured, or purchased by order of either House of Congress or a joint resolution of the two Houses, shall be considered as public documents.[1]

This definition was modified by subsequent Congresses to include statements about printing at government expense and the legal requirements for printing and distribution of the publication:

> Any publication printed at government expense or published by authority of Congress or any Government publishing office, or of which an edition has been bought by Congress or any Government

office for division among Members of Congress or distribution to Government officials or the Public, shall be considered a public document.[2]

The current definition used by the U.S. Government Printing Office in the administration of the federal depository program is:

"Government publication" as used in this chapter, means informational matter which is published as an individual document at Government expense, or as required by law.[3]

There are also as many definitions of *government documents* published by state or provincial governments as there are types of governmental divisions. These definitions can range from brief statements to several paragraphs. For example, in Connecticut *state publication*:

means all publications printed or published by or under the direction of the state or any officer thereof, or any other agency supported wholly or in part by state funds.[4]

In Texas, *state publication*:

means printed matter that is produced in multiple copies by the authority of or at the total or partial expense of a state agency, including a publication sponsored by or purchased for distribution by a state agency or released by a research firm, consulting firm, or other similar private institution under contract with a state agency. The term does not include correspondence, an interoffice memorandum, or a routine form.[5]

Further complications arise as one moves across national and state borders and attempts to define interstate compacts, foreign documents, and international/intergovernmental documents. For instance, the Brussels Convention of 1886 established the exchange of government documents between countries and defined *official publications* as:

official documents, parliamentary and administrative, which are published in the country of their origin; works executed by the order and at the expense of the governments.[6]

Some international and intergovernmental organizations also make distinctions among types of documents based on dissemination (i.e., "internal use" compared to publications or materials available to the public).[7] Examples of such organizations are the United Nations, the Organization of American States, and the publications of most national governments.

In an attempt to standardize a definition for *government documents*, several organizations have published definitions. The American National Standards Institute defines *government document* "as bearing a government imprint." In 1977, the Government Documents Round Table of the American Library Association adopted the following definition:

A government publication/document is any publication in book, serial, or non-book form published by or for a government agency, e.g., the publications of Federal, State, Local, and Foreign governments and of intergovernmental organizations to which governments belong and appoint representatives, such as the United Nations, Organization of American States, and the Erie Basin Commission.[8]

The American Library Association, in its *Glossary*, states:

government publication. Any publication originating in, or issued with the imprint of, or at the expense and by the authority of, any office or a legally organized government or international organization. Often called government document, public document, and document.[9]

In looking through these various definitions, two common elements emerge: a document is something published by or for a government agency and it contains information that should be available to the public.

TYPES OF DOCUMENTS

In his book *The United States Government as Publisher*, LeRoy Charles Merritt identifies six types of documents, based on their functions: legislative; administrative; reportorial; service; research; and informational.[10] These categories assume that a specific agency issues documents on a particular subject for a certain purpose.

Legislative documents are published to further the legislative process of a government. They take the form of bills, hearings, reports, and records of the legislative proceedings. Congressional hearings, the *Congressional Record*, and the British *Parliamentary Debates* are examples of this type of document.

Administrative documents are issued to assist the public administrative functions of government. These documents may be compilations of rules and regulations needed to carry out the intent of the law. Excellent examples of this document type are the *Federal Register, Texas Register*, or a schedule of legislative proceedings such as the *Calendar* of the House or Senate.

Reportorial documents are issued to report on activities for a specific time period, the completion of a particular task, or the results of a decision. Examples are the annual reports issued by government agencies, reports of commissions, and court decisions.

Publications concerned with the welfare of the people come under the category of service. They convey beneficial information to individuals or groups. For example, trade data may help a small business market its product overseas and contribute to the financial health of a country.

The research function covers publications that report on special research projects. These might be the results of research projects by a government agency or technical reports by a government contractor. Examples of this type of document are technical reports of the Environmental Protection Agency, National Aeronautics and Space Administration, or the United Nations.

4 □ **Government Documents in Libraries and Society**

Finally, there are documents that provide an informational function—they are issued to inform the public about government activities or services. Examples in this category are Social Security brochures and directories of government officials, offices, and telephone numbers.

TYPES OF DEPOSITORY COLLECTIONS

The term *depository* refers to library collections that have been established to manage government documents. A depository can acquire its documents from a broad spectrum of governmental and intergovernmental sources, and the financial arrangements for depositories can vary considerably (see chapter 3). Some depositories are "free," in the sense that the library does not pay the issuing agency for the documents. For other libraries, depository status involves a serial commitment to purchase documents. The best source for locating specific depositories, by either state or type of depository, is the *Directory of Government Document Collections and Librarians*.[11]

U.S. Federal Depository Program

In the United States, as the federal government was being formed, Congress authorized the printing of additional copies of the journals of the Senate and House of Representatives for distribution to colleges and universities and historical societies in each state. This was the beginning of a system to make government publications available to the public. In 1895, Congress formalized this distribution by passage of the Printing Act, which established the Federal Depository System under the control of the Public Printer of the Government Printing Office (GPO). This act stated that libraries designated by congressional appointment, the libraries of the executive departments and independent agencies, state and territorial libraries, and libraries of land-grant colleges could be designated as depository libraries. Government publications of the United States were to be placed on deposit in these libraries; in return, the libraries accepted responsibility for making these publications available to the public. Today this program has grown to include over 1,400 federal depository libraries in the United States, with 57,000 titles distributed during 1991.[12]

Similarly, some departments of the U.S. government also administer special depository programs. These programs were established to supplement the GPO depository library system, to ensure that special collections would be available in convenient locations for the public, and to meet heavy demands for the department's publications. For example, the U.S. Census Bureau has a depository program that makes all census publications available to libraries that might not otherwise have these materials for public use. Another specialized depository program is the one administered by the U.S. Patent and Trademark Office. Seventy-five libraries in the United States are involved in this program. The Patent and Trademark Office supplies paper publications, microfilm and microfiche, CD-ROM data and equipment, and access to an on-line system for these libraries. In return, the libraries help the public with patent and trademark research. This program ensures that citizens throughout the United States, not just those in the Washington, D.C., area, have access to the information of the Patent and Trademark Office.

State Programs

For most states in America, there is a state depository program administered by an agency or department of the state. These programs are the result of diligent work by librarians in the various states to have laws passed to legitimize the depository program. The strongest legislation includes definitions of state publications and agencies, requires the program to include all publications issued by the state, provides for centralized and automatic distribution, establishes a system of libraries to serve as depositories, and provides for bibliographic control of the publications. For further information on state programs, see Margaret Lane's book *State Publications and Depository Libraries*.[13]

Municipal Programs

Distribution of the records of cities is usually based on informal agreements between a library (typically the public library) and the local government. Such an arrangement requires diligence by the documents librarian to keep up with political changes in the government and the resulting changes in publishing. Some cities do have ordinances that require city departments and agencies to deposit copies of their reports with a designated library. A few states also include municipal and county documents in their state depository legislation. However, even these programs must be carefully monitored by the library to ensure compliance.

Intergovernmental Programs

There are also many depository programs worldwide, reflecting the work of intergovernmental organizations. The United Nations (U.N.) has a depository system of 300 libraries throughout the world. This system differs from most depository programs in that the libraries are expected to pay an annual fee. Under this U.N. depository agreement, the libraries receive not only the publications produced to disseminate information about the U.N.'s activities, but also those published to support the work of the individual components of the U.N. These libraries also receive regional materials from the commissions in their region.

Within the U.N. family of organizations, there are additional depository programs. For example, UNESCO has a wide system of depository libraries that receive all publications classified as main documents. The Food and Agricultural Organization (FAO) produces many publications and has depository libraries in more than 90 countries. The World Health Organization's (WHO) depository system is limited to one library per country. The European Economic Commission has both Depository Libraries and European Documentation Centers. The Depository Libraries are generally public libraries that are dispersed geographically to allow for wide public accessibility. The Documentation Centers, on the other hand, are located in colleges and universities that provide European studies programs.[14]

Foreign Programs

Most libraries receive foreign documents by exchange rather than through depository programs. The Brussels Convention of 1886, which established the exchange of government documents among countries, has about 90 countries as parties to the agreement. The national libraries of the participating countries usually administer this program in their own countries.

Canada has also established a depository program in the United States. The documents that are placed on deposit come from the *Weekly Checklist of Canadian Government Publications*. The Library of Congress receives all these publications, while the selective depositories can choose from the *Weekly Checklist*.

INTEGRATED VERSUS SEPARATE DOCUMENTS COLLECTIONS

The question of whether to integrate a government documents collection with the main library collection or to keep the collection separate has been debated almost as long as there have been documents in libraries. Further complicating this debate are the many formats in which documents are issued, as collections also may be arranged by format: paper, microforms, audiovisual, computer. There is no single answer to this question. Each library must make its own decision based on its collection size, space, staff size, organization, clientele, and financial resources.

If a library chooses to include its documents in the general library collection, it will have the advantage of related subject materials with a minimum of duplication. With this arrangement, no distinction is made between government documents and other library materials, and one classification system is used for all library materials. It implies that documents are cataloged and classed with all other materials and receive the same level of collection maintenance as do books and serials.

On the other hand, if a library chooses to separate its government publications from the general library collection, it will have the advantage of a unique collection that allows for more staff specialization and in-depth reference service. Another advantage is the lower costs for materials processing, because the library will be able to use the classification system provided by the depository organization. Until very recently, a separate collection also implied that the documents were not cataloged to the same level as other library materials.

However, technological developments are quickly making this debate of integrated versus separate insignificant, as is discussed in chapter 5. With shared computer records, the efficiency of library cataloging has improved, and government documents are now included in more library on-line public access catalogs (OPACs). This development makes the physical location of documents less important, because the catalog provides one source for searching all library materials, through standard cataloging and OPAC conventions.

"FEE VERSUS FREE" DOCUMENTS

Historically, U.S. government documents have been free or available for minimal charges. However, during the Carter administration, the question of "fee versus free" for government information became an important policy issue. This debate over the cost of government information production and dissemination was reflected in the Paperwork Reduction Act of 1980. The act, plus the cost-cutting measures of the Reagan administration, severely curtailed free government information. Some publications ceased to exist, because the agency did not have funds for printing and distribution; others were given to the private sector for publication. Technology has also had an impact on this issue. Agency automation has ensured more efficient information handling and production, but it has also increased the cost of information delivery within libraries, because retrieval software and specialized equipment must be purchased to use the technology to its fullest extent.

The basic question becomes this: If taxpayers are supporting the collection and creation of information, shouldn't they have free access to the information? With this argument, the essential difference between access and dissemination surfaces. Although the information may be distributed through the depository program, unless software and appropriate hardware are also available, the data are unusable. Congress is currently in a debate over the government's role in and responsibility for making information available to the public. Democracies do not function without an informed citizenry. Careful attention must be given to these issues so that a society of information elite is not created. These are seminal issues facing government information librarians in the 1990s, and are issues that will determine the role of government information in libraries and in society in the 21st century.

NOTES

[1] 9 Stat. 2002, sec. 13, approved March 3, 1847.

[2] *Checklist of United States Public Documents, 1789-1909*, 3d ed. (Washington, DC: U.S. Government Printing Office, 1911), vii.

[3] United States Code, title 44, sec. 1901.

[4] Connecticut General Statutes Annotated sec. 11-9b(a). Reprinted with permission. Copyright © 1986 by West Publishing Co.

[5] Texas Government Code Annotated sec. 441.101(4).

[6] Article II, *Convention for Exchange of Official Documents, Scientific and Literary Publications*. Concluded at Brussels, March 15, 1886.

[7] Judith Schiek Robinson, *Tapping the Government Grapevine* (Phoenix: Oryx Press, 1988), 2.

[8] *Documents to the People* 5 (September 1977): 187.

[9]Heartsill Young, ed., *The ALA Glossary of Library and Information Science* (Chicago: American Library Association, 1983), 106. Reprinted with permission.

[10]LeRoy Charles Merritt, *The United States Government as Publisher* (Chicago: University of Chicago Press, 1943), 5-9.

[11]*Directory of Government Document Collections and Librarians*, 6th ed. (Washington, DC: Congressional Information Service, 1991).

[12]U.S. Government Printing Office, *GPO Annual Report 1991* (Washington, DC: U.S. Government Printing Office, 1992).

[13]Margaret Lane, *State Publications and Depository Libraries* (Westport, CT: Greenwood Press, 1981).

[14]Robert W. Schaaf, "Information Policies of International Organisations," *Government Publications Review* 17 (January/February 1990): 49-61.

2

Collection Development

Bruce Morton
Assistant Dean of Libraries
for Public Services
Montana State University Libraries

Collection development is a planning process that encompasses decision making about the selection and retention of information.[1] It is an essentially subjective process that includes the identification, selection, acquisition, and provision of access to information in response to recognized and defined needs.[2] Collection development and management address the core objective of a library—optimizing holdings and respecting patron needs and institutional goals, given limited materials and budgetary resources.[3] Such a process requires forethought, prudence, a breadth and appreciation of knowledge, and a willingness and ability to work cooperatively both intra- and interinstitutionally.

There is a core of collection development truisms that should be laid out at the beginning. Few, for instance, would take issue with the idea that "collection development is much more than the selection and acquisition of materials. It is a decision making process that determines which specific materials will be obtained in terms of subject content, format and other criteria."[4] Or, "one centralized source for the acquisition of all United States government publication has not been attained. Decentralization seems permanently entrenched due to the multiplicity of agencies and their wide use of printing devices...."[5] This is still true more than 35 years after it was written.

Building government information collections has usually been based on the source rather than content or budget. Not only was this unusual when compared to general library collection development, it was completely irrational. Yet for the greater part of the 20th century, this philosophy of collection by producer remained state-of-the-art collection development for government information.

THE LITERATURE

Before the 1980s, little interest was shown in the collection development process for government information collections. The discussion that did take place was one-dimensional in its focus on distribution and acquisition of documents or publications. Hernon and Purcell provide a good overview of the literature of collection development as it relates to government information collections in their 1982 book.[6] In the literature, there are four landmarks on collection development of government documents: the first annual Library Government Documents and Information Conference, sponsored by Meckler Publishing and devoted to the topic of collection development;[7] Morton's publication of a model collection development policy for selective U.S. depository libraries;[8] a theme issue of *Government Publications Review* devoted entirely to the topic of collection development;[9] and the publication of the aforementioned book by Hernon and Purcell. Peter Hernon and Charles R. McClure have been consistent advocates for the building of a body of literature reporting empirical research on collection development topics so that theory can be applied in an intelligent and effective manner. A search of the literature since the early 1980s will find that researchers are heeding this clarion call.

CONCEPTS OF GENRE AND PACKAGE

Government information comes in a variety of generic information packages. Thinking in terms of packages is useful for conceptualizing how the special formats affect government information collection building. Just as one can expect to find characteristically different presentations of information, quite independent of subject matter, in a newspaper, magazine, and book, one also can expect to find characteristic kinds of information in each of the various genres of government information. It is important to know and make distinctions between the various genres as packages in which government information comes and the selection implications each has regarding presentation and content.

The range of generic government information is daunting. All examples listed in figure 2.1 are common to most government publishers and are readily evident in the U.S. depository library and sales programs. It is important that the collection builder not only recognize these kinds of government information as generic packages, but also be able to make correct assumptions about the *nature* of information *content* (this is quite different from subject) of each.

Fig. 2.1. Range of government information genres.

• Annual Reports	• Bibliographies and Lists
• Bills and Resolutions	• Committee and Commission Reports
• Judicial Decisions and Opinions	• Directories
• Audiovisual Materials	• General Information Pamphlets
• Hearings	• Journals and Proceedings
• Laws and Statutes	• Maps
• Newsletters	• Magazines
• Scholarly Journals	• Press Releases
• Research/Investigation Reports	• Rules and Regulations
• Statistical Reports/Compilations	• Executive Communications
• Books/Monographs	

With each of these generic information packages must be considered possibilities of format: sewn binding, perfect binding, staple binding, maps, pamphlets, microfiche, microfilm,[10] videotape, film, audiotape, floppy diskettes, computer tape, and CD-ROM are all available via deposit and commercial sources. Each has its respective implications for storage facilities, environmental requirements, type of handling required, space, accessibility, longevity, and ease of future review for retention and selective disposal (weeding). Also of primary consideration in the selection process should be governmental source: national (e.g., the U.S. Government Printing Office, Her Majesty's Stationery Office, Canadian Communication Group); state or provincial; international (e.g., the United Nations)[11] or intergovernmental (e.g., Organization for Economic Cooperation and Development, European Community, North Atlantic Treaty Organization, or Organization of American States).

For a non-depository or depository acquiring titles on a supplemental basis, consideration of origination, genre, and format factors is a matter of primary focus. However, for depositories receiving publications on deposit, it is difficult to be as discerning in these matters, as selection is usually based on categories that relate to agency of origin and may or may not be related to subject, genre, or format.

PARADIGMS LOST AND REGAINED

United States federal regional depositories are not as oppressed by the negative collection development implications of the present system as are selective depository libraries. This is because the regionals have a statutory obligation to accept all items offered for depository distribution and to maintain nonsuperseded materials in perpetuity. Consequently, they do not have to face the exigencies of collection development and management confronted by the selective depository; the problem for the regional depository is space. The task of managing and developing the selective depository collection in the face of limited space, staff, and budget requires planning and hard decisions. Decisions about money and staffing are usually the purview of a library's administrative officers. However, decisions about effective use of space fall to the librarian—in this case, the documents librarian.

The librarian with responsibility for any deposit collection labors under guidelines prescribed by the depositor. For U.S. federal depositories, there are few guidelines that specifically direct collection development. United States depositories are asked only to maintain a basic core collection available for immediate use. Each library is expected to acquire and maintain "basic catalogs, guides and indexes, retrospective and current, considered essential" to the use of the collection.[12] Libraries are directed to select materials that will be of potential use and responsive to the needs of the local congressional district. It is suggested that they coordinate selections with other depositories in the area to ensure adequate coverage. These guidelines are of the loosest possible sort. Although they were developed with the best of intentions by documents librarians for the GPO, the effort was undertaken during the 1970s, before collection development for government information collections became a matter of serious consideration in the library community.

Because of the looseness of these guidelines, many U.S. federal deposit collections did not *develop* as much as they *accreted*. The guidelines promulgated in 1977 asked the selective depositories to select at least 25 percent of available item classes or provide additional justification for depository status. This concept of critical mass did a disservice to the notion of intelligent collection development. A signal was sent, quite unintentionally, that quantity superseded quality in selection. This should not be the prevailing value in the development of any collection. Fortunately, the revision of the guidelines in 1987 deleted the 25-percent rule.[13] A librarian at a selective depository must continually decide what to accept on deposit as a new deposit item (see chapter 3); what items to delete from deposit subscription; which titles to retain or withdraw; which deposit items to claim or further pursue should they not be available through deposit channels; and finally, which complementary resources to purchase in the commercial marketplace. Such decisions must be based on client and collection analysis. It is imperative that the librarian who has responsibility for developing the government information collection maintain a continual sense of how the collection has developed and is developing (two very different dynamics—the former cumulative and both perpetual) and how the latter can be effectively managed.

IMPLICATIONS OF AUTOMATION FOR COLLECTION DEVELOPMENT

Conceptually, collection development for government information collections has long been reliant on the card catalog apparatus. The process of building and keeping various card files has too often been equated with collection development and management. There has been little sense of relation between these separate card files. The limitations of card stock, drawer, and pull rod kept the process of collection development physically and intellectually separate.

The GPO has required that a depository be able to account for the government information for which it is the custodian. The GPO has traditionally expected that the shelflist would be the mechanism to accomplish this. The shelflist has long been the bibliographic mainstay of government information collections. Often found in nonpublic office areas, shelflists have served as serial check-in devices with continual updating of receipt information. Even in enlightened libraries where shelflists were made accessible to the public, they only marginally served as an access tool, in that they confirmed the presence of a title after bibliographic information was acquired by another means. The card-based shelflist is a dynamic collection development tool only to the extent that it grows. The automated shelflist, in contrast, has the potential of providing enhanced access to government information by call number, agency, key word, or any combination thereof. These same points of access, combined with publication date and date-received fields, provide significant opportunities for collection analysis and monitoring. The automation of the shelflist has been discussed both as practical model and in theory by Morton.[14]

In the card-catalog environment, government information was usually underrepresented until 1976. This was because reliable cooperative cataloging on the major bibliographic utilities was difficult to find. Therefore, cataloging of anything but selected titles meant a laborious and expensive process. Most libraries chose not to catalog most government titles. The result was a doubly segregated government information collection. The materials themselves would be shelved using the archivally based classification of the distributing governmental agency (e.g., SuDoc, Canadian Communication Group, United Nations, European Community), so that there could be no real subject browsing of governmental materials. At the same time, the usual mode of access to government information was through specialized reference materials (e.g., *Monthly Catalog of U.S. Government Publications,* CIS-produced indexes and abstracts, *UNDOC Index,* etc.). In such an environment, it was only natural that both the information user and the librarian would come to think of government information as different and separate from the general library collection. Thus, government information collections were frequently developed of and in themselves, without proper consideration of or relation to other library collections. The primitive technology of the card catalog/shelflist imposed its limitations on processes of thought and access.

Automation, however, permits—even invites—perception of the dynamics of addition, deletion, rejection, and discontinuance as a continuing and fluid process of development, each part of which is intrinsically related to the other parts. The computer provides an instrument by which the process may be understood and monitored and the collection managed. The opportunity to apply the power of the computer is present no matter how a library approaches collection development and management for its government information—there are automated models that can be adopted or adapted. Even simple reliance on an item records file (for U.S. depository libraries) can be automated to the effect of moving from unidimensional perspective to the capability of multidimensional insight.[15] If the shelflist is relied on, it can be computerized to provide features of collection analysis that permit intersection of issuing agency, classification, or item control number with subject or key word. Such an automated shelflist also allows for embedding notification commands so that the librarian is made aware of dates of supersession or dates for withdrawal review.[16] An automated version of conspectus data, for instance, can be annotated with potential weeding or storage areas and can serve as a master plan to guide many years of collection development work.[17]

The advent of automated on-line public access catalogs (OPACs) in the late 1970s and their growing acceptance and implementation throughout the following decades should have a significant effect on collection development for government information. The possibility of integrating Library of Congress cataloging into the library's OPAC in a relatively non-labor intensive manner makes the acquisition of certain classes of government titles or the titles of particular agencies more attractive. One can assume that such titles would be more accessible than when they were in a separate, paper-based bibliographical environment. Another collection development aspect facilitated by an OPAC is the capability of examining holdings on an ad hoc basis from a remote location. The necessity of going to a card catalog separate from the library's main catalog, on a title-by-title or subject-by-subject basis, discouraged use. The consequence was that government information collections grew in a vacuum, without regard to what materials existed in the rest of the library.

Another important consideration in measuring the needs of clientele, which is affected directly by automation, is the presence of local, state, national, and even international networking. In the paper environment, one might have

14 □ Collection Development

calculated the radius of clientele to be commuting distance or the artificial bounds of campus, municipality, or congressional district. However, electronic access transcends such artificialities. If access becomes available to anyone with a modem, then the view of client need must be expanded based on an assessment of who has the means of using the network and what the likelihood is of them using it; locus of the client becomes a considerably reduced factor.

GPO COLLECTION DEVELOPMENT TOOLS

The Government Printing Office (GPO) has created several resources that can be helpful in collection development. All libraries, especially non-depository libraries, will find the GPO's *Sales Publications Reference File* (*PRF*) a valuable collection development tool. The *PRF* is offered as a depository selection item, and it can be purchased from the GPO Sales Office. Although it is available from the GPO in microfiche only, it is also available on-line from DIALOG as the *GPO Publications Reference File*. The *PRF* is an essential collection development tool for depository and non-depository alike. *Books in Print* is to the commercial U.S. book trade as the *PRF* is to the sales publications of the GPO. Also included in the *PRF* are forthcoming and recently out-of-print publications. The sales publications listed in the *PRF* are frequently more current than those listed in the most recent *Monthly Catalog*, which by its nature of production experiences delays.

The *PRF* provides access to GPO publications by SuDoc class, and is particularly useful for surveying publications emanating from a given agency. Subject access to the *PRF* is provided through the Legislative Indexing Vocabulary of the Congressional Research Service of the Library of Congress. A key-word listing is provided in the microfiche version; on-line, the flexibility of key-word, subject, or free-text searching, along with the possibility of boolean combination with publication year, author, or agency of origination, allows for analytical screening of publications available or searching for a particular title.

Publications listed for sale in the *PRF* may by ordered from the central GPO Sales Office or any of its regional bookstores by telephone or mail; the GPO will accept a check for payment in full, a major credit card, or credit to a GPO account. The latter is recommended. Publications also can be ordered via DIALORDER on DIALOG and billing directed to the DIALOG account.

Another valuable collection development tool produced by GPO is its Subject Bibliography Series. These approximately 200 bibliographies list GPO titles on specific popular subjects. These bibliographies are excellent and can be acquired on deposit, from depositories via interlibrary loan, or purchased from GPO. The series has its own index to subjects covered.

Perhaps the most basic collection development tool for U.S. government information is the *List of Classes of the United States Government Publications Available for Selection by Depository Libraries*, published and updated periodically by the GPO. This listing, in SuDoc classification order of all categories of material offered by the GPO to its depositories, is essential for depositories and useful for non-depositories in developing their collections. Because the SuDoc classification scheme mirrors the federal bureaucracy rather than topicality, the list of classes provides an almost taxonomic view of the government that produces information. An appendix to the *List of Classes*, listing items and class stems, has definite collection development applications, especially if subject orientation can be imposed on it. If item numbers are not given a subject orientation, then libraries must base collection development largely upon the provenance of the item categories.[18]

Of course, the ultimate list of GPO publications is the *Monthly Catalog of United States Publications*. This catalog, with its multiple indexes, is intended to include all publications distributed for deposit through GPO's Library Programs Service. The *Monthly Catalog* is itself offered as both a deposit and a sales item. It is, perhaps, more useful as a reference tool than as a collection development tool, because publications listed in any given issue may have been published and distributed many months earlier. The risk is that a title may not be offered for sale at all or, if it has been for sale, the stock may have been exhausted by the time the *Monthly Catalog* is received. It is better to rely on the *PRF*.

Information about the content, availability, and use of the *PRF*, Subject Bibliography Series, *List of Classes*, and the *Monthly Catalog* can be obtained from the nearest U.S. depository library. Locations of depository libraries and their phone numbers can best be obtained from one's state library.

GOVERNMENT INFORMATION IN THE MARKETPLACE

Libraries that do not have depository status must acquire needed government information from the marketplace. Even libraries that do have depository status for particular organizations or agencies may find it necessary to purchase government information.

Although it is sometimes possible to request titles from government agencies and receive them gratis, this is usually the case only when the agency views it as a public service or in its own interest to do so. Such cases are the exception rather than the rule. For U.S. titles, a library may wish to consider paid membership in the Library of Congress's Documents Expediting Project (DocEx). DocEx is a joint effort of the Library of Congress, university, public, and special libraries. It provides its member libraries with certain federal non-depository publications not available through the established channels of the GPO or issuing agencies. Membership cost at the time of this writing ranges from $225 to $750 per year. A library may choose to join at any amount in this range in increments of $25. However, when a particular title is in short supply, members paying the highest amounts will be served first. DocEx offers several services that are particularly useful for collection development efforts. Perhaps most useful is a special request service through which members may request a missed GPO claim, a needed second copy, a paper copy of a title received from GPO in microfiche, or perhaps just a particularly popular item. DocEx also provides special offerings of out-of-print publications via lists of older U.S. documents that are available from DocEx. Another DocEx service is placing its members on appropriate agency mailing lists. Non-depository libraries should examine carefully whether it would be more economical for them to use the GPO's *PRF* to monitor U.S. publications and purchase from GPO Sales, or to subscribe to DocEx services and request publications within the limits of their subscriptions.

16 □ Collection Development

Another governmental quasi-commercial source of important government information is the National Technical Information Center (NTIS), headquartered in Springfield, Virginia. The NTIS sells government titles in a variety of formats. Unlike GPO pricing, which is based on a production cost-recovery formula, NTIS is mandated by its enabling legislation to be self-supporting. Therefore, NTIS prices tend to be more expensive than those of either the GPO or private-sector competitors. Most of NTIS's inventory is comprised of documents on an amazingly broad range of topics produced under federal government contract, most of which find their way into neither the depository distribution program nor the *Monthly Catalog*. NTIS differs from the GPO's sales program in another important way. Whereas GPO titles will go out-of-print, NTIS titles remain in-print in perpetuity, because master copies of documents are maintained in microfiche and paper or microfiche copies can be produced on demand. NTIS titles are accessible via NTIS's *Government Reports Index (GRI)* and *Government Reports Announcements (GRA)*, the latter being companion abstracts to the *GRI*. With the indexing that *GRI/GRA* provides, the librarian can monitor this unique governmental "gray" literature for topics of collection relevance. For those not subscribing to *GRI/GRA*, the database from which NTIS produces *GRI/GRA* is accessible on DIALOG as the NTIS database; the database is also available commercially on CD-ROM. Titles may be purchased directly from NTIS by mail with payment enclosed, by telephone using a major credit card, or by either of these avenues using an NTIS account.

There are also private-sector vendors who specialize in government information. Two stalwarts in this category are the Congressional Information Service (CIS) and Readex, both of which supply U.S. government titles in microformat. CIS particularly lends itself to the kind of analysis that non-depository libraries might do to monitor specific agencies and/or topics, as it publishes what are undoubtedly the very best reference resources for U.S. government publications—the *Index to Congressional Publications* and the *American Statistics Index (ASI)*. Both indexes are also available on DIALOG. The collection development librarian can search these indexes for specific needs, and on the automated version can develop profiles to automatically provide monthly reports and directly place orders with CIS. Bernan Associates is another vendor that is particularly good in supplying international organization and foreign publications.

Libraries that find themselves needing to buy government information in the marketplace will find four other tools especially useful in helping them discern potentially worthy titles. Perhaps the most valuable of these is the annual issue, Number 6, of *Government Publications Review (GPR)*. This final issue of each year is completely devoted to the most important government publications of the previous year. United States federal and state publications are covered, as are foreign nations and international organizations; abstracts are provided. Another notable documents list is that compiled by the Government Documents Round Table (GODORT) of the American Library Association. The GODORT list in recent years has been published annually in *Library Journal*, and copies also may be obtained from the American Library Association. For international documents, *UNDOC* is a likely source for UNIPUB purchases. Finally, the *Public Affairs Information Service Bulletin (PAIS)* selectively indexes government titles from all levels of government and can provide a subject approach for documents collection development.

Acquiring rare and out-of-print government titles is more problematic. It is almost a given that one must know what one is looking for, although an occasional dealer catalog will highlight government documents. The easiest way to target dealers who sell government information of this type is to look in the Yellow Pages of the telephone directory under "rare book dealers"; in the United States, the District of Columbia directory is probably the best place to start. One also might look at the annual *AB Bookman Directory*.

Perhaps the most elusive government information is that produced at the municipal, county, and state or provincial level. Municipal and county-level information usually will not be in state checklists of government information (many states do not have regular checklists), and most state information does not find its way into national bibliographies (those that do include such information are normally federal/state joint efforts). There are some state/provincial depository programs, but compliance is more difficult to enforce than at the federal level (where it is already exceedingly difficult). Consequently, collection development librarians must be extremely attentive to getting on agency mailing lists, monitoring local and regional newspapers for announcements of government information, and then immediately writing to request copies before supplies are exhausted. Collection development at the local and state levels is by its very nature more assertive than document collection development for the national level. In the case of electronic information, it may be necessary to supply blank diskettes or tape to the issuing agency to have a copy of information made.

CLASSIFICATION AND COLLECTION DEVELOPMENT

Convenience is a key element in a provenance-based classification arrangement such as the Superintendent of Documents (SuDoc) classification. Over the years, most documents librarians have seen some utility in keeping the published information emanating from a particular agency together. Actually, the utility was originally perceived by the classification's developers at the GPO. Librarians merely found it easier to use it than to do the original classification that would have been necessary in the pre-cooperative cataloging environment. The utility of the arrangement is inherent in the view that an agency's publications are about the activities of that agency rather than about subjects or things. Therefore, it is deemed useful to be able to see what an agency has been doing by scanning the variety and kinds of information that it has produced in the conduct of its work.[19]

This assumption is tenuous at best. Often the focus of an agency is narrow and there will not be much variation in the topicality of its publications. One might expect a direct correlation between the size and scope of a bureaucratic center of responsibility and the variability of subject matter represented. For instance, department publications would publish on a wide range of topics, while offices or commissions would likely be consistent in publishing within a narrower range. The effect of opting to use the SuDoc classification is that the collection ends up being physically segregated from other elements of the overall subject collection. This can be overcome if bibliographic records are integrated into a central catalog. If not, there will be a considerable reduction in client demand, because knowledge about the collection will be significantly reduced.

Library of Congress (LC) classification is predicated on subjects being grouped physically together—a congregation of the intellectually similar. Since

July 1976, the bibliographic records in the *Monthly Catalog* have been produced by GPO catalogers according to the Anglo-American Cataloging Rules and in the Library of Congress' MARC format; the GPO also joined OCLC at this time. The following year, the Library of Congress began distribution of the computer tapes for the *Monthly Catalog* in MARC II format. These accomplishments have had significant impact on how librarians think about government information. Before the availability of GPO cataloging on the various bibliographic utilities [i.e., OCLC, Research Library Information Network (RLIN), and Western Library Network (WLN)], libraries were far less likely to classify government titles in anything but the SuDoc classification, because it would have been very labor-intensive and expensive. Therefore, the convenience of the SuDoc classification system is not in its provision of easy access based on provenance, but rather on the fact that the shipping lists accompanying publications provided SuDoc classification that needed only to be affixed to the document.

Indeed, although classification is traditionally viewed as an access issue, it is a collection development issue for government information. Classification provides the organizational structure that dictates how the information seeker will view the collection. So too, to some extent, will it determine how the librarian(s) responsible for building and managing the collection view the collection. The SuDoc-organized collection demands two overarching operative archival mind sets, *segregation* and *provenance*. One is forced to think in terms of how the government collection relates to the rest of the collection, while the use of a subject-oriented classification, such as LC or Dewey Decimal, allows for the interfiling of government titles with nongovernment titles based on topicality. The integrative approach invites a view of a holistic collection in which government is another source of information, just like the university press or the professional association.

These two ways of looking at collection development, based on classification, afford collection development opportunities as different as the classification schemes themselves. In the SuDoc classification system, the librarian must either equate originating agency with likely topical interest or equate SuDoc class stems with topicality.[20] Conversely, for the equation of subject areas with SuDoc item classes or originating agencies, the intellectual process must be reversed.[21] In either case, a schematic must be developed that can guide depository selectors. Non-depository selectors can do the same, or can rely on the subject heading section of the *PRF* to guide them to government titles dealing with desired subjects.

ARTICULATION OF POLICY

The formalization of philosophy and process in a policy statement provides a plan that gives guidelines to selectors as to the appropriateness of information on various subjects and in various formats.[22] It is essential for a documents collection to have such a policy and to be included in subject-based policies as appropriate.[23] The policy should be a statement that the library has developed to meet its collection objectives. It should identify priorities established by library staff based on careful and thorough analysis of need. The policy should be intended to provide stability and consistency in the collection development process, as well as a resource that can be employed when tough choices must be made. It will be difficult for a library to develop its collection systematically without a well-reasoned collection development policy that considers the full range of information needs of the community it serves.[24] "The design of a collection development policy ... should involve as many members of the staff as possible, as well as representatives of the constituencies served."[25] The steps for such a design are outlined in figure 2.2.

Fig. 2.2. Collection development design.

- Build the collection based on client needs
  -Produce a client or constituency profile

- Build the government information collection based on identifiable general collection strengths and weaknesses
  -Identify collection strengths and weaknesses

- Maintain a collection that will be responsive to evolving users needs
  - Regularly review item class productivity and title relevance of titles acquired
  - Regularly and expeditiously withdraw titles that are no longer deemed appropriate to the collection

When changes to the selection profile become necessary or desirable, they can be made against a background of an existing selection policy to maintain collection continuity. Policy changes, whether reflecting a new librarian's philosophy or a change in emphasis of organizational priorities, should be based on a logical outgrowth of an earlier development policy rather than developing again from scratch.[26]

Any collection development policy must be reviewed periodically. No policy statement can remain definitive forever, because the library and the parent institution are dynamic organizations undergoing constant change. Policies must be adjusted to be responsive to organizational and client needs. Policy is a tool that should be refined to meet the service goals of the library; the danger in a static collection development policy is that it will eventually thwart service goals.

APPLICATION OF PARADIGMATIC THOUGHT

It is impossible to deal with the tremendous mass of government information in an intellectually adequate manner unless an overarching frame of reference is imposed for the purposes of collection development. Of the two such frames of reference recommended, a subject/format matrix is the more traditional and less labor-intensive. Library staff must decide which formats (e.g., microfiche, computer tape, floppy disk, paper, etc.) will be compatible with the library's ability to accommodate them and the willingness of clientele to use them. In contrast, quite independently, an analysis must be undertaken of the information needs of clientele (whether based on curriculum, business interests, or other). The results of this assessment must be translated into subject areas and the subject interests must be translated into either issuing governmental agencies or classifications of those agencies. Once these two operations have been accomplished, the format desirability should be overlaid on content needs. The choice of format for the overlay is indicative that it should take precedence over subject. It makes no sense to collect formats that either cannot or will not be used, no matter how relevant their subject might be. By way of example, if pamphlets are an excluded format based on assumptions of shallowness, narrowness, and ephemerality, then a pamphlet on a compelling subject such as the pollution of public drinking water would be excluded from acquisition. If CD-ROMs are an excluded format, one would not collect even such a significant item as the *National Trade Data Bank*.

Another paradigm for viewing the development of the government information collection is inherent in the conspectus approach. The term *conspectus* connotes a general review or digest; as the concept has been applied to libraries, it provides both. The conspectus is essentially a survey measuring the depth of past collecting (i.e., the existing collection) and current collecting (i.e., present practice) against best-case scenario aspirations. The conspectus methodology was originally developed by the Research Libraries Group (RLG) as an instrument that could facilitate coordinated collection activity among large academic libraries. However, the conspectus approach has been adapted to use by others (e.g., the Association of Research Libraries, the North American Collections Inventory Project, the Alaska Statewide Collection Development Steering Committee, and the Pacific Northwest Conspectus Project). The conspectus approach to collection development "provides an organized process for systematically analyzing a library collection using standardized definitions."[27] Conspectus assessment and the resultant reports may be used to support collection development in an individual library or cooperating libraries. "The value of the assessment process to the individual library lies in the enhanced ability to measure, describe, and evaluate how well the current collection and acquisition commitment is meeting institutional goals."[28] The documentation produced from the process can serve well as a de facto collection development policy by clearly articulating current and desirable collection levels. The conspectus reports can also "serve as communication tools in budget justification and allocation, in support of accreditation or program evaluation, and in profile definitions for vendor approval plans. However, the great value of the process rests in using the reports in cooperative activities. Among libraries ... comparison profiles can serve as the basis for cooperative collection development projects and resource sharing agreement."[29]

The conspectus uses a breakdown of subjects into very broad subject divisions (e.g., Pacific Northwest Conspectus uses 24 divisions (see appendix 2.1). These broad divisions are then broken into broad subsets, called *categories*, and narrower subsets, called *subjects*, based on either the Library of Congress or Dewey Decimal classifications.[30] Conceptually, subjects form the y axis of the conspectus matrix. The x axis is comprised of a library's current collection (CL), acquisition commitment (AC), collection goal (GL), and preservation commitment (PC).

Acquisition Commitment, or collection level, is the current level of activity at which the collection is being developed and is normally based on recent acquisition information. Collection Goal represents a target level to which a library plans to build its collection in order to meet client needs. Preservation Commitment reflects a library's level of commitment to preserving the intellectual content of the material and/or including a commitment to the conservation of the physical materials in a particular subject area.[31]

Where the x and y coordinates intersect, a conspectus numerical valuation is used to describe synoptically Collection Level, Acquisition Commitment, and Collection Goal.[32]

The conspectus also can help identify materials for storage or withdrawal. For example, when the existing collection is stronger than the current collection intensity in a particular area, this might indicate a diminishing local emphasis on the subject and less use may be inferred, a usual qualification for storage or withdrawal. The conspectus allows selectors to make informed selective disposal decisions by providing information against which to compare knowledge of similar or stronger collections elsewhere.[33]

ACCESS TO WHAT IS NOT HELD LOCALLY

Even the most comprehensive and responsive of collections cannot possibly account for every client need. Therefore, it is imperative, no matter what the level of a library's ambition for the government information collection, that account be taken of opportunities to borrow government information from other libraries. Knowledge of the degree to which government information is included in regional and national bibliographic utilities or in OPACs accessible via computer networks (e.g., Internet) is important, so that the documents librarian can weigh local need against remote availability. With this information, intelligent decisions can be made as to whether temporary or permanent acquisition is more appropriate. Special effort is necessary to keep apprised of the government information holdings and collection development policy in all nearby libraries, especially those that are depositories. It is also useful to know the persons responsible for government information in each of these libraries; they can be helpful in the acquisition of government titles either for addition to the collection or on loan.

INTEGRATION OF COLLECTIONS

Integration of government information in a library's overall collection can be addressed at several levels. At the bibliographic level, one confronts the catalog; at the physical level, location is the operative factor; at the intellectual level, the organizational relationship of the head of collection development and the documents librarian is predominant. McClure, who has long championed the integration of government information into general library collections, suggests that the effectiveness of integration will be determined by the degree to which it is included in the overall philosophy of library collection development. He asserts that integration is largely a matter of attitude rather than physical arrangement.[34]

The purpose of collection development, in terms of service, is to make information resources available to those in need of information. Collection development is a key determinant in the information user's needs being met. Integration of the government information collection development policy into the overall library collection development policy significantly affects bibliographical access, physical availability, and professional support services.[35] The government information librarian who has responsibility for collection development can achieve this goal by working bilaterally with the librarian who has responsibility for the general collection. Another approach is to involve other colleagues who have subject specialties or special departmental responsibilities and bring their expertise to bear in government information collection development decision making. In academic libraries, the government information librarian may consider calling on faculty to help develop the collection profile. Again, integration involves mainstreaming the collection decision-making process; it may or may not also mean physical integration of the government information itself.

A key component for integrated collection development of government information is the provision of information services. Collection development is not performed in a vacuum. A government information collection development process that neither addresses the specific information needs of clientele nor responds to identified weaknesses in the library's larger collection is condemned to be dysfunctional.[36]

ACCOUNTING AND ACCOUNTABILITY

It may seem like belaboring the obvious, but the collection should be able to be described not only expositively, as in a policy statement or conspectus report, but also quantitatively. Data on number of titles, volumes (pieces), microforms, maps, annual rates of acquisition and withdrawal, and circulation and in-house use aid planning and budgeting for space, shelving, and equipment needs. For libraries that have not in the past collected such data, nor wish to collect it in the future, there are formulas that will provide fairly accurate extrapolative estimates.[37] Statistical data not only give additional insight on the ebb and flow of any dynamic collection to those charged with collection development, but also serve managers well when it comes time to respond to the inevitable surveys (biennially from GPO, annually from the Association of College and Research Libraries, etc.). More immediate uses of good collection data include charting of growth rates and space occupied, projecting space needs, and planning for the purchase of additional cabinetry and shelving, not to mention giving credibility to annual reports, budget requests, and defenses of program and budget.

It is also a good idea to work closely with the library's acquisitions unit to monitor government information acquisition statistics, so that the growth in this area of the collection is reflected in overall collection growth statistics. A library risks losing sight of the importance of government information in the total collection because much of it may not be purchased. Likewise, circulation department records regarding the circulation or reshelving/refiling of government information should be monitored and documented to give credence to assertions that the collection is being used and to provide subject-based collection development information. If there is an automated circulation system, consideration should be given to the kinds of reports that might be generated to provide valuable detailed insight into the use of the government information collection. Special attention should be given to monitoring and documenting the use of microform documents.[38]

Statistical data relating to the government information collection will prove useful as well for insurance purposes. Insurance premiums are calculated on the estimated value of a collection; this is usually extrapolated based on an average cost per title or volume. Even U.S. federal depositories, which technically serve as custodians of materials that continue to belong to the U.S. government, are responsible for insuring the government's property on the same basis as the rest of the general collection.[39] If some disaster should occur and the catalog or shelflist were to be destroyed or damaged, the collection and statistical profile of the collection might be the only remaining basis on which to calculate loss.

CONCLUSIONS

One must conclude that collection development for government information collections will continue to become more challenging. It is safe to assume that the output of information by governmental agencies will continue to increase. However, more of the government information output will manifest itself in an increasing variety of electronic formats, and less of it may appear through standard depository arrangements.[40]

Collection development librarians will need to become ever more mindful not only of the sources and content of this information, but also of the computer technologies, telecommunications technologies, and inherent costs that will make it accessible and usable. Traditionally, cost in collection development has been an up-front purchase or subscription price. Acquisitions were based on budgeting the fiscal resources available; in deposit arrangements, the traditional cost was usually embedded in salaries, space, and supporting equipment for the documents collections. Client expectations were largely based on what was available on the premises—in the collection.

In the brave new world predominated by electronic government information, cost will be a far more significant factor and far more nebulous and difficult to budget. It is envisioned that electronic government information in the future will be delivered via satellite transmission, requiring an ability to receive, download, select or pre-select, edit, and store the information transmitted. Government information will be available via interactive networks, whereby libraries will have access to databases housed at government agencies and from which they will be able to download information. And, of course, more electronic on-demand products will be available, including tapes, disks, and CD-ROMs.[41] All of these scenarios have serious implications. In an on-demand environment, client expectations are formed by possibility rather than collection. Indeed, much government information will be available only on an on-demand basis electronically. The effect of this on collection development will be to force librarians to become knowledgeable about what information is available and through which electronic conduits; to do cost-benefit analyses on the hardware and

24 □ Collection Development

software support systems required; and to remain informed as to what other libraries are doing about electronic government information, so that cooperative access may complement the concept of active or passive cooperative collection building.

Collection development has long been the stepsister of acquisitions—not to be bothered with because there was neither time nor staff. One got what one needed. What did one need? One knew it when it was requested or one saw it. Collection development was a topic about which effete articles were written. Collection development was something that big libraries received grants to undertake. Now the importance of government information, its universality in terms of topic, its increasing value and expense, and its escalating production all assure that government information collection development has moved from being something that could not afford to be done to something that cannot afford *not* to be done by all libraries.

NOTES

[1] Peter Hernon and Charles R. McClure, *Public Access to Government Information: Issues, Trends, and Strategies* (Norwood, NJ: Ablex, 1988), 116.

[2] Nancy Powell, comp. and ed., *Pacific Northwest Collection Assessment Manual*, 3d ed. (Salem, OR: Oregon State Library Foundation, January 1990), 1.

[3] Ronald L. Larsen, "The Library as a Network-Based Information Server," *EDUCOM Review* (Fall/Winter 1991): 39.

[4] Charles R. McClure, "An Integrated Approach to Government Publication Collection Development," *Government Publications Review* 8A (1981): 5.

[5] Jerome K. Wilcox, "The Acquisition of Government Publications," *Library Trends* 3 (April 1955): 404.

[6] Peter Hernon and Gary R. Purcell, *Developing Collections of U.S. Government Publications* (Greenwich, CT: JAI Press, 1982), 28-38.

[7] See Peter Hernon, ed., *Collection Development and Public Access of Government Documents: Proceedings of the First Annual Library Government Documents and Information Conference* (Westport, CT: Meckler, 1982).

[8] See Bruce Morton, "Toward a Comprehensive Collection Development Policy for Partial U.S. Depository Libraries," *Government Publications Review* 7A (1980): 41-46.

[9] See *Government Publications Review* 8A, no. 1 (1981).

[10] Microform government information presents unique collection development issues in terms of usability, preservation, and selective disposal. For discussion of collection development issues relating specifically to microform, see Charles R.

McClure, Vicki W. Phillips, and John B. Phillips, "Microformatted Government Publications," *Government Publications Review* 8A (1981): 127-33; and Bruce Morton, "New Management Problems for the Documents Librarian: Government Microfiche Publications," *Microform Review* 11 (Fall 1982): 254-58.

[11]See Peter I. Hajnal, "Collection Development: United Nations Material," *Government Publications Review* 8A (1981): 89-101.

[12]See "Guidelines for the Depository Library System," as adopted by the Depository Library Council to the Public Printer, October 18, 1977, sec. 4. For a model of cooperative collection development between depositories, see J. Randolph Cox and Bruce Morton, "Cooperative Collection Development Between Selective U.S. Depository Libraries," *Government Publications Review* 9 (May-June 1982): 221-29.

[13]"Guideline for the Depository Library System (revised 1987)," in *Instructions to Depository Libraries* (Washington, DC: U.S. Government Printing Office, 1988), sec. 4-6.

[14]Bruce Morton, "Implementing an Automated Shelflist for a Selective Depository Collection: Implications for Collection Management and Public Access," *Government Publications Review* 9 (July/August 1982): 323-44.

[15]See Bruce Morton, "An Items Record Management System: First Step in the Automation of Collection Development in Selective GPO Depository Libraries," *Government Publications Review* 8A (1981): 185-96; see also Margaret T. Mooney's description of the University of California at Irvine's PC-based depository item numbers database in *Administrative Notes* 7, no. 8 (November 1986), in the "Readers Exchange" column.

[16]See Morton, "Implementing an Automated Shelflist."

[17]Ferguson, et al., "The RLG Conspectus: Its Uses and Benefits," *College and Research Libraries* 43 (May 1988): 202.

[18]Hernon and Purcell, *Developing Collections*, 116.

[19]Jay W. Rea, "Assessing Documents Collections," in Powell, *Pacific Northwest Collection Assessment Manual*, 50.

[20]See Hernon and Purcell, *Developing Collections*, 69-84; and Powell, *Pacific Northwest Collection Assessment Manual*, 67-82 for examples of such approaches.

[21]See Hernon and McClure, *Public Access*, 119 for an example.

[22]Charles R. McClure, "An Integrated Approach," 5.

26 □ Collection Development

[23]For examples of policies, see Bruce Morton, "Toward a Comprehensive Collection Development Policy for Partial U.S. Depository Libraries," *Government Publications Review* 7A (1980): 41-46; Cox and Morton, "Cooperative Collection Development"; Hernon and Purcell, *Developing Collections*, 137-208; and Depository Library Council to the Public Printer, *Federal Depository Library Manual* (Washington, DC: U.S. Government Printing Office, 1985). In the latter source, see sec. 2, a brief overview of collection development policy; sec. 3, "Suggested Core Collection: Small/Medium Public Library"; sec. 4, "Suggested Core Collection: Small Academic Library"; and sec. 5, "Suggested Core Collection: Law Library."

[24]Hernon and Purcell, *Developing Collections*, 10.

[25]Ibid.

[26]*Federal Depository Library Manual*, sec. 2, 1.

[27]Powell, *Pacific Northwest Collection Assessment Manual*, 3. The Alaska project attempted to adapt the RLG Conspectus for use on all types of libraries.

[28]Ibid. 1.

[29]Ibid. 1-2.

[30]At the time of this writing, there is no readily available LC to SuDoc classification conversion table. However, in the *Pacific Northwest Collection Assessment Manual*'s Class Number Comparison Tables, there are conversion tables for "Dewey Decimal to SuDoc" and for "Dewey to LC," so one can extrapolate backward between these tables to establish equivalent classes for a LC to SuDoc conversion. It should be noted that the SuDoc classification is provenance-based, while LC and Dewey Decimal are subject-based; thus, SuDoc classes will change as agencies appear, disappear, or change their place in the bureaucracy. Therefore, only the most recent edition of the conversion tables should be used, and even then 100 percent accuracy cannot be assured.

[31]Powell, *Pacific Northwest Collection Assessment Manual*, 5.

[32]See ibid. 6-7; developed by the Alaska Statewide Collection Development Steering Committee, adapted from the *RLG Collection Development Manual*, 2d ed. The collection level indicators employed and their numerical codes are:

0 = Out of Scope

1 = Minimal Level
  1a = Minimal Level, Uneven Coverage
  1b = Minimal Level, Even Coverage

2 = Basic Information Level
  2a = Basic Information Level, Introductory
  2b = Basic Information Level, Advanced

3 = Study or Instructional Support Level
  3a = Basic Study or Instructional Support Level
  3b = Intermediate Study or Instructional Support Level
  3c = Advanced Study or Instructional Support Level

4 = Research Level

5 = Comprehensive Level.

[33] Anthony W. Ferguson, Joan Grant, and Joel S. Rutstein, "The RLG Conspectus: Its Uses and Benefits," *College and Research Libraries* 49 (May 1988): 202.

[34] Charles McClure, "An Integrated Approach," 6.

[35] Hernon and McClure, *Public Access*, 115; see page 130 for a discussion of indicators of bibliographic access, physical availability, and professional support service.

[36] Hernon and McClure, *Public Access*, 136.

[37] See Catharine J. Reynolds, "How Many Government Publications in a Linear Foot?" *Documents to the People* 7 (May 1979): 96, 99; Keyes D. Metcalf, *Planning Academic and Research Library Buildings* (New York: McGraw-Hill, 1965), 393; and U.S. Government Printing Office, "1991 Biennial Survey," 10.

[38] See Morton, "New Management Problems."

[39] See Memorandum of GPO General Counsel, "Responsibility of Depository Libraries to Insure Their Depository Collection," dated 12 January 1984.

[40] See *GPO/2001: Vision for a New Millennium* (Washington, DC: U.S. Government Printing Office, 1991), 6, 12.

[41] See *GPO/2001*, 20, 35-36. Such methods of dissemination are already in GPO's strategic planning.

APPENDIX 2.1
COLLECTION LEVEL INDICATORS

Developed by the Alaska Statewide Collection
Development Steering Committee (used with the permission of
WLN Bibliographic Information Services).

Pacific Northwest Collection Assessment Manual,
3d Edition.

Use these codes for determining collection level, acquisition commitment, and collection goal.

0   *Out of Scope*: The library does not collect in this subject.

1   *Minimal Level*: A subject area in which few selections are made beyond very basic works. A collection at this level is frequently and systematically reviewed for currency of information. Superseded editions and titles containing outdated information are withdrawn.

1a *Minimal Level, Uneven Coverage*: Few selections are made and there is unsystematic representation of subject.

1b *Minimal Level, Even Coverage*: Few selections are made, but basic authors, some core works, or a spectrum of ideological views are represented.

2   *Basic Information Level*: A selective collection of materials that serves to introduce and define a subject and to indicate the varieties of information available elsewhere. It may include dictionaries, encyclopedias, access to appropriate bibliographic databases, selected editions of important works, historical surveys, bibliographies, handbooks, and a few major periodicals. The collection is frequently and systematically reviewed for currency of information.

2a *Basic Information Level Introductory*: The emphasis at this level is on providing resources that introduce and define a subject. A collection at this level includes basic reference tools and explanatory works, such as textbooks; historical descriptions of the subject's development; general works devoted to major topics and figures in the field; and selective major periodicals. The introductory level of a basic information collection is only sufficient to support patrons attempting to locate general information about a subject or students enrolled in introductory level courses.

2b *Basic Information Level Advanced*: At the advanced level, basic information about a subject is provided on a wider range of topics and with more depth. There is a broader selection of basic explanatory works, historical descriptions, reference tools, and periodicals that serve to introduce and define a subject. An advanced basic information level is

Appendix 2.1 □ 29

sufficient to support students in basic courses as well as supporting the basic information needs of patrons in public and special libraries.

3   *Study or Instructional Support Level*: A collection that is adequate to impart and maintain knowledge about a subject in a systematic way but at a level of less than research intensity. The collection includes a wide range of basic works in appropriate formats, a significant number of classic retrospective materials, complete collections of the works of more important writers, selections from the works of secondary writers, a selection of representative journals, access to appropriate machine-readable data files, and the reference tools and fundamental bibliographical apparatus pertaining to the subject. At the study or instructional support level, a collection is adequate to support independent study and most learning needs of the clientele of public and special libraries, as well as undergraduate and some graduate instruction. The collection is systematically reviewed for currency of information and to assure that essential and significant information is retained.

3a *Basic Study or Instructional Support Level*: The basic subdivision of a level 3 collection provides resources adequate for imparting and maintaining knowledge about the basic or primary topics of a subject area. The collection includes the most important primary and secondary literature, a selection of basic representative journals/periodicals, and the fundamental reference and bibliographic tools pertaining to the subject. This subdivision of level 3 supports lower division undergraduate courses, as well as some of the basic independent study needs of the lifelong learner and the general public, with coverage at all appropriate reading levels.

3b *Intermediate Study or Instructional Support Level*: The intermediate subdivision of a level 3 collection provides resources adequate for imparting and maintaining knowledge about the basic or primary topics of a subject area. The collection includes a broad range of basic works in appropriate formats, classic retrospective materials, all key journals on primary topics, selected journals and seminal works on secondary topics, access to appropriate machine-readable data files, and the reference tools and fundamental bibliographic apparatus pertaining to the subject. This subdivision of level 3 supports undergraduate courses, including advanced undergraduate courses, as well as most independent study needs of the clientele of public and special libraries. It is not adequate to support master's degree programs.

3c *Advanced Study or Instructional Support Level*: The advanced subdivision of level 3 provides resources adequate for imparting and maintaining knowledge about the primary and secondary topics of a subject area. The collection includes a significant number of seminal works and journals on the primary and secondary topics in the field; a significant number of retrospective materials; a substantial collection of works by secondary figures; works that provide more in-depth discussions of research techniques, and evaluation; access to appropriate machine-readable data files; and reference tools and fundamental bibliographic

30 □ Collection Development

apparatus pertaining to the subject. This level supports all courses of undergraduate study and master's degree programs as well as the more advanced independent study needs of the patrons of public and special libraries.

4   *Research Level*: A collection that includes the major published source materials required for dissertation and independent research, including materials containing research reporting, new findings, scientific experimental results, and other information useful to researchers. It is intended to include all important reference works and a wide selection of specialized monographs, as well as a very extensive collection of journals and major indexing and abstracting services in the field. Pertinent foreign language materials are included. Older material is usually retained for historical research and actively preserved. A collection at this level supports doctoral and other original research.

5   *Comprehensive Level*: A collection in which a library endeavors, so far as is reasonably possible, to include all significant works of recorded knowledge (publications, manuscripts, other forms), in all applicable languages, for a necessarily defined and limited field. The level of collection intensity is one that maintains a "special collection"; the aim, if not the achievement, is exhaustiveness. Older material is retained for historical research with active preservation efforts.

3

Acquisition of Government Information Resources

Carolyn C. Sherayko
Head, Original Cataloging
Indiana University

and

Diane H. Smith
Chief of Reference and Instructional Services
The Pennsylvania State University

Similar to most other materials that enter a library, government information resources arrive through all types of arrangements and avenues. Many are the result of depository arrangements, either paid or free. Some are purchased by the library's acquisitions department; others are requested for free by the documents librarian through letters to issuing agencies. Some arrive because of cooperative exchanges established at some time in the library's history. Others are simply sent to libraries because someone once was on an agency mailing list. Finally, some documents arrive on the doorstep because a grateful library user was cleaning out an office or closet and thought the library could use the titles. Whatever the source, whether intentionally sought or acquired through serendipity, the decision to acquire and retain a publication should be based on the collection development policy of the library, as discussed in chapter 2. This chapter explores the possible strategies and sources that might be used to acquire documents from all levels of government agencies.

UNITED STATES DOCUMENTS

As is often stated, the United States government is one of the most prolific publishers in the world. However, acquiring these publications sometimes takes a good deal of persistence and detective work. Within most libraries, the key determinant of whether the library will have a federal publication is whether the item in question is a *depository* title. This term usually refers to the automatic distribution of publications to designated libraries. Within the United States, the largest depository program is managed by the Government Printing Office (GPO). All other federal publications are known generically as *non-depository*. However, many other federal agencies, such as the Department of Energy and the National Aeronautics and Space Administration, have also established depository programs. For the sake of simplicity, these programs are considered in this chapter as non-depository publications.

Acquisition of GPO Depository Publications

A key feature of the GPO depository system is that, unless designated a "regional" depository, a library may select the amount and types of material it wishes to receive on deposit.[1] In order for the GPO to keep track of which depository library has selected which publications from the vast amount of material published, it has devised a system of distribution based primarily on categories of documents, rather than on individual titles. The basic component of this system is the *item number*, a number assigned by the GPO to a group of publications produced by a department or issuing agency.

Item numbers represent categories, such as "annual reports," "general publications," "bulletins," and "circulars," that correspond to the form designations used in the SuDoc classification system. Item numbers also can represent other common categories of documents, such as "environmental impact statements," or even specific monographic series, periodical titles, or groups of closely related publications. Usually, when the library selects an item number, it does not know which specific titles nor how many titles will be received as a result of that item selection. Because of constraints in the GPO's automated system, only a limited number of item numbers can be used. The GPO has dealt with this problem by adding new titles or categories to existing item numbers. Therefore, over time it is possible that a library will receive titles it had not initially chosen and does not want. Two alternatives are then open to the depository: it may either deselect the entire item number and withdraw the unwanted titles (as depository regulations permit after five years of ownership), or it may continue to receive all items distributed under the item number.

Newly established depository libraries make selections of item numbers based on a file of 3-by-5-inch cards supplied to the library by the GPO. This file, usually called the *item card file*, is arranged in item number order. For libraries that have long been depositories, these item cards have been sent over the years to facilitate selection. Currently this file consists approximately of 6,900 active items and occupies 12 to 15 standard card-catalog drawers. Each card contains the item number, the name of the department and issuing agency, the "title" of the item(s), and the SuDoc classification number stem(s) associated with each "title."[2] Cards produced in the last 10 years also include annotations written by GPO staff to describe the items to be distributed. Unfortunately, these annotations tend to be very general and of little help in collection development.

Publication activity within the government is ever-changing, and the item numbers reflect this. New item numbers are added to the basic file through "Surveys" sent out by the Government Printing Office. The Surveys include new item cards to be added to the file, a description of the category of material being offered under the item number, and a computer scan sheet, on which the library records a yes or no response to the item number. Besides selecting or not selecting an item, the depository sometimes may choose the format in which to receive the publications (paper or microfiche).

Libraries that wish to stop receiving publications distributed under an item number may notify the GPO of this decision any time by using an "Amendment of Selections" card. However, if a library wishes to add an item number not offered on a survey, it may do so only once a year, when it reviews the items-selected computer printout sent out by the GPO each spring.[3] This computer printout is a management tool used by the GPO to check its distribution records. It contains all item numbers available for selection from the GPO; a "y" (i.e., "yes") is placed beside each number that an individual depository library has selected, according to the GPO's records.

For two reasons, it is essential that the depository librarian review this list carefully and make corrections as necessary. First, the GPO uses this information to acquire publications throughout the year. For instance, if 200 libraries chose item 354-D, then anytime a publication described by that item number is printed, the GPO places a "rider" on the print order to print 220 additional copies for its program (200 for distribution and 20 for claims). Second, in May 1985, the GPO installed an automated "lighted bin" system in which depository shipping boxes are arranged on shelving units according to depository library number. Over each box is a light. When a GPO employee packing boxes enters the item number on a keyboard at the end of the shelving unit, a light comes on over every library's box that has selected that item number. The yearly computer printout tells the library how this lighted bin system has been programmed. Every time a library adds or deletes an item number from its selections, the program running the bins has to be updated. Because of this frequent manipulation of data, discrepancies do occur. Any mistakes on this list will be reflected in mistakes in distribution, and a library may find itself receiving unwanted titles and not receiving selected titles.

Receiving GPO depository documents in the library

On most days, one or more boxes of documents will be delivered to a depository. The number of boxes shipped to any library depends on its selection rate and mail service. Some days there may be no boxes and on other days the library can be deluged. Federal holidays also dramatically affect receipts. Even if a library selects only a few items, the GPO guarantees that a box a week will be sent to every depository. Each box contains an assortment of documents based on the recent printing activity at the GPO. The contents of the boxes are listed on a *shipping list* that is included in the shipment.[4] The shipping list contains a record of all documents that were packed as part of a single shipment. The list, arranged by item number, includes brief title information and SuDoc classification numbers for all publications in that shipment. Each shipping list is given a sequential number (e.g., 92-0119), and separate shipping lists are sent for paper, microfiche, and electronic-format documents. Shipping lists also may contain special notices that should be given to the documents librarian. The GPO uses these notices to communicate a variety of information, including new categories of publications added to existing item numbers.[5] Besides the regular shipments, the GPO frequently sends large sets, microfiche, or individual oversize documents in single packages that are referred to as *separate shipments*. These are listed on separate shipping lists mailed with regular shipments. Frequently libraries will keep records, in either notebook or card format, noting shipments received and date of receipt. Through this recordkeeping, one can easily identify entire shipments missing, discern standard lag times between shipment and receipt, and even track titles back to specific shipments, if documents and shipping lists are date-stamped upon receipt.

Because the shipping list references all documents included in a shipment, the individual depository library must check the item numbers on the shipping list against its computer printout of selection. (Regional depository libraries do not have to do this, as they should receive every document sent out through the depository system.) If the library selected an item number that appears on the shipping list, but the publication was not received, the library should claim the publication from the GPO. This is done by circling or highlighting the missing publication on the list, completing the claim form at the bottom of the shipping list, and mailing the list back to the GPO.[6] Some depository libraries even transmit claims to the GPO by telefacsimile (fax) to speed up the process. The library should retain a photocopy of the shipping list for its records and maintain a count of the number of claims; information about the number of claims is a question on the GPO's Biennial Survey.

Unfortunately, because of the limited print runs of documents, claims are often not filled, regardless of the method used to transmit them. For libraries west of the Mississippi, the issue of claims is problematic. Because of mail deliveries, these libraries frequently receive shipments much later than their eastern counterparts. If they claim through mail, the time lag between receipt and claim may very well mean that the GPO cannot honor the claim, particularly because the GPO acquires only 20 copies for claims purposes.[7] Over the years there has been great dissatisfaction within the depository community about the GPO's efforts and ability to fill claims. Similarly, there has been a good deal of suspicion within the GPO that libraries are claiming titles they had not actually selected. Further streamlining and modernization of the GPO's automation system should decrease this problem in the future.

A different acquisitions problem occurs when the GPO knows that it does not have enough copies of a document to send to all the depository libraries that have selected that item number. In this case, the GPO chooses randomly which libraries will get the publication. For those that will not receive the publication, the GPO issues a *rain check*, a piece of paper included in the depository shipping box that was to have contained the publication. In fact, depositories rarely later receive the documents for which the rain checks are issued. Libraries may wish to keep the rain checks in a folder or notebook, in SuDoc classification number order, to determine why a publication was not received, should a question arise about a title. If a library is loading records into its on-line catalog based on item selection, maintaining this type of record is essential for catalog maintenance. Such a title listing may also prove helpful in further acquisitions efforts.

Exchange lists

In addition to direct deposit from the GPO, exchange of documents is another way to acquire depository publications. There are currently three official ways to exchange documents. The first is by reviewing the *offers* list that a regional library may produce. According to the *Guidelines*, all selectives must inform their regional if they wish to discard a title. Should the regional not wish to acquire the publication, it can, if it provides such a service, offer the title statewide through a state-based "needs and offers" list. A second way to exchange publications is through the quarterly *Needs and Offers* list that is distributed to all depository libraries by the GPO and is based on the lists that selectives have sent to their regionals. The third exchange method that has recently developed is through postings on listservs, such as GovDoc-L. It is not uncommon to see offers of duplicate titles on these electronic discussion lists.

Non-Depository Publications

Acquisition of U.S. federal publications that are neither available through depository status nor distributed by the GPO can be done in several ways. These strategies range from direct purchase to sending letters to agencies requesting a free copy of the publication. The success rate depends in large part upon the subject matter of the document, the number of copies printed, and the reason the publication did not fall into the standard GPO distribution.

The first and most obvious way is to try to purchase the publication. If the title is a current imprint, the best place to look is in the *Publications Reference File* (*PRF*) to determine if it is now or ever was available through the GPO. If the item is in stock, then the options are to apply the purchase against a depository account that the library may have at the GPO or to send out a standard library order through the acquisitions department. The second place to check is against the holdings of the National Technical Information Service (NTIS). If the item can be located in *GRA* and *GRI*, then a purchase order to NTIS is appropriate.

But what if an item is in neither NTIS nor GPO stock? The next avenue is to consider the type of information contained in the publication. If it is statistical or congressional, perhaps a microfiche copy can be acquired from Congressional Information Services (CIS). If it is noted as non-depository within the *Monthly Catalog*, perhaps it can be found in the Readex non-depository collection. If it is based in the social sciences or education, perhaps it can be located within the ERIC database. If the library is a member of DocEx, a purchase request to that organization might be appropriate. In each of these cases, the librarian must apply knowledge and judgment about government publishing practices to help identify a likely purchase source.

A most productive way to get publications recently mentioned in the media is to call the agency and see if free copies are available. Usually the agency is happy to mail a copy that day. This is particularly useful when looking for congressional materials. A phone call to a local congressperson's office can net a wealth of information. Through this technique, the library acquires a needed publication in a timely and cost-effective manner. Similarly, one can write to an agency and ask for a publication. However, the time taken to write and wait for a reply will probably prove more expensive in the long run.

Acquiring documents through agency mailing lists is another possibility. One way to have one's name added to such lists is to write a letter to the Publications Office or Information Office listed in standard agency directories. Scanning catalogs that are published by agencies may also reveal information about free publications or mailing lists. Federal agencies are required to survey periodically that their mailings are being used. Once on a mailing list that provides documents appropriate to the collection, one must be careful to respond to any agency queries about remaining on the list.

36 ☐ Acquisition of Government Information Resources

A fourth approach might be to become a depository for a specific agency, such as the Department of Energy, the National Aeronautics and Space Administration (NASA), the Census Bureau, or the Patent and Trademark Office. Although many agencies have had these programs for years, in the cost-cutting 1980s many have fallen by the wayside, languished, or become extremely costly to the libraries involved. One should carefully consider the obligations of such depository status and all costs before agreeing to this means of document acquisition.

Fugitive and Quasi-Governmental Publications

Although, theoretically, most government publications are supposed to be offered to the GPO for distribution, in reality many that are not printed at the GPO's facilities evade the system. These resources, called *fugitive documents* by the library community, are actively sought by GPO and Joint Committee on Printing (JCP) personnel. Alerting these staffs to titles can frequently help to get the publications into the system. If this tactic does not work, a direct approach to the issuing agency or the private information vendor selling the documents may be the only avenue for acquisition. Sometimes there are publications of which the GPO is well aware, but that it cannot distribute. These documents are usually exempt from distribution because of statutory language or regulations that allow the agency to sell the item. Examples of this type of publication are many of the Library of Congress monographs and serials. When the GPO is alerted to these publications, it uses *Administrative Notes* to explain why the item in question cannot be distributed under Title 44 of the U.S. Code.

A third document type not distributed by the GPO are materials published by quasi-governmental agencies, a listing of which can be located in the *U.S. Government Manual*. Publications of agencies, such as the National Academy of Sciences and Amtrak, fall into this category. Again, the only option for acquiring these publications is through purchase.

UNITED NATIONS DOCUMENTS

The worldwide United Nations (U.N.) depository system disseminates the publications of the United Nations, as well as the documentation of the United Nations Conference on Trade and Development, the United Nations Development Programme, the United Nations Industrial Development Organization, and the U.N.'s various regional commissions. United Nations publications are particularly valuable in analyzing worldwide economic, social, and political conditions.

Acquiring U.N. Depository Publications

The *Instructions for Depository Libraries Receiving United Nations Materials* outlines the specific categories of publications that "full" and "partial" depositories are entitled to receive. A U.N. depository library will receive all *Official Records* of the main organs of the U.N.; sales publications; periodicals available on subscription; volumes of the United Nations Treaty series; and memos of the regional commission covering the area in which the library is located. A depository library also may choose the language (English, French, or Spanish) in which it wishes to receive publications. In addition, full depositories receive "all other generally distributed documents and publications ... whether printed, reproduced by offset, or mimeographed—if available in the language chosen by the depository."[8]

The *Instructions* also indicate the categories that libraries are not entitled to receive automatically. Examples of non-depository publications include materials from specific organizations, such as the International Court of Justice and the United Nations Children's Fund; reprints of documents already deposited; and some sales publications that are issued and distributed by commercial publishers. For these publications, the depository must contact the agency or publisher and purchase directly.

Receiving U.N. Documents in the Library

United Nations depository documents arrive in the library either in boxes or shrink-wrapped, often without shipping or packing lists. Because of the lack of certainty about which U.N. documents are distributed in any given shipment, claiming is a difficult activity for a depository library. First, the depository must determine which documents *should* have been deposited, by identifying which documents were actually *issued*. One does this by checking several sources against the depository's record of holdings. The most important source, and the one to check first, is *UNDOC: Current Index*, particularly the sections on "Official Publications" and "Sales Publications." Other sources to check are the *United Nations Publications*, the *Daily List of Documents Issued at Headquarters*, and the *United Nations New Publications*, a monthly listing of titles. When determining the new publications issued and possibly distributed, the depository librarian must always keep in mind the categories of publications the library is entitled to receive, as explained in the *Instructions for Depository Libraries*. In addition, *UNDOC* often specifies "not for deposit," and the *United Nations Documentation News* publishes a list of "Publications Not Deposited."

If the library ascertains that it did not receive a publication that it should have, it may claim the document using the special depository claim form PS.16.[9] Although a depository has up to two years to claim publications, an effort should be made to claim as quickly as practical, as the U.N. does not keep large inventories of its publications. In libraries with relatively small documents staff, decisions on how much effort should be put into the labor-intensive claiming process associated with U.N. documents must be carefully considered.

Acquisition of U.N. Publications by Non-Depository Libraries

Even if a library is not an officially designated U.N. depository, it is quite possible to build a strong U.N. documents collection through purchase. The options available are varied, including purchase of single titles, periodicals, and series and the establishment of standing orders for U.N. publications by category (e.g., all mimeographed documents, all *Official Records*) and format (paper or microfiche). Possible vendors of these documents include UNIPUB, the U.N. Sales Office, and the Readex Corporation. As happens with depositories, the frequent absence of packing lists makes determination of what should be coming through standing orders difficult, and the librarian will have to determine how much time is to be spent in checking that items were received. For further information on sources and types of standing orders available, consult the most current *United Nations Publications Catalogue*, *Directory of U.N. Serial Publications*, the *UNIPUB Standing Order Catalog*, the *U.N. Catalogue of Documentation in Microfiche*, *United Nations New Publications*, and the current *Readex International Documents Catalogue*. It should be noted that standing orders cannot be placed for all U.N. agency publications; most of these agencies produce their own publications catalogs. Consulting these catalogs and purchasing title-by-title may be the only alternative.

INTERNATIONAL GOVERNMENTAL ORGANIZATION (IGO) DOCUMENTS

Many international government organizations, besides the United Nations, have depository arrangements with various libraries around the world. Each has its own set of rules and procedures for receiving and claiming documents available through their depository programs. "IGO Depository Collections in U.S. Libraries: A Directory and Analysis," by Willis F. Cunningham, contains information that would be helpful for any librarian dealing with an IGO depository in locating another depository for the same type of material.[10]

If a library is not a depository of a particular IGO agency, and there is interest in the IGO's documentation, purchasing from a standard vendor of IGO publications is the best route. UNIPUB and Manhattan are two of the major distributors of these publications. Consulting the *Europa Yearbook* under the name of the organization will provide information on the types of publications issued. A final alternative for smaller IGOs (e.g., OPEC, PAU) is to write to the organization, requesting any free publications or sales catalogs available. For further information on acquiring IGO publications, consult Peter Hajnal's *International Information: Documents, Publications and Information Systems of International Governmental Organizations*.[11]

CANADIAN FEDERAL DOCUMENTS

The depository distribution of Canadian government publications is similar in many ways to the U.S. GPO's depository program. It too is based on a system of designated libraries and has a high level of selectivity; some libraries receive all publications issued through Supply and Service Canada and some select the individual publications they will receive.

For selectives, there are two basic tools: the *Weekly Checklist of Canadian Government Publications* and the *Special List of Canadian Government Publications*.[12] However, unlike the GPO program, the Canadian program is much more labor-intensive for the librarian selecting titles. The *Weekly List* contains two sections—one for legislative publications and one for departmental publications—and lists brief bibliographic information on all documents for sale or on deposit. Depository publications may be selected by checking the appropriately numbered box on the order form at the back of each *Weekly List* and returning it within 50 working days. Depository libraries must request to be put on a mailing list for serial publications. When new serials appear in the *Weekly List*, subscription instructions precede the new listing. For other serials, such as annual titles, the librarian must remember to select the newest edition each year. Items in the *Special List* must be requested individually from the issuing agency. There is no order form.

Selective depository libraries should maintain a file of publications ordered. A useful arrangement for this file is by the catalog number, because this number is usually printed in the publication. It should also include the title of the publication and the number of the *Weekly List* or *Special List* from which the document was selected. If a depository publication is not received, the library may claim it; however, this requires a letter for each missing item. Supply and Services provides no specific claim form.

OTHER FOREIGN DOCUMENTS

The acquisition of foreign documents is problematic at best. Few countries have the type of established depository program that one finds in the United States or Canada. The primary hurdles facing any library are (1) timely identification of an item through collection development sources and (2) the identification of a distributor of publications within that country, either a government agency or an established book dealer.

Several patterns in government information distribution have developed worldwide. Some governments have a centralized national publisher, such as Her Majesty's Stationery Office (HMSO) in Great Britain. Some foreign governments have many national publishers, no doubt to encourage a semblance of free-market economy within the country. Still others have privatized government publishing activities and have given responsibility for government document sales to private firms. In other cases, there is no official publications distribution channel, and one must depend upon book dealers who actively seek out government publications and offer them through catalogs. (For example, Leishman and Taussig and Hogarth Representatives send agents to Africa on buying trips to locate African publications, including government publications.) Whatever the arrangement, it is usually up to the documents librarian to determine the best source for purchasing a publication. An excellent current source for potential distributors is the recent CIS publication *Guide to Official Publications of Foreign Countries*.[13]

Another alternative is to acquire microfiche collections of documents from private vendors. Options available range from buying whole collections of publications (e.g., British documents from Chadwyck Healey) to purchasing specific publications based on subject (e.g., foreign census data from Research Publications). Again, the best source for locating publishers that provide such services is the CIS *Guide*.

There are other means of acquiring foreign publications that are less reliable and more work than standard library ordering, but may be more fruitful in developing a foreign documents collection. The first method works best in an academic environment in which one has faculty traveling abroad. It is frequently possible for researchers to buy publications and maps abroad and ship them back to the library. This approach assumes that the faculty member is knowledgeable about the collection's needs, is willing to do the work, and that your accounting and auditing system can handle the reimbursement procedure. A second approach is to develop "exchange" relationships with foreign distributors. These types of arrangements are difficult to maintain, but may prove valuable in certain circumstances. Discussion with the library's acquisitions department is a first step in pursuing such an approach.

STATE GOVERNMENT DOCUMENTS

The variety of state depository arrangements within the United States makes generalizations about acquisition of state government documents difficult. Some state depository systems require the library to select individually the documents it wishes to receive. In these cases, the depository library needs to create records to track publications requested, those received, and those that need to be claimed or acquired by other means. In other state systems, the depository gets what is sent, and there is no claiming opportunity. For libraries that are not depositories, acquiring documents involves all the same strategies and resulting pitfalls as for federal documents. Letters to agencies frequently will garner free publications; mailing lists can be productive; and paid acquisitions may be the only possible way to attain resources. For further information on specific state depository systems and the acquisition of state documents, see Margaret Lane's *Selecting and Organizing State Government Publications* and her *State Publications and Depository Libraries*.

LOCAL DOCUMENTS

The acquisition of local documents is totally dependent upon the librarian's awareness of current events in the community. Becoming known as an advocate for open information access, following newspaper accounts, and watching locally televised government meetings are some of the best ways to find out when a publication has been produced and where it is available. Talking to local government employees about the library becoming a depository of local publications is an obvious avenue for acquisition. Explaining the value of having public access to such publications is one powerful argument in such discussions. Providing one copy to the library is also much cheaper than providing multiple copies to interested citizens. If copies are available for purchase, following news accounts will help identify when a document has been produced. In most situations, only a few copies will be published, so responding quickly to the appearance of a document is essential. If an item is out of stock and essential to the collection, another alternative is to get permission to photocopy the document.

CONCLUSION

As was discussed both in this and the previous chapter, acquisition of government information resources is a challenging undertaking. Many techniques can be employed, depending upon the materials sought. However, given the expense in acquiring these documents, one should be certain the acquisition patterns match collection development aspirations.

NOTES

[1] A "regional" depository must receive and retain permanently one copy of all U.S. documents issued through the depository system. A "selective" library may choose to receive as few or as many items as appropriate for its situation.

[2] The "title" may be an actual title or a working title. The "stem" is the part of the classification number preceding and including the colon. For example, the stem for the annual report of the Department of Agriculture is "A 1.1:"

[3] The note at the top of each shipping list tells the library the dates of selection under which the GPO is distributing documents. Keeping detailed records of dates of selection and deselection of item numbers can be especially helpful for the depository. If the library chooses to use a vendor service to include bibliographic records for U.S. government documents in its on-line catalog, having these records complete makes the profiling process much more accurate.

[4] A limited category of material is sent to the depository by direct mail from the printer and does not appear on any shipping list. The library has to rely on its serial check-in records to determine whether there are missing issues that should be claimed. These titles are:

Business America
Commerce Business Daily
Congressional Record (daily edition)
Daily Treasury Statement
Daily Weather Maps
Federal Energy Guidelines, FERC Reports
Federal Energy Guidelines, Statutes and Regulations
Federal Register
ICC Register
Internal Revenue Bulletin
List of CFR Sections Affected
Monthly and Seasonal Weather Outlook

Monthly Statement of the Public Debt of the United States
Monthly Treasury Statement of Receipts and Outlays of the US Government
Morbidity & Mortality Weekly Reports
Weekly Compilation of Presidential Documents

[5] In addition to the shipping lists, *Administrative Notes*, the newsletter of the Federal Depository Library Program, has become a very important source of information about changes in item numbers, availability of publications, changes and additions to the SuDoc classification system, and notification of publications that must be removed from the depository system by order of the issuing agency. This newsletter is distributed to every depository library, but is not listed on the shipping lists.

[6] In early 1993, the guidelines changed to reflect budgetary constraints within the GPO. "Effective March 1, 1993 libraries may claim only those publications distributed in paper from a core list of items and only regionals may claim microfiche distributed by LPS. All libraries will be able to claim microfiche that are distributed by one of LPS'[s] microfiche contractors." *Administrative Notes* 4:3 (Feb. 15, 1993), 1-2.

[7] Although the GPO tried to acquire 20 additional copies, it was not successful. Three of the additional copies were designated for exchange programs, thereby decreasing the number of copies actually available for claims.

[8] *Instructions for Depository Libraries Receiving United Nations Material* (New York: United Nations Secretariat, 1981, 1986 updates), 2-3.

[9] Additional copies of the claim form must be ordered on PS.16 as well.

[10] Willis F. Cunningham, "IGO Depository Collections in U.S. Libraries: A Directory and Analysis," *Government Publications Review* 18 (1991): 371-97.

[11] Peter Hajnal, *International Information: Documents, Publications, and Information Systems of International Governmental Organizations* (Englewood, CO: Libraries Unlimited, 1988).

[12] *Weekly Checklist of Canadian Government Publications; Special List of Canadian Government Publications* (Ottawa).

[13] *Guide to Official Publications of Foreign Countries* (Bethesda, MD: Congressional Information Service, 1990).

4

Bibliographic Control and Access

Carolyn C. Sherayko
Head, Original Cataloging
Indiana University

Bibliographic control of government documents embodies several different concepts and results in consideration of several basic organizational choices relating to a documents collection. Bibliographic control, in its standard definition, "covers a range of bibliographic activities: complete bibliographic records of all bibliographic items as published; standardization of bibliographic description; provision of physical access through consortia, networks, or other cooperative endeavors; and provision of bibliographic access through the compilation and distribution of union lists and subject bibliographies and through bibliographic service centers."[1] This chapter focuses on bibliographic control of government documents via physical access in the local library's documents collection.[2]

CHOICE OF MEANS OF BIBLIOGRAPHIC ACCESS TO DOCUMENTS

One of the first decisions to make is how to inform patrons that the library owns a particular document and how to ensure that patrons looking for information on a topic have access to the potential resources to be found in government documents. Bibliographic control of documents in libraries has evolved over the years. Unlike most library materials that were controlled by standard cataloging practices, documents have experienced a number of stages in bibliographic control. These stages have included local processing procedures, dependency on externally produced catalogs in either print or electronic formats, and full cataloging.

Separate Access

Before the 1980s, if a library chose not to include documents in its primary catalog, but rather to provide separate access, the means to implement this decision were limited. Most libraries relied on a combination of card catalogs developed and maintained by the documents department, shelflists of holdings, and printed bibliographies and catalogs.[3] Each of these options had significant limitations. The card catalogs were usually not developed following standard cataloging practices and required the user to know that a separate catalog must be consulted. Similarly, the shelflist and index approaches required complete dependence on a trained and knowledgeable documents staff.

44 □ Bibliographic Control and Access

Integrated Access

With the development of computerized, national databases of bibliographic records, beginning with OCLC in 1971, and with the steadily increasing implementation of on-line catalogs in all types of libraries during the 1980s, documents librarians continued to advocate that their library administrations reconsider the earlier decisions to exclude documents from the library's catalog. In 1976, the U.S. Government Printing Office (GPO) began cataloging all publications listed in the *Monthly Catalog of United States Government Publications* through OCLC, giving further impetus to this movement. After that, a significant amount of complete cataloging was available to libraries at a much lower cost than if the cataloging had to be done in-house.

Various studies have reported that the amount of machine-readable cataloging on the utilities is both significant and increasing, as more libraries fully catalog their documents.[4] Although Margaret Mooney's 1989 article focused on the time lag between the receipt of a U.S. depository publication and its appearance in the printed *Monthly Catalog of United States Government Publications*, she reported that 97.9 percent of the U.S. documents in her study of 1,800 titles had been cataloged by the GPO within 6.3 months of receipt.[5] A little over 2 percent had not been cataloged by the GPO by the end of two years. (Mooney did not indicate if cataloging had been provided by other OCLC member institutions for this 2 percent.) In another, more inclusive report in 1987, Pennsylvania State University reported finding cataloging records on OCLC for between 83 percent and 93 percent of all documents received (state, United States, United Nations, foreign, and international) within six months of receipt in the Documents Section.[6]

Evidence suggests that it is now feasible to integrate bibliographic control of documents into the library's standard bibliographic access to other types of materials. For most libraries, it should be immaterial whether this mode of access is in the card or on-line catalog environment; libraries large enough to have a separate documents collection are also likely to perform their cataloging activities through a bibliographic utility that provides either cards or machine-readable records.

Having made the decision to integrate bibliographic control and access, the next question is one of staffing. Who will be responsible for the procedures of transferring cataloging records from the utility and for cataloging materials without records? Traditionally the acquisition and processing point for government documents has been the documents department. This meant that the processing routines were separate from the library's regular procedures for new receipts. However, the decision to integrate document bibliographic control forces a reconsideration of this arrangement.

What is the best decision for how to process documents? Various models exist, and the method chosen should be based on what works best for the individual library. One model would require all acquisition and technical processing to be done by the library's technical services unit. In this scenario, documents would be treated exactly like all other materials in the library, receiving the same bibliographic access set by national standards, but classified according to the notation scheme(s) chosen for the documents collection. The opposite scenario would be to have all technical processing for documents completed within the documents collection, including original cataloging. Between these options lie all the variations possible for differing libraries and situations. The key to making an integrated approach work is the development of trust and communication between the documents department and the technical services unit of the library. Whether all processing takes place in technical services, or in the documents department, or a combination of both, each group should understand and respect the activities, standards, and constraints inherent in the situation of the other.

Computerized Access

A relatively recent improvement to documents bibliographic control has been the development of computerized files. OCLC provided the first widely available computerized access to bibliographic information about documents. One could search by corporate body, personal name, title, ISBN, ISSN, and later by document classification number to identify specific government publications. Because holdings cataloged by libraries varied widely, government documents from all levels of government formed part of the database. In some libraries today, the documents department maintains a public access OCLC terminal for patron use. In other libraries, OCLC access is limited to library personnel in the documents department, in technical services, and interlibrary lending.

Both DIALOG and BRS began to provide access to U.S. documents (from 1976 to the present) through on-line bibliographic database searching when the archive tapes of GPO-OCLC cataloging were made available through the Library of Congress Cataloging Distribution Service. Key-word and descriptor searching increased the scope of retrieval to facilitate identification of documents on a particular topic. On-line database vendors continue to make bibliographic and textual information more available, as more producers enter the market. The major drawback to this type of increased access has been that most libraries are unable to support the costs of searches for patrons and have had to charge a fee to subsidize the service.

CD-ROMs

In the mid-1980s, several commercial producers of indexes of bibliographic information began to exploit the new CD-ROM technology. The availability of machine-readable cataloging records for U.S. documents led to the production of several variations of the *Monthly Catalog of United States Government Publications* on CD-ROM.[7] Some of the major indexing companies and microform publishers of government publications have also made some of their bibliographic products available in this format (e.g., *CIS Masterfile*).

Although CD-ROM products are increasingly available, they tend to be electronic versions of print publications. The actual amount of indexing coverage of government publications has not increased substantially. Nevertheless, CD-ROM products are viewed as an improvement in bibliographic access.[8] Primary benefits of using them are the ease and flexibility of searching and the fact that there is no cost to the patron, unlike an on-line database search. The drawbacks for the library are the monetary investment required for equipment, particularly if the library acquires more than one CD-ROM product, and the multiplying number of search commands and strategies that must be mastered by patrons and librarians for successful retrieval. A further drawback to choosing either on-line database access or CD-ROM access for government documents is that neither of these options provides a link to the holdings of the local documents collection. An intermediary step in the form of a local shelflist or documents catalog is still necessary.

Local databases

Another option for providing computerized bibliographic access to documents is the creation of local databases using database software packages on a microcomputer.[9] Many choices of such packages are available in the neighborhood computer store, and many more are available as "freeware" or "shareware." A library that decides to provide this type of access must plan carefully for the data elements to be included in each record to ensure consistency in format for commonly recurring elements, such as government corporate body names. Also, a library will want to investigate the equipment needed (e.g., a local area network and microcomputers) to support local database access for patrons and documents staff.

CHOICE OF CLASSIFICATION SCHEMES

As already discussed in chapter 2, the concept of "provenance" is a primary tenet of all work with government documents. The originating source of the item has a bearing on the methods by which it is acquired by the library, its physical location within the library, and often, its bibliographic treatment. If the choice within the library is to maintain documents in a separate collection, decisions must be made about the physical arrangement of the material.

An established documents collection may use several classifications, depending on the scope of the collection—whether it contains federal, state, local, international, or other national governmental documents. The creation, expansion, or reclassification of a documents collection requires decisions on the choice of a classification scheme or schemes. To save both patron and library staff time, it helps to choose a system that is understood by patrons; is a comprehensive arrangement by provenance or by subject; is easily applied locally; and is simple to maintain and update. Because on-line catalogs are becoming part of the everyday access to documents collections, an additional factor in choosing a classification is its adaptability to machine indexing and retrievability.

Several standard, widely used classification/notation systems are available for documents. In addition, numerous specialized classification schemes have been developed to provide an archival arrangement for a collection of government documents or to accommodate special subject collections that might be composed primarily of such publications.

Superintendent of Documents Classification System

Attributed to Adelaide R. Hasse, and codified by William Leander Post of the Government Printing Office Library in 1904, the Superintendent of Documents Classification (SuDoc) is the most widely used notation system for U.S. government documents.[10] The basic philosophy behind the classification is to provide a shelf arrangement that reflects the structure of the United States government and, within that structure, to provide sub-arrangement by type of publication. It is only of secondary importance that this sub-arrangement results in a limited subject grouping of publications.

The SuDoc classification scheme, which is an alphanumeric system, employs mnemonic letters to represent the major departments, independent agencies, and branches of the federal government; numbers to represent issuing agencies within the primary divisions; numbers to represent form of the publication, and numbers or "Cutter numbers" to represent the specific publication. The alphanumeric sequences are separated by meaningful punctuation.

The mnemonic letters that begin the notation are based on the significant word in the name of the agency, such as "A" for the Department of Agriculture or "PrEx" for the Executive Office of the President. Following this are numbers representing subordinate agencies within the department or branch, with the number "1" usually reserved for the secretary's or administrator's office. Other subordinate agencies are assigned in sequence. For example:

A1. Agriculture Department.

A13. Forestry Service.

A57. Soil Conservation Service.

In practice, no attempt is made today by the Government Printing Office, when assigning numbers to new agencies within departments, to maintain the original alphabetic arrangement of the subordinate bodies. Each alphanumeric assigned is followed by a period to separate it from the form designation.

The form designations are intended to represent commonly occurring types of publications produced by the various departments and agencies. In the earlier history of the classification system, these numbers were limited to:

1 Annual reports

2 General publications[11]

3 Bulletins

4 Circulars

As the complexity of the federal government grew, the need for additional form designations also increased. Additions were made in the 1950s and again in 1985. These are:

5 Laws

6 Regulations, rules, and instructions

7 Releases

8 Handbooks, manuals, guides

9 Bibliographies and lists of publications

10 Directories

11 Maps and charts

12 Posters

13 Forms

14 Addresses, lectures, etc.

Other numbers beyond these are assigned in sequence to represent monographic series, serials/periodicals, or other logical groupings of publications issued by an agency. The form designation is separated from the remainder of the classification number by a colon.

Depending upon the type of publication, the type of notation following the colon may either be numeric or alphanumeric (a Cutter number). This notation is intended to represent the specific item. The Government Printing Office prefers to assign a numeric designation if one is printed on the document. Often these will be the numbering within the monographic series or the volume/issue number/date of the serial issue. If no numbers are apparent, the tendency is to assign a Cutter number based on a significant word in the title.

Using this outline so far, a document entitled *Tree Identification Handbook* issued by the U.S. Forestry Service might be assigned a SuDoc number as follows:

A 13.8:T 8
A Department of Agriculture
13. Forestry Service
8: Handbooks, manuals, guides
T 8 Cutter number for "trees"

Beyond these basic principles, other notational devices have been used to increase the flexibility of the SuDoc classification system. The slash (/) is often used in the form designation to place closely related series next to each other on the shelves. It is also used to indicate date of publication as part of the class number. For example, the hypothetical document in the preceding example might have been re-issued in 1992. Its classification number then would be:

A 13.8:T 8/992[12]

The SuDoc Classification System made the transition to the on-line environment in 1976 when the Government Printing Office began cataloging publications through the bibliographic utility OCLC. A special MARC[13] field (tag 086) was implemented in 1980 in which to record classification numbers for government documents. The SuDoc number is searchable in the major bibliographic utilities in the United States (OCLC, RLIN, and WLN). Most vendors of the current generation of on-line public access catalogs (OPACs) also provide call-number searching that includes the SuDoc classification number. Frequently, it is possible to "browse" a call number range in the catalogs; therefore, patrons can "see" what is likely to be on the documents shelves.

One drawback to SuDoc number browsability is the inability of most OPAC call-number indexes to sort and display the number as it really is shelved. This problem is not specific to SuDoc numbers, but it is typical of machine sorting of numbers. Compare the following displays:

Shelf Arrangement	OPAC Call Number Item
C 1.1:992	C 1.1:992
C 1.2:C 3	C 1.11:25
C 1.11:25	C 1.2:C 3

A method for making the transition from such an OPAC display to the shelf to find the publication has to be part of documents bibliographic instruction.

Another drawback is that SuDoc numbers change as agencies change. Therefore, a series of publications (e.g., census publications) may be found sprinkled through the C's, reflecting organizational changes in government. In those instances, it is necessary to reclass earlier documents, use dummies or shelf notes to direct users to earlier/later class numbers, or note in the processing records the change in classification.

Most U.S. government depository libraries choose to adopt the SuDoc classification scheme. There are two practical advantages to this decision; the documents arrive in the depository with the SuDoc numbers already assigned to the individual items by the Government Printing Office, and the primary reference works used with U.S. documents cite these numbers.

For a non-depository library's collection, one would need to consider the size of the documents collection and the planned method of bibliographic access before deciding to adopt this system. As the SuDoc classification is rarely printed on the document itself, the librarian must decide whether the shelf arrangement provided by SuDoc is worth the extra staff time and effort it will take to wait for the item to appear on a bibliographic utility or in the *Monthly Catalog of United States Government Publications,* or to assign a local SuDoc number. Another classification system that allowed for the integration of U.S. documents into the library's general collection or for the integration of all levels of government publications within a single scheme might be more appropriate.

United Nations Series Symbol

Similar to other types of government documents, publications of the United Nations consist of a variety of administrative, legislative, and informational materials. The Documents Control Section at U.N. headquarters has the responsibility of assigning the Series Symbol number to each document. Other U.N. agencies that also issue documents assign appropriate Series Symbol numbers as well. For the most part, the Series Symbol number is printed on each United Nations document.

The United Nations Series Symbol classification system is primarily an archival/accession number order scheme, although there is some provision for indicating the type of publication within the class number.[14] The system is alphanumeric, consisting of an acronym for the issuing body and subordinate bodies, a form division, and a consecutive number indicating the specific publication. In addition, further qualifiers may be included at the end of a classification number. The components of the number are separated by slashes (/).

Typical of symbols for issuing bodies are:

E/ECE/AGRI/-	E/	Economic and Social Council
	ECE/	Economic Commission for Europe
	AGRI/	Committee on Agriculture
A/AC.105/-	A/	General Assembly
	AC.105/	105th Ad Hoc Committee (i.e., Committee on Peaceful Uses of Outer Space)

A peculiarity of the Series Symbol system is the presence of "constructed" numbers, that is, Series Symbols that have had the first element intentionally omitted by the Document Control Section or other issuing body when printed. An example of this might be "ECE/AGRI/-," instead of "E/ECE/AGRI/-." Libraries using the U.N. Series Symbol classification for shelving United Nations documents should become familiar with instances when this is likely to occur, to avoid the creation of separate shelving locations for publications of the same issuing body.

Similar to the Superintendent of Documents Classification System and many other archival notation schemes, the Series Symbol contains an indication of the type of material. For example:

- INF. Information series
- RES. Resolutions
- SR. Summary records
- WP. Working papers

This notation is usually followed by a number to indicate the specific publication. There may also be an abbreviation indicating that the document is an addendum, revision, or corrigendum (e.g., "Add.," "Rev.," or "Corr.").

This classification system makes no attempt to keep together the various issues of a serial or the individual documents in a monographic series. The emphasis is on the accession order. For example, "E/ECE/AGRI/WP.25/Rev.1" might represent the first revision of the 25th working paper of the Economic Commission for Europe's Committee on Agriculture. Likewise, regularly occurring documents associated with each session of the General Assembly would be given separate numbers, because the session number takes precedence in the Series Symbol notation (e.g., "A/37/" represents documents of the 37th Session of the General Assembly, "A/38/" the 38th Session, etc.). Libraries using the U.N. Series Symbol classification for access to their U.N. documents collection must make adjustments in this system to accommodate these documents in the on-line catalog. It would not be an efficient use of staff time or computer storage space to have individual records for each issue, not to mention the difficulties that display of these nearly identical records would cause for patrons.

In discussing United Nations documents, one should mention the United Nations Sales Publications Numbers that are also found printed on the documents. The Sales Publications Numbers are acquisitions control numbers assigned to U.N. documents of general interest that are sold to the public. They consist of a letter indicating the language of the item, a two-digit code for the year of publication, a Roman numeral corresponding to one of seventeen subject categories, and an accession number. Some libraries with a small collection of U.N. documents made up primarily of general-interest publications might find this a preferred shelving arrangement over the U.N. Series Symbol number.[15]

Department of Supply and Service Catalogue Numbers (Canada)

In 1984, the Documentation Section of the Canadian Government Publishing Centre published an "Outline of Classification." Its introduction delineated some issues surrounding use of the Supply and Service catalogue numbers as classification numbers for Canadian documents.[16] This classification system was introduced in the 1953 *Canadian Government Publications: Consolidated Annual Catalogue*. Its purpose, then as now, was to provide numbers for the procurement, distribution, and acquisition processes for Canadian government publications by indicating, in a coded format, the issuing agency and other unique information identifying the documents.

Like other classifications based on provenance, the application of this system is subject to the frequent changes in the structure of the government, which in turn leads to inconsistencies and overlaps in the classification. A further complication of the Canadian situation is that the classification number is often assigned without the publication in hand, from incomplete information, before the document is published. Therefore, the catalogue number printed on the document may not coincide exactly with the number that would have been assigned according to the guidelines of the classification system.

52 □ Bibliographic Control and Access

After acknowledging these difficulties, the Documentation Section proposed several ideas to establish a more cohesive application of the system. Among these were principles for assigning two-letter codes for each department or first-level agency; creating a sequential numbering pattern to represent issuing agencies; providing form designations based on type of publication; and standardizing the representation of specific publications. The proposals also included a methodology for representing language and format of the document.

These principles result in a classification number that would be similar to the Superintendent of Documents system. For example, publications issued by Agriculture Canada would be assigned class letter "A" (or, as in the proposals, "AG"). This would be followed by a number representing either the overall administrative activity or a subordinate unit. There would be five "places" to this basic classification—two letters for the department (positions 1-2) and three digits (positions 3-5) for the subunits and the form designation. The subunits would be represented in position four with "0" used for the department as a whole and "1" used for the remainder. The form designations proposed were:

1. Administrative information (e.g., annual reports, regulatory agenda, Cabinet discussion papers, etc.)

2. Annuals and directories

3. Periodicals

4. Series

5. Reports of inquiries

6. Conference proceedings

7. (left open)

8. Monographs (1) (i.e., books or substantial booklets)

9. Monographs (2) (i.e., pamphlets)

Within these forms, distinct groups of documents would be assigned a sequential accession number. Therefore, a typical departmental publication might have a classification number such as:

AG101-1/   AG   Agriculture Canada

                 10   the department as a whole

                 1   an administrative information item

                 -1   accession sequence

The slash (/) divides the basic classification from the specific item information. In the preceding example, the specific information would be the year, and the

Choice of Classification Schemes ☐ 53

number would be completed as "AG101-1/1992." The *Outline of Classification* also proposed that an indicator of language and format could be added. Thus, the French microform version of this document would be assigned "AG101-1/1992FM."[17]

For either a Canadian documents depository or a non-depository collection of Canadian government publications, the choice of using the Supply and Service catalog number as a shelving method is appropriate. The system groups documents by administrative issuing agency, and it provides a sub-arrangement by format and by limited subject groupings due to the scope of the agencies' missions. Moreover, the classification number is printed on the publication as well as in the various selection and reference tools. Cataloging records for Canadian government publications are increasingly available on the national bibliographic utilities, and frequently the Supply and Service catalog number is included in the MARC 086 field, usually prefaced by "DSS Cat. no." The availability of these sources means staff time does not have to be spent on searching for an appropriate number before the item can be processed and made available.

Library of Congress and Dewey Decimal Classifications

Most documents librarians should be familiar with the basic principles of shelf arrangement under the Library of Congress (LC) and Dewey Decimal Classification (DDC) systems; these are the two primary means of organizing general library collections in the United States. Both classifications are based on a systematic arrangement of knowledge into subject groupings, with further divisions of the groupings by chronology, geography, ethnic group, or more discrete subject divisions.

Throughout the LC classification schedules, there are provisions for grouping government documents in a specific classification number under the topic (e.g., HD171-HD183). Until the mid-1970s, LC further attempted to group documents together through means of reserved Cutter numbers, the "A" Cutters, that could be used in combination with any classification number.[18] Since then, the policy has been that documents would not be treated as a separate category of materials, unless the classification schedule itself contained provisions for documents.[19] This change in concept reflected the principle that documents should be classed with the appropriate subject matter, regardless of provenance. This same principle exists in the Dewey Decimal Classification, although there are some provisions for classing documents such as administrative reports or legislative materials together.

The arrangement of a documents collection on archival principles is a longstanding practice among libraries. However, an arrangement by subject, employing either of the LC or DDC systems, could be appropriate and might be a better choice in certain libraries. If the same classification were used for documents as for the general library collection, patrons would have only to understand the difference in location to find desired material, and staff time would not have to be spent in developing and maintaining a local classification system.

CODOC

Among the "standard" classification schemes in existence, the shelving notation used in the CODOC system holds a unique position: it is accession-number-order based, was designed specifically to be used in a computer context, and was developed by an agency other than a publisher or distributor of government documents. The CODOC system is not only a classification system, but also encompasses a software program that creates a bibliographic database of documents records.

First developed in 1966 at the University of Guelph in Canada,[20] the system employs alphanumeric codes to represent the level of government and the issuing body, a date of publication code, and a Cutter number for the title. For serial publications, the date of publication code is omitted, thus keeping individual issues together by title. This classification and the information on which it is based are then put into computerized form to create a database that is accessible through KWOC (keyword-out-of-context) indexes. A typical example might be:

```
US    U.S. Dept. of Agriculture. Tree Identification Handbook.
A     Washington, D.C., 1992
92T8
```

Locally Developed Classification Schemes

This section contains a selected bibliography of published classification schemes intended for use with government documents. Some of the classification schemes were designed to be used with documents from all levels of government; others are limited to a particular level or subject focus. An excellent analysis of many of these classification systems can be found in Russell Castonguay's *A Comparative Guide to Classification Schemes for Local Government Documents Collections* (Westport, CT: Greenwood Press, 1984).

Archival classification schemes

Heenan, Thomas. "Classification of Local Publications." *Special Libraries* 65 (February 1974): 73-76.

Holdsworth, H. "An Arrangement for Government Publications." *East African Library Association Bulletin* 1 (January 1962): 15-25.

Jackson, Ellen Pauline. "A Notation for a Public Documents Classification." In *Library Bulletin* no. 8. Stillwater, OK: Oklahoma Agricultural and Mechanical College, 1946.

MacEachern, J. H. "The Documents Shelving Notation of the Legislative Library, British Columbia, Canada." In *The Bibliographic Control of Official Publications*, edited by John E. Pemberton, 71-86. Oxford: Pergamon Press, 1982.

Miller, Ann E. "Notation for the Arrangement of Official Publications in the La Trobe University." In *The Bibliographic Control of Official Publications*, edited by John E. Pemberton, 9-21. Oxford: Pergamon Press, 1982.

Miller, J. Gormly. "Classification of Local Municipal Documents." *Library Journal* 64 (December 1939): 938-41.

Newsome, Walter L. "The University of Virginia's Documents Classification System." In *The Bibliographic Control of Official Publications*, edited by John E. Pemberton, 109-24. Oxford: Pergamon Press, 1982.

Pease, Mina. "The Plain 'J': A Documents Classification System." *Library Resources and Technical Services* 16 (Summer 1972): 315-25.

Rettig, James. "A Classification Scheme for Local Government Documents Collections." *Government Publications Review* 7A (1980): 33-39.

Reynolds, Catherine J. "The University of Colorado Classification System for Documents of International Intergovernmental Organizations." In *The Bibliographic Control of Official Publications*, edited by John E. Pemberton, 99-107. Oxford: Pergamon Press, 1982.

Siler-Regan, Linda, Charles R. McClure, and Nancy Etheredge. "Non-SuDocs Classification: A New Procedure." *Library Resources and Technical Services* 20 (Fall 1976): 361-72.

Swank, Raynard. "A Classification for State, County, and Municipal Documents." *Special Libraries* 35 (April 1944): 116-20.

Subject-based schemes

Gavryck, Jacquelyn, and Sara Knapp. "State Secrets Made Public." *Library Resources and Technical Services* 17 (Winter 1973): 82-92.

Glidden, Sophia H., and D. G. Marchus. *Library Classification for Public Administration Materials*. Chicago: American Library Association, 1942.

MacMillin, Frederick N. *Library Classification for Special Collection on Municipal Government and Administration*. Madison, WI: League of Wisconsin Municipalities, 1932.

National League of Cities/United States Conference of Mayors. *The NLC/USCM Library Classification System: Index for an Urban Studies Collection*. Washington, DC: National League of Cities/United States Conference of Mayors, 1970.

Pemberton, John E. "Official Publications in a New Bibliothecal Context." In *The Bibliographic Control of Official Publications*, edited by John E. Pemberton, 147-72. Oxford: Pergamon Press, 1982.

Sessions, Vivian S. "The City Planning and Housing Library: An Experiment in Organization of Materials." *Municipal Reference Library Notes* 37 (November 1963): 269-83.

Shillaber, Caroline. *A Library Classification for City and Regional Planning.* Cambridge, MA: Harvard University Press, 1973.

Accession-order-based schemes

Hajnal, Peter I. "Organization of Publications of the European Communities in the University of Toronto Library." In *International Documents for the 80s: Their Role and Use,* edited by Theodore D. Dimitrov and Luciana Marulli-Koenig, 149-56. Pleasantville, NY: UNIFO, 1982.

State government classification schemes

Hartman, Ruth D. "Bibliography of Classification Schemes Used for State Documents Collections." *Documents to the People* 3 (March 1975): 23-25; "Supplement 1." *Documents to the People* 4 (September 1976): 23-24.

"Section 5: Source Codes—Source Codes for Government Document Classification Number (086)." In *OCLC-MARC Code Lists,* 5:4. Dublin, Ohio: OCLC (Rev. 8512).

NOTES

[1] Heartsill Young, ed., *The ALA Glossary of Library and Information Science* (Chicago: American Library Association, 1983), 21.

[2] A few of the manuals that give an historical perspective on bibliographic control and access to government publications are Ellen Jackson, *A Manual for the Administration of the Federal Documents Collection in Libraries* (Chicago: American Library Association, 1955); Rebekah M. Harleston and Carla J. Stoffle, *Administration of Government Documents Collections* (Littleton, CO: Libraries Unlimited, 1974); Yuri Nakata, *From Press to People: Collecting and Using U.S. Government Publications* (Chicago: American Library Association, 1979); Brenda Brimmer, et al., *A Guide to the Use of United Nations Documents* (Dobbs Ferry, NY: Oceana, 1962); Peter I. Hajnal, *Guide to United Nations Organization, Documentation & Publishing for Students, Researchers, Librarians* (Dobbs Ferry, NY: Oceana, 1978); Margaret T. Lane, *Selecting and Organizing State Government Publications* (Chicago: American Library Association, 1987); and Yuri Nakata, Susan J. Smith, and William B. Ernst, Jr., *Organizing a Local Government Documents Collection* (Chicago: American Library Association, 1979).

[3] Numerous handbooks exist to help the librarian understand the range of printed bibliographies, catalogs, checklists, and location aids to assist in the identification of government documents. Many of these are listed in the bibliography of this book and throughout the various chapters.

[4]A sampling of these studies include: Alice Harrison Bahr, "Cataloging U.S. Depository Materials: A Reevaluation," *College and Research Libraries* 47 (November 1986): 587-95; Cynthia E. Bower, "OCLC Records for Federal Depository Documents: A Preliminary Investigation," *Government Information Quarterly* 1 (1984): 379-400; Roseann Bowerman and Susan A. Cady, "Government Publications in an On-line Catalog: A Feasibility Study," *Information Technology and Libraries* 3 (December 1984): 331-42; Mary Ann Higdon, "Federal Documents Processing with OCLC: The Texas Tech Experience—Planning, Utilization, the Future," in *Government Documents and Microforms* (Westport, CT: Meckler, 1984); Margaret S. Powell, Deborah Smith Johnston, and Ellen P. Conrad, "The Use of OCLC for Cataloging U.S. Government Publications: A Feasibility Study," *Government Publications Review* 14 (1987): 61-76; Sharon Walbridge, "OCLC and Government Documents Collections," *Government Publications Review* 9 (1982): 277-87. The focus of most of these studies has been on U.S. documents. One would expect, however, that similar results might hold for all types of documents. Further investigation is needed.

[5]Margaret T. Mooney, "GPO Cataloging: Is It a Viable Current Access Tool for U.S. Documents?" *Government Publications Review* 16 (1989): 259-70.

[6]Carolyn C. Jamison [Sherayko], "Automating Documents Processing Activities: Variations on a Theme at Penn State," *Documents to the People* 15 (December 1987): 226-28.

[7]Currently on the market are: GDCS—Government Documents Cataloging Service by Auto-Graphics, Inc.; Government Publications Index on Info Trac by Information Access Company; GPO CAT/PAC by MARCIVE, Inc.; and on SilverPlatter by SilverPlatter Information, Inc. For reviews of the *Monthly Catalog* versions, see: Jim Walsh and Mallory Stark, "The Monthly Catalog of United States Government Publications: One Title, Many Versions," *Government Information Quarterly* 7 (1990): 359-70; Charles A. Seavey, "Three CD-ROM Versions of the GPO Database: A Comparison, with an Editorial Observation," *Documents to the People* 19 (June 1991): 116-17.

[8]Some vendors of the *Monthly Catalog* on CD-ROM are now including "temporary records" that will be replaced by the full record on later issuances of the disk. These temporary records are taken from the shipping lists and include only the information that can be found there; however, their inclusion makes the CD-ROM product much more current. This development may help solve the dilemma of receiving documents before bibliographic records are available.

[9]Examples of local databases created for documents access include: Karen A. Becker, "Using FINDER Information Storage and Retrieval Software for Government Documents," *Library Software Review* 9 (January/February 1990): 14-17; Diana Gonzalez Kirby, "Using a Bibliographic Database Management System to Improve Access to State Government Posters," *Library Software Review* 9 (January/February 1990): 10-13; Chris Kiser and Clyde Grotophorst, "GOVDOX: A Government Documents Check-in System," *Library Software Review* 7 (January/February 1988): 42-43; Dave Obringer, "Beyond Technical

Services: Using a PC-based Database to Create a Government Documents Holding List," *Library Software Review* 11 (January/February 1992): 9-10; Louise Stwalley, "A Microcomputer Catalog For Municipal Documents," *Government Publications Review* 16 (1989): 63-72; Ronelle H. H. Thompson, "Managing a Selective Government Documents Depository Using Microcomputer Technology," *CRL News* 50 (April 1989): 260-62; Suzanne Wise, "Automating Government Documents Check-in Using PC File:db," *Library Software Review* 10 (July/August 1991): 258-61.

[10] Many good explanations of the application and history of the SuDoc Classification System are available. Primary among these are the *GPO Classification Manual: A Practical Guide to the Superintendent of Documents Classification System* (Washington, DC: U.S. Government Printing Office, 1986-); John Andriot, "A Practical Guide to the Superintendent of Documents Classification System," in *Guide to U.S. Government Publications* (McLean, VA: Documents Index, 1990), v-xxviii; Yuri Nakata, *From Press to People* (Chicago: American Library Association, 1979), 69-74; Rebekah M. Harleston and Carla J. Stoffle, *Administration of Government Documents Collections* (Littleton, CO: Libraries Unlimited, 1974), 19-27; and Ellen Jackson, *A Manual for the Administration of the Federal Documents Collection in Libraries* (Chicago: American Library Association, 1955), 36-47.

[11] "General publications" is a broad grouping that encompasses the majority of miscellaneous publications that do not belong to a specific bibliographic series or other identifiable category of publications emanating from a government agency.

[12] Note that the first digit of the year is dropped. This is a long-standing convention used for the representation of a date in a SuDoc number. One may expect a change in Government Printing Office usage with the beginning of the 21st century.

[13] *MARC* stands for "machine readable cataloging" and is a communications format developed by the Library of Congress that allows recording of bibliographic information in an electronic format. It is composed of a series of numeric field tags (e.g., 086 -Government Documents Classification Number, 074 -Item Number, 100 -Personal Author Main Entry, etc.) that may be divided into subfields.

[14] Explanations of the U.N. Series Symbols and the Sales Publications Numbers may be found in *United Nations Document Series Symbols, 1946-1977: Cumulative List with Indexes* (New York: United Nations, Dag Hammarskjöld Library, 1978); *United Nations Document Series Symbols, 1978-1984* (New York: United Nations, Dag Hammarskjöld Library, 1986); and Mary Eva Birchfield, *The Complete Reference Guide to United Nations Sales Publications 1946-1978* (Pleasantville, NY: UNIFO, 1982).

[15]*Instructions for Depository Libraries Receiving United Nations Material* (New York: United Nations Secretariat, 1981) makes suggestions on shelf arrangement in Section XI, "Maintenance of the Collection."

[16]*Government of Canada Publications. Outline of Classification*, 4th ed. (Ottawa: Canadian Government Publishing Centre, 1984), iii-14.

[17]In current practice, it seems that many of these proposed guidelines are being followed when the Supply and Service catalogue number is assigned, with some variations—the use of a dash instead of a slash to separate general from specific information, for example.

[18]A detailed explanation of this can be found in Richard H. Schimmelpfeng and C. Donald Cook, eds., *The Use of the Library of Congress Classification* (Chicago: American Library Association, 1968), 135-61.

[19]"Library of Congress Classification, Government Documents," *Cataloging Service Bulletin* 121 (Spring 1977): 19.

[20]The original description of the notation system can be found in Margaret Beckman, Sara Henderson, and Ellen Pearson, *The Guelph Document System* (Guelph, Ontario: University of Guelph Library, 1973). Updates on the developments in the system have appeared regularly in the library literature. Two recent articles are Virginia Gilliam, "CODOC in the 1980s: Keeping Pace With Modern Technology," in *New Technology and Documents Librarianship*, edited by Peter Hernon (Westport, CT: Meckler, 1983), 89-97; and "The CODOC System: An Update for the Mid-1980s," *Government Publications Review* 14 (1987): 465-69.

5

Bibliographic Processing

Carolyn C. Sherayko
Head, Original Cataloging
Indiana University

Bibliographic processing of government documents really begins with the two decisions of method of access and classification discussed in the last chapter. No matter how a document arrives in the library or what means of access to this information is chosen, several activities must be performed before the document is ready and waiting on the shelf for someone to discover its usefulness. This chapter covers those standard processing routines. The activities discussed do not have to be performed in the sequence in which they are presented. Local needs and workflows will determine the order in which various functions are performed.

PROCESSING ROUTINES

Processing routines are activities, in addition to the intellectual effort undertaken to provide bibliographic control and access, that prepare materials for use by library patrons. Many of these activities relate directly to preparing physical materials for shelving, but they may also include statistics-keeping necessary for annual reports and analyses of the collection.

Ownership Stamps

The *Guidelines for the Depository Library System for U.S. Government Publications* specify that "[e]ach publication in the shipment should be marked to distinguish it from publications received from other sources. Each publication should be marked with the date of the shipping list or the date of receipt."[1] Generally, this marking has taken the form of an ownership stamp that includes the library name, the word *depository*, and a date. Some state depository programs may also have similar requirements for distinguishing materials, depending upon their legal requirements. For the sake of simplicity, the stamp should be general enough to be used with all depository publications, yet specific enough to satisfy marking guidelines unique to a library and its depository obligations. If the library chooses, non-depository documents can either be marked with the same stamp used for materials in the general collection, or be marked with a stamp resembling the depository stamp, but minus the word *depository*.

Labeling

Regardless of the classification systems chosen for the documents collection, a number has to be recorded on the piece to facilitate retrieval from its shelving location. In labeling the document, one should be careful not to cover up any pertinent information that might be needed by the patron or the cataloger.

Because many documents are paperbound, one of the simplest labeling methods is to write the classification number in pencil or pen in the upper left corner of the "front" cover. This is usually the best location, because it is the first part of the document seen upon pulling it from a shelf.

However, writing on the document may not work on all types of document covers. Other labeling options include SE-LIN labels or pressure-sensitive labels.[2] Most library supply catalogs offer a variety of labeling products. The SE-LIN labeling system requires a special attachment to a standard typewriter and rolls of labeling stock. Because of its strong adhesive backing, this method is especially suitable for hardcover printed materials, plastic binders, pasteboard containers, or CD jewel boxes. The label stock is thick, however, so attaching a SE-LIN label to a flimsy document, such as a leaflet or a single sheet map, is likely to be unsatisfactory. If the library uses the SuDoc classification scheme, the U.N. classification scheme, or similar systems in which the number can be long, a standard method of dividing the number into units also needs to be used to fit the number vertically on the label.

Pressure-sensitive labels are a less expensive and more flexible labeling option. A variety of labels are available, in many different widths and lengths, from library vendors or office supply stores. Foil-backed labels will even stick to clothbound, hardcover documents. The classification number can either be handwritten or typed on the label with this option. One disadvantage to these labels is that the adhesive can dry out, causing the label to fall off the document after some time, if not used in an optimal preservation environment.

Pre-printed pressure-sensitive labels for United States depository documents are available commercially through Bernan Associates' DECK service and MARCIVE's Shipping List Service (SLS). Based on the depository shipping lists, these services provide a label containing the SuDoc classification number for each document on the list, a 3-by-5-inch card printed with the classification number, and bibliographic information from the shipping list that may be used in a manual shelflist. Such services may be tailored to match the library's item selections. Because the documents and the labels do not arrive together, an extra step is needed to match the depository boxes or items with the label shipments before processing can be completed.

Special formats, such as maps, microfiche, floppy disks, and CDs, present different labeling challenges. Again, the simplest method of recording the classification number on a map is to write it directly on the piece in a consistent location. However, if one chooses to affix a label to the map and the individual sheets are to be stored flat in drawers, care should be taken to vary the location of the label on the map, as all the labels will add thickness to the maps. This will be especially noticeable if the label is always applied in the same spot. Eventually this practice will prevent maps from lying flat in the drawer and will limit the number of maps that can go into a drawer.

On microfiche, there is frequently a little blank space left in the header in which to write the classification number assigned to the fiche (if the number is not already printed on it). If there is room, this can be done with an ultrafine-point acid-free permanent marker. One has to consider legibility for patrons and consistency of location of call numbers in making the decision to label the fiche directly. An alternative is to file each fiche or group of fiche in acid-free envelopes and to label the envelopes with classification numbers and other needed information. The obvious drawback to this is the likelihood that fiche will not always be put back into the correct envelope. A compromise between these alternatives is to label the envelope fully and to mark the fiche with a portion of the same information, or perhaps the last digits of a barcode number applied to the envelope.

The safest way to label floppy disks and CDs is to label the container in which they are stored. One should not apply a label directly on a disk unless there is a space intended for that purpose. It is possible that labels applied elsewhere on the disk will come off while inside the computer and cause damage. If one must label a CD, care should be taken to use a marker that will not harm the disk's surface.

Preparation for Circulation

The increasingly automated environment in libraries has brought barcoding to documents. Most libraries with on-line circulation systems use some sort of computer-scannable label to replace the card and pocket or multipart circulation form. Documents collections that use automated circulation must make decisions on the placement of barcodes on the documents. The key principle is consistency of location. This consistency aids efficient circulation operation because the desk attendant does not have to hunt for the barcode. Additional principles are similar to those for affixing other types of labels (i.e., do not cover pertinent information and do not apply labels where the additional thickness is likely to disrupt storage).

Many libraries also have electronic security systems to protect materials from theft. The format of some documents may prevent applying this security treatment, but documents should be protected in the same way as other library materials.[3]

Statistics

All libraries keep track of collection growth, not only to facilitate space planning, but also to report to various annual library collection surveys. The Association of Research Libraries' *ARL Statistics* and the U.S. Department of Education's Integrated Postsecondary Education Data System (IPEDS) are widely known. Each includes instructions for counting government publications collections.

The tradition of treating documents separately in libraries and the perceived ephemeral nature of their format have led to a lack of consistent standards for reporting holdings. The American Library Association Government Documents Round Table's (GODORT) Committee on Statistical Measurement has grappled with this issue for many years. Most documents collections count items by the physical piece, despite the item's bibliographic nature—whether a multipart monograph, single monograph, map sheet, floppy disk, or serial issue. The reporting requirements on the U.S. Government Printing Office Biennial Survey of depository libraries fostered this methodology. In the 1991 Biennial Survey, depositories were asked to supply the number of pieces added during a typical week for paper, microfiche, and map sheets. The Survey also asked for the pieces (paper, microfiche, and map sheets) withdrawn during the previous year.[4] By comparison, the 1990-1991 ARL survey asked for a *volume* count of government documents classified and included in the library's catalogs, as well as a piece count of microforms and any documents not included elsewhere.[5] The volume count was to be based on a formula that estimates the number of equivalent volumes in one linear foot of documents. The instructions were explicit that the volume count was different from a piece or title count. Alternatively, the IPEDS survey for 1990 asked for a *title* count of documents not cataloged and shelved with the regular collection of the library. For documents in microformat, IPEDS requested both title and piece counts.[6] As shown by these examples, as more documents are added to on-line catalogs, a standard methodology for statistics-gathering will have to be designed. This standard, including volume, title, and piece counts, will become increasingly appropriate for government publications, not only to be able to report the size of the collection in a consistent manner for the national surveys, but also as useful data in computer capacity and shelving need estimates.

CATALOGING

This discussion of the cataloging of government publications makes two assumptions: first, that integrating documents into the library catalog is an economically feasible activity; and second, that the catalog is an automated one. There has been a revolution in the world of government publishing and bibliographic access within the last 10 years. The reports in library literature to date suggest that more documents collections are applying new technology to all aspects of their activities. Unlike the paper/card file practices well documented in previous manuals on government publications administration,[7] there is as yet no clear direction on what is the best way to incorporate documents into the on-line environment. The number of librarians asking, via numerous electronic bulletin boards, for advice on adding documents to their on-line catalogs is evidence of the need for more sharing of experience. As much as the library community sometimes disdains "how-we-do-it-good" articles, this is a case in which they are needed.

MARC-Speak

The lingua franca of most automated library catalogs is the MARC communications format. No records are created, loaded, manipulated, or displayed in an on-line catalog without some reference to MARC tags or the MARC format. MARC (*ma*chine-*r*eadable *c*ataloging) development began in the 1960s, when the Library of Congress (LC) wanted to take advantage of emerging computer technology to share LC cataloging in machine-readable form. MARC is a coding system that allows computer manipulation of bibliographic data. Understanding the basics of (and specifics of) the MARC format is helpful for librarians in planning the inclusion of documents in the on-line catalog (see figures 5.1 and 5.2). This understanding makes it easier to talk to vendors and technical services librarians about one's needs and expectations regarding documents records.

Fig. 5.1. MARC terminology.

Basic definitions for the terminology associated with a MARC record.[8]

Leader: A data string at the beginning of a bibliographic record with fixed length of 24 characters that provides information for processing the record.

Directory: A data string following the leader that specifies the locations of tags and fields within the record.

The Leader and Directory form the "behind-the-scenes" part of a MARC record. It is this portion that encodes much of the information that helps a computer index and retrieve the record efficiently.

Fields: Groups of one or more data elements defined and manipulated as a unit, such as the 245 (Title) and 001 (Record number). Each field is identified by a tag.

Tags: Labels for fields. For example "245" is the tag for the title field.

Indicators: Two characters at the beginning of each field except for control fields. Indicators provide additional information about the field.

Subfields: Data elements within fields. Each subfield is defined by a subfield code, which is composed of a delimiter ... and a single character. The symbol used for the delimiter varies from system to system.

As computer systems have developed, the MARC communications format has been adapted to fit the needs of the users of each system. USMARC is the standard iteration of the format as documented by *USMARC Formats for Bibliographic Data*.[9] Major bibliographic utilities, such as OCLC and RLIN, have each developed a version of MARC, in which variations occur mostly in the fixed field and application of the local variable fields allowed by USMARC. Individual on-line systems have also developed specific applications of the MARC format (e.g., NOTIS/MARC).

Generally, the fields of a record are spoken of as two groups—the fixed field and the variable fields—though the fields in both groups are composed of information that will change from record to record. Figure 5.3 is a typical display of an

(Text continues on page 68.)

Fig. 5.2. Selected list of MARC fields.

"Authors":
- 100 Main entry - personal name
- 110 Main entry - corporate name
- 111 Main entry - conference or meeting
- 130 Main entry - uniform title heading
- 700 Added entry - personal name
- 710 Added entry - corporate name
- 711 Added entry - conference name
- 730 Added entry - uniform title heading

Titles:
- 240 Uniform title
- 245 Title statement
- 740 Added entry - title traced differently

Series:
- 400 Series statement - personal name/title
- 410 Series statement - corporate name/title
- 411 Series statement - conference or meeting/title
- 440 Series statement - title
- 490 Series untraced or traced differently
- 800 Series added entry - personal name/title
- 810 Series added entry - corporate name/title
- 811 Series added entry - conference or meeting/title
- 830 Series added entry - uniform title heading

Subjects:
- 600 Subject added entry - personal name
- 610 Subject added entry - corporate name
- 611 Subject added entry - conference name
- 630 Subject added entry - uniform title
- 650 Subject added entry - topical heading
- 651 Subject added entry - geographic name

Description:
- 250 Edition statement
- 255 Mathematical data area (maps)
- 260 Publication, distribution, etc. (Imprint)
- 300 Physical description
- 310 Current frequency (serial)
- 362 Dates of publication and/or volume designation
- 500 General note
- 504 Bibliography/discography note
- 507 Scale note for graphic material (maps - pre-AACR2)
- 538 Technical details note (computer files)
- 565 Case file characteristics note (computer files)

Standard numbers:
- 010 Library of Congress Control Number (LCCN)
- 020 ISBN
- 022 ISSN
- 050 LC call number
- 090 Local call number

Fig. 5.3. OCLC/MARC record.

```
Copyright 1978-1992 OCLC Online Computer Library Center, Inc.

Screen 1 of 2
NO HOLDINGS IN UPM - FOR HOLDINGS ENTER dh DEPRESS DISPLAY RECD SEND
OCLC: 20579746      Rec stat: n Entrd: 891101       Used: 900104
Type: a Blb lvl: m Govt pub: f Lang: eng Source: d Illus: a
Repr: b Enc lvl: I Conf pub: 0 Ctry:  dcu Dat tp: r M/F/B: ^0
Indx: 0 Mod rec:    Festschr: 0 Cont: b
Desc: a Int lvl:    Dates: 1988,1988
  1 010
  2 040      CUY $c CUY
  3 007      h $b e $c o $d b $e m $f b--- $g b $h a $i c $j a
  4 086 0    GA 1.13:PEMD-88-22
  5 049      UPMM
  6 245 00   Domestic terrorism $h [microform] : $b prevention efforts
in selected federal courts and mass transit systems : report to the
chairman, Subcommittee on Civil and Constitutional Rights, Committee on
the Judiciary, House of Representatives / $c United States General
Accounting Office.
  7 260      Washington, D.C. : $b The Office, $c [1988]
  8 300      116 p. : $b ill. ; $c 28 cm.
  9 500      Cover title.


Screen 2 of 2
 10 500      Running title: Domestic antiterrorism efforts at selected
sites.
 11 500      Distributed to depository libraries in microfiche.
 12 500      "June 1988."
 13 504      Includes bibliographical references.
 14 500      "GAO/PEMD-88-22."
 15 500      "B-229893"--P. [1].
 16 533      Microfiche. $b [Washington, D.C.] : $c Suptdocs, GPO, $d
1988. $e 2 microfiches : negative ; 11 x 15 cm. -- $f (GAO report ; B-
229893)
 17 650  0   Terrorism $z United States $x Prevention.
 18 650  0   Local transit $z United States $x Security measures.
 19 650  0   Courthouses $z United States $x Security measures.
 20 650  0   United States marshals.
 21 710 10   United States. $b General Accounting Office.
 22 740 01   Domestic antiterrorism efforts at selected sites.
```

Fig. 5.4. MARC fields in document records.

---

027 Standard Technical Report Number (STRN)
Field containing the number assigned to a technical report by the National Technical Information Service (NTIS) according to ANSI Standard Z39.23-1983. Only these numbers appear in Field 027.
    Ex.:   027 $a METPRO/ED/SR-77/035

037 Stock Number
Field containing acquisition information such as stock number, and acquisition source.[10]
    Ex.:   037 $a 240-951/147 $b GPO
            037 $a 001689 E $b Vienna Tourist Board

074 GPO Item Number
MARC field developed specifically for recording the U.S. Government Printing Office item number used by the depository distribution program. In older MARC records the item number is often found in Field 500 (General Note).
    Ex.:   074 $a 334-C-1
            074 $a 277-A-2 (microfiche)

086 Government Document Classification Number
Field containing the classification number officially assigned to a government document by the appropriate government agency at any level (e.g., state, national, international). When the field contains classification numbers other than the SuDoc or the Government of Canada, Department of Supply and Service catalogue numbers, the source of the classification is included in a subfield. Locally assigned numbers would not be recorded in Field 086.
    Ex.   086 0 $a HE 20.6209:13/45
          086 $a HEU/G74.3C49 $2 ordocs

088 Report Number
Field for recording all other technical report numbers.
    Ex.:   088 $a EPA-6001/2-76-224

500 General Note
Not a field typically containing documents information, but a frequent location of GPO Item Numbers and report numbers.
    Ex.:   500 $a "GAO/AFMD-91-17"
           500 $a Item no.: 1063-H

536 Funding Information Note
Not a widely applied field; however, if a publication is the result of funded research, this information may appear in Field 536, including contract, grant, or project numbers.
    Ex.:   536 $a Sponsored by the Advanced Research Projects Agency through the Office of Naval Research. $b N00014-68-A-0245-0007 $c ARPA Order No. 2616

949 Local Processing Information
OCLC/MARC field used by the U.S. GPO to indicate that the record is an "availability" record.[11] This field is not part of the master record in OCLC and would not be transferred in the course of routine cataloging, but does appear in any OCLC-MARC Subscription Service tapes.

OCLC/MARC record. Bibliographic description of government publications differs little from bibliographic description of other types of publications. Usually there is an "author,"[12] a title, publication information, and a physical description. With varying frequency of occurrence, the cataloging record may also contain notes, subject headings, series statements, additional access points for authors or corporate bodies, and other pertinent information. Figure 5.4 contains a brief outline of the MARC fields associated with the parts of a bibliographic record that are of special interest to documents librarians.

When discussing documents bibliographic records in the on-line catalog, one should consider the importance of these fields for the operations of the documents collection. Is indexing of the information in these fields necessary? Would keyword searching be sufficient for the retrieval of information contained in these fields? Furthermore, are there bibliographic policy issues (e.g., always including a specific field on documents records no matter what the cataloging data source) that should be explored?

Changes regularly take place in the MARC format as needs develop. Discussions began in the 1980s on "format integration" (that is, the merging and consolidation of the individual formats for books, serials, visual materials, maps, computer files, music, and archives/manuscripts).[13] A more recent development is the move toward representation of "multiple versions" on a single bibliographic record (e.g., the print document and its microfiche version). In 1992, the Library of Congress published its interim decisions on implementation of the recommendations developed at the Multiple Versions Forum in 1989.[14] This will simplify the cataloging of U.S. documents in cases in which the GPO has entered a bibliographic record for the paper, but the depository library received the microfiche version.[15] Instead of the local library having to create a new record for the fiche or having to teach patrons to look in two locations to determine if the needed item is owned, the information about the microfiche version can be added to the original print record.

Monographs and Serials

Typically, the distinction between monographs and serials[16] and the numerous title changes associated with serials was not of great importance to documents collections constrained by a paper-file environment. In moving to the on-line environment, where the rules of bibliographic description laid out in *Anglo-American Cataloguing Rules*, 2d edition, revised (*AACR2R*), and the *Library of Congress Rule Interpretations* (*LCRIs*) apply, this distinction comes into focus and becomes critical. Before further processing takes place, this basic categorization (monograph versus serial) should be determined. The rationale is one of saving effort and avoiding confusion. One would not want to catalog individually a publication that belonged to an already established bibliographic record (e.g., a single issue of a serial). Also, current cataloging rules require a separate bibliographic record each time the serial *title* changes. In the paper-file environment, new records were frequently created only when the class number (e.g., SuDoc) changed.

If an item has a numeric or chronologic designation (e.g., a volume number, issue number, or date), appears to be intended to continue indefinitely, and bears a title common to all issues, then it is likely to be a serial. Words in the title such as "newsletter," "bulletin," "journal," "yearbook," "annual," "monthly," "quarterly," etc., imply continuation and may be an indication that the publication is a serial. One should catalog based on that premise rather than on the item's call number, if one has been assigned by the government body distributing the item. This definition for determination of the seriality of a publication applies to other physical formats as well, including microfiche, maps, and electronic information.

Bibliographic Record Acquisition — One-by-One

One of the basic ideas behind the development of bibliographic utilities, such as OCLC, RLIN, and others, was to provide an economic and effective means of sharing cataloging records among libraries. Until these utilities matured, the Library of Congress had been the major source of cataloging data outside the local library. If LC had not cataloged an item, the library had to bear the cost of producing original cataloging.

The feasibility of cataloging documents increased dramatically with the development of these utilities, particularly when the U.S. GPO began entering cataloging data into OCLC in 1976. Libraries that had been cataloging government publications—whether state, local, federal, international, or foreign—were then able to share these records so that other libraries could take advantage of them. Even now, in 1993 (for state, local, international, and foreign government publications), there is no other means of obtaining cataloging for one's collection.[17] The procedure for capturing a bibliographic record from a utility is to search the new receipts one by one and transfer any matching records to the local system. If no matching record is found, the library may choose to provide original cataloging for the item, either at the full or minimal level of bibliographic description, and to contribute this record to the utility to which the library belongs.

Creating a local record on-line, either as a circulation record or as a provisional cataloging record, provides an alternative to original cataloging. The desirability of this alternative depends on the retrievability of the information contained in these types of records by one's local system. As it is unlikely that these records will be included in a common database provided by one of the utilities, a disadvantage of this option is the limited availability of the information to other libraries that acquire the same publications.

Research is needed into the costs of one-by-one record creation. Pricing structures of some utilities now provide incentives to libraries contributing original cataloging records, while lowering the cost of using an existing record. Does this incentive make original cataloging of documents more cost-effective for a library? How much cataloging data is available for government publications from various types of governments? During the last decade, many state libraries have undertaken the cataloging of publications issued by the state agencies and have contributed these records to one or the other of the utilities. How comprehensive and widespread is this coverage? There have always been libraries that cataloged foreign and international government organization publications as part of their general collections. Has this amount increased significantly? Record creation and shelflist maintenance in manual systems also have a cost that has not been measured. How does this cost compare with the searching, matching, transfer, and/or original cataloging costs in an on-line system using a bibliographic utility?

Bibliographic Record Acquisition — Tape Loads

For United States government publications, machine-readable magnetic tape services form an alternative to the one-by-one method. Current vendors of these services are OCLC, Inc., and MARCIVE, Inc. The premise of both services is to supply the cataloging records produced on OCLC by the U.S. GPO, comprising either the entire file from 1976 to the present or portions of that file, based on a profile of the individual library's federal document collection.

The profile consists of providing the vendor with a list of item numbers selected by the library, including the dates of selection or deselection of the item. A library may also make profile decisions based on the SuDoc classification number stem. Besides the bibliographic records on tape, in a format suitable for loading into most automated library systems, these services also can provide card sets, shelflist cards, and call number labels, and can attach the library's holdings symbol to the bibliographic record in the OCLC database for interlibrary loan purposes.[18]

The seeming ease with which a large number of records can be acquired without much labor investment, and the relatively low cost for these services, have made them attractive to the documents community. However, there are drawbacks. When the first libraries loaded these tapes, it became immediately apparent that there were problems with the quality of the cataloging. Some of these problems were caused by GPO catalogers' misunderstanding of the rules for bibliographic description and subject analysis; some by the changes caused in the formation of access points under *AACR2R*; and some by the lack of a clear understanding of the technicalities of tape production.[19]

In 1987, MARCIVE, Inc., in cooperation with librarians at Louisiana State University, Rice University, and Texas A&M University, began a project to address the bibliographic control issues in the "cleanup" of the GPO tapes. By 1989, the cleanup process had resulted in a database of about 225,000 records, with nearly 78,000 records deleted from the original tapes.[20] Efforts continue to monitor the database as it is produced by MARCIVE to assure the quality of the tape products.

The twin issues of matching the records received on tape with a library's actual holdings and the time lag between receipt of the publications and receipt of the cataloging records also cause concern among documents librarians choosing this method. Because the profiling of records is based on the item number, there will be cases when the library receives a cataloging record for a publication that should have been received under that item number, but was not (because of a rain check or claim). Other likely mismatches include recently deselected or added item numbers and incorrect or missing item numbers in the cataloging record (MARC field 074). Research reported in 1990 indicated a 93.4 percent rate of exact matches between bibliographic records received on tape and actual publications.[21] By most standards, this rate is within acceptable norms; however, the *Guidelines for Depository Libraries* require a depository to maintain a record of each publication received, down to the piece level. To meet this guideline, the library must devise a way—automatically or manually—to match each incoming tape record with the document itself.

The time lag between receipt of the document and receipt of the tape catalog record creates an additional complication in the matching process. Several studies have shown that the time lag between receipt and cataloging availability is three to six months.[22] A methodology for recording receipt of the publication must be used until the record is available on-line. Libraries have dealt with this time lag in several ways, and as yet no standardized, universally adopted procedure has emerged. Some libraries create manual shelflists or databases of new receipts and then match cards acquired from the tape vendor against the shelflist or database. Unless the shelflist or database is marked or arranged by receipt date, this method will catch only items for which the catalog records are received. It will not identify publications for which there is no vendor cataloging record. Another approach involves holding new receipts in a special area and searching the individual publications against each new tape load. This avoids the problem of the previous method, but hinders access to newly received documents, which are more likely to be in high demand. An alternative is to barcode the documents upon receipt and apply a duplicate barcode on the shipping list next to each entry. When records are loaded, the entries on the shipping list can be searched and matched.

On-line systems usually allow for the creation of records locally, either in the circulation module, the cataloging module, or both. Another possibility for managing the time lag occurs when one creates a local record upon receipt, then overlays the record with the incoming tape record. The problem here is one of developing a matching algorithm. Systems with automatic overlay functions usually depend on the System Control Number (MARC field 001) or another unique numeric field, such as 010 (LC Control Number) and 020 or 022 (ISBN or ISSN), for the match. Most frequently, the only unique number associated with U.S. documents is the SuDoc classification number. A matching algorithm based on this number may require programming modifications to the local system software.

Much more research into the costs associated with profiling a collection, maintaining the records necessary to satisfy GPO requirements, and matching receipts with incoming tapes is needed. Then, the comparison of cost should be made between the one-by-one methodology and tape loads to determine which is most effective for current processing of U.S. government publications.

Retrospective Conversion

To date, few large-scale retrospective conversion projects for government documents collections have been reported in the literature. Several libraries have converted their U.S. documents collections by loading the GPO tapes from 1976 to a locally determined cutoff date. With this approach, the problem of matching actual holdings to records loaded remains. Some libraries have solved this by "smart barcoding" the collection (i.e., taking advantage of local system programming to produce a barcode for each bibliographic record added to the database, then physically applying those barcodes to the publications). The leftovers would most likely be items that are now missing from the collection or were never received. Publications not receiving barcodes in this manner would be candidates for other retrospective conversion projects. Other libraries merely load the records and match with holdings as items circulate.

In 1990 to 1992, the University of Kentucky conducted a hit-rate study of pre-1977 imprints from the U.S. Department of Agriculture, the Department of Interior, and the Smithsonian Institution as preparation for applying for retrospective conversion grants. The sample of documents included in the study was randomly selected from the *Checklist of United States Public Documents, 1789-1970: A Dual Media Edition of the U.S. Superintendent of Documents Public Documents Library Shelf Lists*, in which documents are listed according to the status of the originating issuing agency (i.e., currently active as a unit of government or no longer active or "dead"). Each publication in the sample was checked in the OCLC database to determine the existence of cataloging copy. However, no evaluation of the completeness or quality of these records was undertaken as part of this study. Preliminary indications are that there is a 59 percent hit rate for "dead" agencies.[23] These preliminary statistics are encouraging and suggest that retrospective conversion projects for pre-1976 United States documents are feasible.

CLASSIFICATION

Chapter 4 discussed the principles behind choosing classification schemes for government publications collections. The system(s) chosen will determine when in the technical processing workflow the numbers should be assigned to individual publications. If the classification system is based on the provenance of the document, it is easier to assign the classification number early in the process, before the bibliographic record is created (e.g., in the case of the U.S. depository, United Nations, Canadian, and some states, the classification number arrives with the document). If the system is subject-based, the classification number may not be assigned until after the bibliographic record is developed (e.g., in the Library of Congress system). The following sections deal with issues unique to the SuDoc classification that are important for documents librarians to consider.

Locally Assigned SuDoc Numbers

United States documents collections frequently contain many publications not received through the GPO Depository Library program. The GPO recommends two ways of locally assigning SuDoc numbers so that these publications may be filed with others from the same agency.[24] If the publication would usually be assigned an existing class stem,[25] the library could assign that stem with an appropriate Cutter number, and place an "x" at the end of the number to differentiate it from a number assigned by the GPO. If there is no appropriate existing class stem, the library may create one by adding a "slashed-on" number to a similar stem and then completing the number.

Class Corrections

Over the years, dependence on the *Monthly Catalog of United States Government Publications* for identification and retrieval of U.S. documents has created a situation in which the "correctness" of the SuDoc number is a concern. The classification number assigned and distributed on the shipping list with the documents is sometimes incorrect. Often this error will have been found before the *Monthly Catalog* is printed; therefore, the number that appears in the *Catalog* does not match the number that the library put on the document when it was received. Following publication of an issue of the *Catalog*, the GPO may also identify other classification errors. The GPO has tried to rectify these errors in two ways: (1) by publishing shipping list corrections; and (2) by publishing the "Corrections for Previous *Monthly Catalog*" in the prefatory pages of each *Monthly Catalog* issue. Shipping list corrections and *Monthly Catalog* corrections contain classification and item number distribution errors of varying degrees of significance for retrieval. Standard practice among depository librarians has been to make these corrections on the documents, the shelflist or card catalog, and in the printed *Monthly Catalog*; some in the past even made corrections on the original shipping list.

The development of CD-ROM versions of the *Monthly Catalog* and the distribution of GPO cataloging on tape have added a new complication to the decision of whether to make all the class corrections that the GPO identifies. Presently, the extent to which CD-ROM producers make the classification corrections is unclear. However, tape vendors are beginning to experiment with providing update tapes that include the corrections.

It is possible, as more documents collections go on-line, that the accuracy with which the SuDoc number listed on the shipping list matches the *Monthly Catalog* number will become less important. It seems in this scenario that the most serious error would be a duplicate class number. Checking for this at the time of record input, or later through a batch duplicate call number error report generated by the local on-line system, would be logical options. However, errors in the SuDoc stem (that portion of the number up to the colon) should still be corrected, as discrepancies in this area affect the archival arrangement of the collection.

Reclassification

Before the SuDoc classification scheme became the standard, many libraries developed their own arrangements. However, in the typical course of events, these libraries switched from the local system to SuDoc and undertook a major reclassification project. These projects involved identifying a SuDoc number for each document in the collection and remarking the piece and the shelflist or card catalog. Figure 5.5 includes many bibliographies and finding lists that contain SuDoc numbers helpful in such a reclassification project.

Fig. 5.5. Finding Aids for SuDoc Classification Numbers.

1789-1909	Checklist of United States Public Documents, 1789-1909. 3rd ed. rev. and enl. Washington, DC: U.S. Government Printing Office, 1911.
1789-1909	CIS Index to U.S. Executive Branch Documents, 1789-1909: Guide to Documents Listed in Checklist of U.S. Public Documents 1780-1909, Not Printed in the U.S. Serial Set. Washington, DC: Congressional Information Service, 1990-91.
1789-1970	Checklist of U.S. Public Documents, 1789-1970. Washington, DC: U.S. Historical Documents Institute, 1975.
1789-1976	Cumulative Title Index to United States Public Documents, 1789-1976. Arlington, VA: U.S. Historical Documents Institute, 1979-82.
1833-1969	CIS US Congressional Committee Hearings Index, 23rd-91st Congresses, 1833-1969. Washington, DC: Congressional Information Service, 1981-85.
1895-1924	Monthly Catalog of Government Publications with Superintendent of Documents Classification Numbers Added, 1895-1924. Arlington, VA: Carrollton Press, 1975.
ca.1900-1989	Guide to U.S. Government Publications. Donna Andriot. 1990 ed. McLean, VA: Documents Index, 1990.
1924-	Monthly Catalog of United States Government Publications Washington, DC: U.S. Government Printing Office.
1910-1924	Documents Office Classification Numbers for Cuttered Documents, 1910-1924. Mary Elizabeth Poole and Ella Frances Smith. Ann Arbor, MI: University Microfilms, 1974.
-1969	CIS US Congressional Committee Prints Index: From the Earliest Publications Through 1969. Washington, DC: Congressional Information Service, 1980.
-1976	Documents Office Classification. Mary Elizabeth Poole. 5th ed. Arlington, VA: U.S. Historical Documents Institute, 1976.
1970-	CIS Index to Publications of the United States Congress. Washington, D.C.: Congressional Information Service, 1970-.
1960s-	American Statistics Index. Washington, D.C.: Congressional Information Service, 1973-.
1977-	GPO Sales Publications Reference File (PRF). Washington, DC: U.S. Government Printing Office.
1979/81-	Out-of-Print GPO Sales Publications Reference File. Washington, DC: U.S. Government Printing Office.
Current	List of Classes of United States Government Publications Available for Selection by Depository Libraries. Washington, DC: Depository Administration Branch, Library Division, Library Programs Service, U.S. GPO.

Another type of reclassification decision involves serials with a publishing history that spans different issuing agencies. In the SuDoc system, each time the issuing agency changes, the classification number also changes. This means that a single serial may be located in several places within the documents collection. In the early 1970s, there was a heated debate in *Library Resources and Technical Services* over whether the library should reclassify serials to the most recent SuDoc number.[26] Most commentators supported not reclassifying, because of the amount of staff time it would take to relabel the documents and the shelflists or card catalogs and the time it would take to shift collections to make room. Reclassifying also would disrupt the archival intention of the classification in keeping all publications of an agency together.

It is possible that the structures for representing serial holdings in on-line catalogs will reopen this debate. Some library system configurations assume that all issues of a serial title will have the same call number, and they structure holdings records accordingly. Documents librarians are beginning to raise the question of how to handle split runs in this situation. For now, the solution will depend on the individual library catalog. One hopes that documents librarians using a particular type of on-line catalog will share information and ideas so that standard practices for that catalog can begin to emerge.

SPECIAL ISSUES

Several problems in documents processing remain largely unsolved. These problems exist because (1) the focus has been on acquiring bibliographic access; (2) the issue has not received the analysis necessary to resolve it; (3) or the medium of publication is rapidly changing and all issues have not been fully defined. This section attempts to outline these situations. As automation is applied to more documents collections, other issues are likely to be identified.

Serials Control

Even though the vast majority of government publications is serial in nature, few articles have appeared in the literature regarding serials control for government publications. In 1985, Mary Sue Stephenson and Gary R. Purcell wrote an analysis of on-line serials control systems then available for documents serials check-in.[27] Since then, many on-line catalogs have developed serials control modules through which a library can display bound and unbound receipts of issues. Subscription agents such as Faxon, Ebsco, and others have also developed on-line check-in systems that can be functionally integrated with automated catalogs. In addition, some vendors have developed stand-alone personal computer-based check-in systems. Database management software, such as that used for producing item card files, can also be adapted to perform serial holdings functions.

Two factors should remain uppermost in the librarian's mind when choosing serials control methods. First is the ability to communicate holdings directly to the patron. If there is a serials control module in the on-line catalog, this is the most efficient method. Unless the PC-based methods are connected in a LAN, a staff intermediary will be required before the patron can learn whether a specific issue is held. A second consideration is the ability to record each piece. This is particularly important for U.S. documents management to meet the GPO requirement of a holdings record to the piece level.

Serials Within Series

A monographic series frequently contains one or more serial titles. Usually cataloging agencies have "analyzed" the series, creating a separate monographic format record for each monograph title within the series and a serial format record for each serial title. Each bibliographic record (monographic and serial) will have a MARC field 4XX that contains information about the monographic series. This seems to serve the patron well, as there is then access by the specific title of the monograph or serial as well as access by the series name and number.

There are several monographic series issued by the United States government that contain serials. These have had a variety of treatments in both bibliographic description and classification. This varied history of practices and GPO policies has made "serials within series" a problematic issue for documents librarians. The Current Population Reports series is a ready example. When the GPO began cataloging this series, it treated it bibliographically as described in the preceding paragraph, yet continued to classify it according to the monographic series numbering (e.g., C 3. 186:P-20). This meant that the individual issues of a serial within this series, such as *Fertility of American Women*, would be intermixed on the shelf with other titles in the same series. In an attempt to change this situation and in response to comments from the documents community, the GPO began to assign unique SuDoc numbers to these serials (e.g., C 3. 186/10:1990 [*Fertility of American Women*, 1990]). This brought the individual publications together on the shelf, but meant a decision on reclassification of the earlier volumes to the new number. In recent years, the GPO has sometimes reverted to the original numbering system of the series, while continuing to analyze each series according to its bibliographic format.

The documents librarian must decide how this issue should be treated in the on-line catalog. If the serials control or holdings display information is flexible enough in the local system, one can catalog the serial as it should be, use the SuDoc classification number that brings the serials together on the shelf, and display for the patron the individual issues of the serial as well as their numbering within the monographic series. If the system is not sufficiently flexible, one must decide which access points are most important and teach reference staff to deal with those "quirks" in the system.

Electronic Formats

The most recent development of concern in technical processing for documents librarians is the growing distribution of government information in electronic format. Catalogers increasingly discuss the concept of cataloging journals, electronic journals, bulletin boards, and even other library catalogs available on the networks, in addition to the more "traditional" publications distributed on floppy disk, magnetic tape, and CD-ROM.

Fields specifically designed to contain data about electronic publications expand the USMARC format to accommodate these types of publications. Therefore, creation of a bibliographic record is possible, although the completeness of a record often depends on the equipment available to the cataloger. Many electronic publications require that the disk or CD be loaded with appropriate hardware and software before the cataloger can describe fully the system requirements and the scope of the information contained. Printed documentation also helps in this process. Unfortunately, much of the electronic information currently being distributed often arrives in the documents collection without documentation of any type, and frequently also without the software necessary to load and manipulate the data. This in turn affects the cataloging of the item in hand.

To provide the best bibliographic access for patrons, it is important that electronic publications be included in the library catalog along with other types of documents, though effective use is likely to require intervention by the documents librarian. As more experience with this material develops, more sophisticated ways of providing access are likely to emerge.

NOTES

[1]*Guidelines for the Depository Library System* (Washington, DC: U.S. Government Printing Office, 1988), point no. 5-2.

[2]Several automated library systems have a label-producing capability as part of the bibliographic processing module. If documents are to be entered into the online catalog, it might be worthwhile to use this feature, if available.

[3]The *Guidelines* make this explicit for U.S. documents. See chapter 6, appendix 6.1, of this book for text of these guidelines on this point.

[4]*Administrative Notes* 12 (January 15, 1991): 19.

[5]"ARL Statistics, 1990-91, Instructions for Completing the Questionnaire," 1-2.

[6]"IPEDS, Integrated Postsecondary Education Data System, Academic Libraries, 1990."

[7]The texts listed in chapter 4, note 3, contain detailed descriptions of paper files used to control documents collections.

[8]Walt Crawford, *MARC for Library Use: Understanding Integrated USMARC*, 2d ed. (Boston: G. K. Hall, 1989), 8.

[9]U.S. Library of Congress, *USMARC Formats for Bibliographic Data* (Washington, DC: Library of Congress, 1988).

[10] In 1991, the GPO agreed to routinely put the NASA Technical Report number—a number frequently used by patrons and which is not a standard report number by the Z39.23-1983 definition—into the MARC 037 field.

[11] *Availability record* is the term used by the GPO for "piece-level cataloging records for individual issues of serials or volumes of multipart monographs. For example, there will be an availability record in the *Monthly Catalog* and on the GPO tape for each issue of an annual report, but each of these records has the same OCLC control number and is derived from a single OCLC record." "Definitions ... 6/24/89," *Administrative Notes* (June 1989).

[12] *Author* here is used in the general sense to mean any personal, corporate, or governmental body or conference name associated with the creation of the intellectual content of a work. For the sake of simplicity, "uniform titles" (the standardized title by which a work is known) have been grouped with authors.

[13] Fuller discussions of this can be found in Walt Crawford, *MARC for Library Use: Understanding Integrated USMARC*, 2d ed. (Boston: G. K. Hall, 1989); and Deborah J. Byrne, *MARC Manual: Understanding and Using MARC Records* (Englewood, CO: Libraries Unlimited, 1991).

[14] "Linking Bibliographic Records for Microreproductions to Records for Originals (Monographs)," *Cataloging Service Bulletin* 55 (Winter 1992): 38-42.

[15] From 1977 to 1992, GPO policy required cataloging "the archival version of a publication in the original format in which it was published" rather than the format in which it was distributed to depository libraries. The change to cataloging microreproductions was announced in March 1992 in "Cataloging Policy Changed for Documents Converted to Microfiche," *Administrative Notes* 13 (March 31, 1992): 9.

[16] *Serials* is the generic word used to describe publications such as journals, periodicals, magazines, newspapers, annual reports, proceedings, numbered monographic series, etc.

[17] RLIN began loading records from the United Nations Bibliographic Information System (UNBIS) in October 1991, corresponding to the data contained in the print products *UNDOC: Current Index* and the monthly *Current Bibliographic Information*. The records are in MARC format, but lack many data elements, such as personal or corporate authors, series statements, notes, and Library of Congress subject headings.

[18] For information on the details of the specific services offered by each vendor, interested libraries should contact OCLC, Inc., and MARCIVE, Inc., directly.

[19] Judy E. Myers, "The Government Printing Office Cataloging Records: Opportunities and Problems," *Government Information Quarterly* 2 (1985): 27-56; and Carolyn C. Jamison [Sherayko], "Loading the GPO Tapes: What Does It Really Mean?," *Government Publications Review* 13 (1986): 549-59.

[20]Myrtle Smith Bolner and Barbara Kile, "Documents to the People: Access Through the Automated Catalog," *Government Publications Review* 18 (1991): 51-64.

[21]Margaret T. Mooney, "Matching Library Holdings Against GPO Tapes: Issues, Concerns, and Solutions," *Government Publications Review* 17 (1990): 424.

[22]Margaret S. Powell, Deborah Smith Johnston, and Ellen P. Conrad, "The Use of OCLC for Cataloging U.S. Government Publications: A Feasibility Study," *Government Publications Review* 14 (1987): 61-76; Michael A. DiCarlo, "U.S. Government Document Collections and the IOLS," in *Proceedings of the Conference on Integrated On-line Library Systems* (Canfield, OH: Genaway & Associates, 1984), 195-200; Cynthia E. Bower, "OCLC Records for Federal Depository Documents: A Preliminary Investigation," *Government Information Quarterly* 1 (1984): 379-400; Margaret T. Mooney, "GPO Cataloging: Is It a Viable Current Access Tool for U.S. Documents?" *Government Publications Review* 16 (May/June 1989): 259-70.

[23]Private communications of May 28, 1992, and June 5, 1992.

[24]"Locally Assigned SuDocs Numbers," in *A Practical Guide to the Superintendent of Documents Classification System*, edited by Jorge E. Ponce (Washington, DC: U.S. Goverment Printing Office, 1985), 49.

[25]The *List of Classes of United States Government Publications Available for Selection by Depository Libraries* (Washington, DC: U.S. Government Printing Office) contains the most current listing of SuDoc class stems. New stems are added in the "Update to the List of Classes" in *Administrative Notes*. Mary Elizabeth Poole's *Documents Office Classification*, 5th ed. (Arlington, VA: U.S. Historical Documents Institute, 1976) contains stems assigned to older documents.

[26]R. M. Simmons, "Handling Changes in Superintendent of Documents Classification," *Library Resources and Technical Services* 15 (Spring 1971): 241-44; Irene Shubert, "Superintendent of Documents Classification," *Library Resources and Technical Services* 15 (Fall 1971): 547; LeRoy Schwarzkopf, "Comments on 'Handling Changes in Superintendent of Documents Classification' by R. M. Simmons," *Library Resources and Technical Services* 16 (Winter 1972): 95-75; Jack W. Lyle, "Utilizing the Superintendent of Documents System Without Reclassification," *Library Resources and Technical Services* 16 (Fall 1972): 497-99; R. M. Simmons, "SUDOCS Classification," *Library Resources and Technical Services* 17 (Summer 1973): 354-56; LeRoy Schwarzkopf, "Reply," *Library Resources and Technical Services* 17 (Summer 1973): 356-58; Jai L. Yun, "SUDOCS Classification—More," *Library Resources and Technical Services* 17 (Summer 1973): 358-59; LeRoy Schwarzkopf, "SUDOCS Classification—More," *Library Resources and Technical Services* 17 (Summer 1973): 359-60.

[27]Mary Sue Stephenson and Gary R. Purcell, "The Automation of Government Publications: Functional Requirements and Selected Software Systems for Serials Control," *Government Information Quarterly* 2 (1985): 57-76.

6

Collection Maintenance

Sandra K. Peterson
Documents Librarian
Government Documents Center, Seeley G. Mudd Library
Yale University

Most depository program agreements and guidelines outline the depository library's responsibilities for care and maintenance of the collection. The U.S. Government Printing Office (GPO) most clearly articulates what is expected in its guidelines, *Instructions to Depository Libraries* (see appendix 6.1):

> As a minimum standard for the care and maintenance of depository property, the Government Printing Office insists that the maintenance accorded to depository materials be no less than that given to commercially published publications.[1]

The United Nations Secretariat, the Canadian Communications Group-Publishing, and the European Communities Office for the Official Publications also include a statement to the effect that all materials received on deposit be processed, *kept in good order*, and made accessible to the public.

This chapter addresses the practical aspects of maintaining a government publications collection, including space planning, stack maintenance, special materials and publication patterns, preservation techniques, weeding procedures, and collection maintenance recordkeeping.

ORGANIZATION

Earlier chapters of this text outlined the arguments for separate versus integrated collections and any other resulting variations. The need to maintain materials is the same no matter how the collection is organized. Government publications present some unique maintenance problems because they are a mix of large and small pamphlets, books, and periodicals, with an unusually high percentage of materials in pamphlet format. Also, when the Superintendent of Documents (SuDoc) classification scheme is used, the classification number for a single title may have changed many times to reflect government reorganizations. Each of these factors has an impact on collection maintenance and planning.

Closed Stacks

Some libraries use closed or limited-access shelving areas because the space allocated for government publications is inappropriate for public access. Closed stacks have some advantages. They usually reduce the number of misshelved or misplaced publications and the need for periodic shelf-reading. Also, fewer return shelves are needed. Special shelving arrangements, such as for oversize documents, changes in classification numbers, or mixed formats (fiche, paper, diskettes), are easier to maintain and explain to staff than to the casual user. However, there are two major disadvantages to a closed-stack arrangement. First, it is very expensive to have stack attendants for retrieval available during all the hours the collection is open. Second, users lose the browsing capability that is provided by an open-stack arrangement. Browsing is a factor in access even for those collections classified by the Superintendent of Documents or United Nations provenance-based classification scheme.

Open Stacks

As suggested, open stacks allow users direct access to the materials and reduce the cost of retrieval for libraries. However, open stacks for government documents do require special accommodations. To assist users in retrieving materials from open stacks, guides and signs are extremely important. The Superintendent of Documents classification scheme organizes materials in a manner different from most book classification schemes, and the length and complexity of the numbers tend to intimidate users. A copy of the Superintendent of Documents classification scheme poster, available from the U.S. Government Printing Office, posted near the stacks will help the user understand the scheme. It is useful to create and post maps of the stack areas, with pointers to any special shelving areas (e.g., oversize materials). Stack range guides with the beginning and ending classification numbers for each range are also helpful.

The collection should be shelved in exact shelflist order. This is especially important in open stacks. However, most collections have some special shelving arrangements. Examples include oversize, reference, and current periodicals. Also, titles may be in two or more formats—paper, microform, or electronic. When the classification numbers change, earlier or later issues of a title may be shelved in a different location. These variations should be noted on the volume, in the shelflist, in the on-line catalog, and on the shelf with dummies or shelf holders.

Aids for Stack Maintenance

The mix of pamphlets, books, and periodicals that are found in government documents stacks is more easily shelved when a variety of shelf aids are used. Aids include:

- pamphlet boxes or files—plastic, metal, or fiberboard
- pamphlet binders

82 □ Collection Maintenance

- acid-free folders
- cork-bottom (non-slide) bookends, both small and large, preferably with a flange for additional support
- spring-wire book holders that attach to the shelf above.

Large bookends constructed of heavy-gauge steel with a flange are recommended for use with large, heavy volumes, such as the decennial census volumes.

Maintaining the order of large paper sets, such as the House and Senate documents and reports or the *Current Industrial Reports*, is easier when the sets are filed in appropriately labeled pamphlet boxes or files; they are also easier for the user to retrieve if filed in this manner. Extremely small items, such as *Statistics in Brief*, if placed in labeled acid-free folders, are less likely to be damaged or disappear from the shelves.

Ideally, in open stacks, one shelf in each stack range is designated as a return shelf. Use different colored shelves if possible, or use tape to color-code return shelves. At a minimum, provide a return truck or shelf, clearly labeled as such, near the entrance/exit of the stack areas.

Space Planning

The reorganization of government agencies, and the subsequent changes in classification numbers, as well as the creation of new agencies, create a challenge for space planning. Other factors, including the requirement to retain publications for at least five years, the heavy use of pamphlet files that add to space requirements, and the unusual proportion of oversize materials that reduces the number of shelves per section, have an impact on the shelving space needed for government publications.

To determine the overall growth of the collection and to project the amount of shelving space needed, establish a "pieces per linear foot" count for your collection. Count and measure daily all materials that are permanently added to the collection (exclude slip laws, slip treaties, and paper House and Senate documents and reports that can be discarded in preference to a permanent volume later). Divide the number of pieces received by the number of linear feet added to obtain the pieces per linear foot count. In 1979, Catharine Reynolds established a standard for the regional depository collection at the University of Colorado as 52 pieces per linear foot.[2] Although this figure is often used in space planning for government documents, the count for collections may vary depending upon the types of material the library selects.

SPECIAL PATTERNS OF PUBLISHING

United States federal government agencies, as well as foreign and international governments, publish in a variety of patterns that require special handling and that make them exceptions to the rule of retention for at least five years. These special patterns include cumulations, superseded editions, and transmittals or supplements.

Cumulations

Indexes are one of the best examples of a cumulative publication—for instance, the annual index that supersedes the monthly, bimonthly, quarterly, or semiannual indexes. Examples of titles with indexes that cumulate include the *Monthly Catalog of U.S. Government Publications*, the *Monthly Checklist of State Publications*, the *Weekly Compilation of Presidential Documents*, and *Resources in Education*. Sometimes the entire volume, both index and abstracts, is cumulated on a regular or irregular basis (e.g., the five-year cumulations of the *EPA Publications Bibliography*).

Another type of cumulation is a title in which preliminary or advance releases are replaced by a cumulated volume. Examples are slip laws, slip treaties, slip opinions, House and Senate documents and reports, and advance data sheets, such as those for the *Vital Statistics of the United States*.

Superseded Editions

United States federal selective depositories have the option of retaining only the latest edition of some titles. Appendix C of the *Instructions to Depository Libraries* lists specific titles for which superseded editions may be discarded. Local needs and historical collections, as outlined in a collection development policy, may dictate retention, but the list in Appendix C serves as a guide to what is superseded and may be withdrawn. Shelflist and bibliographic records should be revised to reflect the withdrawal of superseded materials.

Other depository collections (United Nations, European Community, etc.) do not address superseded editions directly. Many United Nations "mimeographed" documents are republished in the supplements or annexes to the *Official Records*. Each issue of *UNDOC: Current Index* contains a list. In this instance, withdrawal is a time-consuming process, and it adds an additional step to the retrieval process.

Transmittals, Errata, and Supplements

Another pattern of publishing is the loose-leaf volume that is updated with supplements, transmittals, or errata sheets. The replaced pages may be discarded. Upon receipt of a supplement, transmittal, or errata sheet, the basic volume should be removed from the shelf and the updated pages filed or the pen-and-ink changes made. Most supplements and transmittals are accompanied by an instruction sheet detailing the pages to be removed or replaced. Some volumes have a sheet on which to record the date when the transmittal or supplement is filed. In the absence of such a sheet, the cover sheet from the transmittal can be filed in the front of the volume to indicate that the transmittal has been filed. It is important to record which transmittals and supplements have been filed and to be certain to file them in order of publication.

84 □ Collection Maintenance

Transmittals and supplements frequently create problems in the depository for one or more reasons:

1. Supplements and transmittals are received for which there is no basic volume;

2. Supplements and transmittals are received in a different format from the basic manual, or vice versa; and

3. Supplements and transmittals are missed or skipped.

In 1982, the U.S. Government Printing Office offered an explanation and directions to the depository libraries regarding basic manuals and their updates. The explanation was that by the time the GPO identifies and surveys a title to determine the number of depository copies needed, the basic manual often has already been printed. Until a depository count is determined from the survey, Library Programs Service (GPO) orders only two copies. Thus, copies of the basic manual may not be available to depository libraries until the agency reissues a consolidated reprint or a new basic manual. Meanwhile, transmittal sheets will be sent to depository libraries. The GPO suggested that in such cases, an effort be made by the depository library to purchase the basic manual from GPO Sales.[3] The GPO's suggestion may not be a viable alternative for many titles. For example, in 1991 a subscription to the three basic volumes for the *General Wage Determinations Issued Under the Davis-Bacon and Related Acts* totaled nearly $1,000. When basic manuals are incomplete (missing transmittals or supplements), place a notice on the front cover indicating that the volume is incomplete and/or not updated. For sources citing to legal issues, this is particularly important.

Other methods for handling transmittals without basic manuals are to request a copy directly from the agency (sometimes successful); to request a copy from Documents Expediting Service (for members only); or to shelve transmittals and supplements with the note: "no basic manual available." Librarians must decide, based on their users, how much time can be spent in pursuing the basic manual and whether it is really used. If it is not used, it might be best to deselect the title, if that can be done without affecting other titles on that item number.

Changes in technology may be the solution to incomplete or missing manuals. Agencies have begun issuing manuals that require updating on compact disc; for example, the Occupational Safety and Health manuals and the *Federal Acquisitions Regulations* are now available on CD-ROM. If this becomes a trend, such publications would guarantee a complete manual and would eliminate the filing time needed in the library.

SPECIAL HANDLING REQUIRED

Documents collections contain information in many formats, including microfiche, maps, posters, diskettes, compact discs, cassette tapes, and videos. To preserve, secure, and provide access to nonbook materials, special handling is required.

Microfiche

Fifteen years ago, the Government Printing Office began distributing depository publications in microfiche. Depositories receive microfiche through other depository programs as well as by purchase. There are three types of microfiche: diazo, vesicular, and silver halide. It is essential that you know what type(s) your library is receiving. As it is not easy to tell them apart by sight, it is best to ask the distributing agent or the company from which you purchase the materials. The Government Printing Office distributes diazo microfiche. It can withstand patron use and high temperatures and should be stored in acid-free containers or file cabinets. Silver halide microfiche are preferred for their archival quality, but the archival quality is achieved when the microfiche is infrequently used. Frequent use with ungloved hands will wear this type of microfiche quickly. Silver halide microfiche should never be interfiled with diazo or vesicular microfiche and ideally should be stored in separate cabinets.

Microfiche received from depository programs usually requires no additional labeling if the library uses the classification or accession number that appears in the microfiche headers (i.e., Superintendent of Documents, UN Series Symbol, Queen's Printer) for filing. Occasionally the GPO distributes agency-produced microfiche that do not have standard header information, that is, the Superintendent of Documents classification number is not included. Or the microfiche header may simply contain incorrect information (title, report number, classification number). Corrections can be typed onto acid-free microfiche labels or strips and placed over incorrect information. The labels may have to be cut so that they do not obliterate any other vital information on the microfiche header. GPO fiche arrives in acid-free envelopes and libraries are required to stamp each piece with the depository stamp. Stamp-pad ink with a pH value of no less than 7.0 should be used for this purpose.

Maintaining a microfiche collection is facilitated by the generous use of guides in file drawers. Guides that explain a special filing order and guides directing users to another format (paper or electronic) are also useful. A supply of acid-free "microfiche in use" cards, with signs encouraging users to put one in each time a microfiche is removed, will simplify the refiling process. Format indicators—a stamp or code—should be included in shelflist and on-line catalogs. When the collection contains several different microform sets, it is helpful to color-code each set; use matching colored labels on the microfiche drawers where the collection is stored and on the indexes that provide access to the collection.

Maps

When the Geological Survey and the Defense Mapping Agency mapping programs were brought into the federal depository program, government documents librarians became more aware of the maps in their collections. Depository collections have always included maps; in fact, historical collections contain some very valuable charts and maps.

86 ☐ **Collection Maintenance**

Depository librarians have several options: selectively house maps in the library's map collection; acquire the supplies, skills, and equipment necessary to house them in the documents area; or employ some combination of the first two methods. The first step is to identify the maps in the collection (see appendix 6.2)—current receipts as well as historical holdings.

Maps should be stored flat in acid-free map folders, preferably in map cases or drawers. Approximately 50 maps can be stored in each folder, with a maximum of 250 maps per map drawer. If map cases are unavailable, then storing them flat in acid-free folders on folio shelves is another option. The map folders should be labeled with their contents. The classification number should be written on a lower corner of each map, in a standard location. The word "map" should be placed either above or below the classification number; shelflist and/or catalog records should carry the same notation.

When storing maps flat is not an option, folding them and storing them in legal-sized file cabinets should be considered. Fold maps so that any identifying writing is on the outside, thus reducing the amount of folding and unfolding necessary. Stewart suggests folding coastal charts in an accordion style with the printed surface exposed.[4]

Many depositories have extensive collections of historical maps that have been folded and stored as books on shelves. After identifying these, consult with map curators and preservation specialists to establish preservation priorities and to learn preservation techniques. Professional restoration is expensive, but in-house preservation is possible. In 1988, Jones-Eddy and Zwinger detailed their library's effort in preserving maps.[5]

Posters

Posters, like maps, should be stored flat. To protect them from dust, store them in acid-free folders, either in map drawers or on folio shelves. Label the folders and write the classification number in a standard location on the piece. As with other materials in special locations, annotate the shelflist and catalog records, place a shelf holder in the stacks, and label the item with the special location. Item numbers for posters are listed in appendix 6.3; however, an occasional poster will be distributed under other item numbers. Some libraries have created special finding aids for poster collections.[6]

Nonprint Materials

The number and type of nonprint materials in documents collections have increased in the last two years. Some nonprint materials are published as separate entities, accompanied by documentation, and some are published as a part of a printed book or journal. Libraries are handling nonprint materials in many different ways.

The option most frequently noted for disks or cassettes that accompany printed material is to separate the disk from the book or periodical. If it is possible, and if the library has the resources to do so, a back-up copy is created. The master disk is stored in a secure location within the department (reserve shelves, for example); the back-up copy circulates; and the book or periodical is shelved as usual, but with a notation indicating that a disk is available. The catalog record should also indicate that supplementary material is available. Filing units for diskettes are available from most microcomputer supply vendors.

Compact disks are frequently shipped in a plastic compact disc case (*jewel box*). Labels with the classification numbers can be placed on these cases and the disks filed in a box, file cabinet, or the like. Compact disk storage units designed to hold several hundred disks are available from microform storage vendors.

PRESERVATION

Government documents collections are vulnerable to the same elements that affect other parts of library collections: heat, humidity, light, dust, insects, people, and acidic paper. Although many factors that affect the collection cannot be controlled, appropriate maintenance will slow or retard deterioration. The supplies that assist in maintaining shelf order—pamphlet files and boxes, pamphlet binders, acid-free folders, and bookends—also help preserve the collection and are readily available from library supply companies. Special archival and preservation products are available from the companies listed in appendix 6.4.

Since the mid-19th century, most government publications have been printed on acidic paper. Public Law 101-423 established a national policy on acid-free permanent paper. This law requires the Public Printer, the Librarian of Congress, and the Archivist of the United States to devise mechanisms to implement the law. Depository librarians may expect that future volumes of titles of historical significance (for example, the *Foreign Relations of the United States*) will be printed on acid-free permanent paper.

Vacuuming and Cleaning

Dust and grime contribute to paper deterioration. Thus, vacuuming and cleaning materials is one way to preserve publications. Begin a cleaning project with a portable vacuum, One-wipe dust cloths[7] (or Endust and a soft cloth), cheesecloth, and a book truck.

Working from the top shelf downward, remove all books from each shelf and wipe the shelf clean with One-wipes or a cloth sprayed with Endust. Vacuum the top of each book with the vacuum brush nozzle fitted with cheesecloth; work from the spine outward. Check the cheesecloth frequently and remove any cumulation of dust or other matter. Wipe the three edges of the book and the spine with One-wipe or the Endust-treated cloth. Carolyn Horton's *Cleaning and Preserving Binding and Related Materials* provides more information on cleaning materials and is applicable to documents collections.[8]

Repairs

Even with the best maintenance, repairs are sometimes necessary. Very few supplies are necessary to make basic repairs. Linen tape can be used to reinforce torn bindings, and transparent document repair tape mends torn pages; both are available from archival and preservation suppliers (see appendix 6.4). Regular tape should never be used for repair; it is acidic and contributes to the deterioration of the paper.

Binding

The GPO *Guidelines* specify that government publications be maintained in the same manner as other parts of the collection. In most libraries, maintenance includes a mix of in-house pamphlet binding and commercial binding. Criteria and policies regarding binding should be outlined in a written policy. If available, use the general library's policy as a model. General criteria are:

- level of use;
- value or historical significance; and
- retention policy (Is it superseded or replaced by microform? Is it a periodical? Is the title indexed in commercial indexing and abstracting services?)

Preparation and Records

Establish a binding pattern (cover color, print color, frequency, and format of spine information, including volume and date pattern and any special instructions that apply to all volumes) for each serial title to be bound. Frequency of binding is determined by the number of issues published per year. The ideal thickness of a volume is 1.5 inches. The information on the spine includes the agency, title, classification number, and variant data (volume and date or issue number). Any additional information that enables the user to identify the correct volume without removing it from the shelf also should be printed on the spine. Examples include the accession numbers in *Resources in Education*, patent numbers in the *Official Gazette of the Patent Office*, and treaty numbers in the United Nations Treaty Series. Once a pattern has been established, most commercial binders can provide preprinted bindery slips and/or authority cards showing the established format.

Notes on serial check-in records, whether manual or on-line, should indicate the frequency with which issues are to be pulled for binding. Most on-line systems provide the option of charging volumes out to the bindery and discharging them upon return.

To prepare a title for binding, divide it into units that measure approximately 1.5 inches (follow the established pattern unless frequency, size, etc., has changed). If the back cover contains no print, remove the back covers of all issues except the last one in each binding unit; this reduces the bulk of the volume and the shelf space required. When a cumulative index exists, remove the weekly, monthly, quarterly, etc., indexes from the individual issues. Place the issues in order and tie or band together (the binder may provide more specific instructions).

Bind or Replace with Microform

If a title is available in microform, it is sometimes better to replace paper copy with microform than to bind. Factors to consider in making this decision are:

How complete is the paper volume?
—How much time and effort would be required to acquire the missing parts or issues?
—Are missing issues or parts a recurring problem?

What is the content of the title?
—Does it contain illustrations, color photographs, maps?

On what quality of paper is the title printed? How often is the title used?

When a high level of effort is required to complete a paper volume (United Nations *Official Records*, for example) or when the quality of the paper is poor (*Federal Register*), microform replacement may be justified. In contrast, if the content of the title does not convert well to microformat (e.g., it has illustrations, maps, or photographs), then binding the paper volume may be the best option. The availability of a specific title can be discerned from the most recent issue of *Guide to Microforms in Print*.[9]

Government Documents as Rare Documents

Government publications received through depository programs are usually free of charge. Those that are for sale are priced inexpensively, so it is sometimes a surprise to documents librarians to discover that their collections contain many volumes of historical significance and of monetary value. For example, the Congressional serial set (U.S. House reports, Senate reports, House documents, Senate executive documents and reports, and Senate and House miscellaneous documents) issued since the early 19th century contains reports of western explorations and surveys, catalogs of exhibitions and expositions, and reports and proceedings of organizations chartered by the U.S. government, such as the American Historical Association and the Girl Scouts of America. The Coast and Geodetic Survey, the National Museum, and the Bureau of American Ethnology, among others, produced many publications that contain reports, some with illustrations and maps, that are now found with some frequency in antiquarian book dealers' catalogs.

What makes something rare? Quinlan[10] identifies several characteristics that make publications of value; they include text, subject matter, illustrations, provenance of the piece, physical characteristics, binding, paper, scarcity of the item, and date and place of publication.

The first step in protecting and preserving valuable collections is to identify the rare documents. Seavey,[11] Hasse,[12] and Schmeckebier[13] list specific volumes that are now considered rare. Two librarians are compiling a packet of materials designed to help librarians identify rare items in their collections. This packet will be distributed to depository librarians late in 1992. Colleagues, including rare books librarians and map curators, antiquarian book dealer catalogs, and auction records are all helpful in identifying rare documents and in establishing value.

Once identified, two options are available for protecting the volumes from loss, mutilation, and deterioration. One can either remove the materials to closed or limited-access stacks within the documents collection, or transfer them to a special collections area. The advantages that transfer to a special collections area provides are usually a controlled environment, in terms of heat and humidity, and the expertise of colleagues who have been specifically trained to handle rare materials. Such transfers require the cooperation of other library units in effecting changes in bibliographic records, negotiating the space required, making the physical transfer, and providing public access as required by depository agreements. In 1985, the Rare Books and Manuscripts Section of the American Library Association published guidelines on the selection of general collection materials for transfer to special collections;[14] these guidelines are useful for documents librarians considering such transfers.

WEEDING

Collection development and evaluation, including the development of criteria for weeding, were discussed in detail in chapter 2. Collection evaluation for depository libraries includes both deselection of item numbers and weeding or withdrawal of specific titles. Item numbers may be deselected any time throughout the year by sending an "amendment of selections." Usually when the library deselects an item number, a decision is made regarding the existing holdings, that is, whether to withdraw selectively or withdraw all of them. Beyond the determination of criteria for *what* to weed, depository librarians must consider *when* to weed, *how* to weed, and *how to dispose* of materials weeded.

When Can You Weed?

Chapter 10 of the GPO's *Instructions to Depository Libraries* addresses disposition of materials that are part of the U.S. federal depository program. General principles to remember are:

1. All items remain the property of the federal government; libraries cannot materially benefit from the disposal of depository holdings.

2. Depository libraries not served by a regional depository library cannot weed (exceptions noted later).

3. All depositories must retain materials received on deposit for at least five years. Permission to withdraw after that time must be received from the regional depository library serving the state or region.

United States federal depository libraries may dispose of secondary copies of any publication without permission from the GPO or the regional depository library. Secondary copies are defined by the GPO as unrequested documents (those received but not selected); superseded documents (including preprints); and duplicates (including reprints).

Categories of superseded publications are enumerated in section G of chapter 10 of *Instructions To Depository Libraries*, and a list of specific titles appears in appendix C of the *Instructions*.

Canadian federal government depositories must, as a rule, retain all monographs and serials permanently.[15] Exceptions are Statistics Canada serials, which must be retained for only 10 years, and parliamentary publications that are either cumulated or replaced by other publications. Most international intergovernmental organizations with depository programs do not address the disposition or withdrawal of depository publications. The assumption is that, unless replaced by another format or cumulated in another volume, the depository publications received will be retained indefinitely.

How to Weed

The weeding process may be initiated by the deselection of an item number, by the need for space, or by an evaluation of the collection on a regular schedule, whether agency-by-agency or class-by-class. Within each classification number, weeding may be done by publication or receipt date, circulation and in-house use, or a title-by-title review. These methods should be a reflection of criteria outlined in a written collection development and evaluation policy, as discussed in chapter 2.

Volumes to be withdrawn are listed on a discard list. Most regional depository libraries have established form and format guidelines, as well as a timetable, for the preparation of discard lists. In general, the information required is the SuDoc classification number (if used), agency, title, date of publication for monographs, or holdings (volumes or numbers) for serial or series titles. Once permission to withdraw has been received from the regional depository library, the library's bibliographic and holdings records must be revised to show the withdrawal of the titles or holdings. Libraries whose holdings are reflected in an on-line catalog may have to coordinate the withdrawal of publications with the cataloging department. Besides revising the shelflist and cataloging records, a notation regarding deselection and withdrawal should be made to the item number record, either manual or electronic. In 1988, Wilson wrote a detailed procedure for weeding the partial depository.[16] To forestall any questions or problems later, stamp "discard" over any property or depository stamp on each publication when it is physically removed from the shelf for withdrawal.

Disposal of Materials

Librarians cannot materially benefit from the disposal of depository holdings, but what may be one library's trash may be another's treasure. Consequently, after receiving permission for withdrawal from the regional depository, discard lists may be sent to the editor of the GPO *Needs and Offers List*. *Needs and Offers* is distributed to all federal depository libraries. However, the selective depository must be prepared to hold the publications for at least 3 to 6 months—the time it takes for publication and distribution of the list, plus the 45 days allowed for libraries to make requests.

Other avenues for disposal include discard lists prepared by the regional depository and circulated to the selective depositories within a state or region. Listservs, such as GovDoc-L, UN, Int-Law, and EC, are another avenue for offering materials withdrawn or duplicates received to other libraries.

Duplicate copies acquired by purchase or gift may be sold to dealers, offered as duplicates to users, or contributed to the library's annual book sale. Appropriate dealers can be identified in the latest editions of the *American Book Trade Directory* or *Literary Market Place*. A list of government documents dealers was compiled by Dow in 1988.[17] When all avenues for disposal to other libraries have been exhausted, publications may be destroyed; some may be appropriate candidates for recycling.

AUTOMATION OF COLLECTION MAINTENANCE RECORDS

The microcomputer now provides the librarian with opportunities for managing the depository collection that did not exist with manual records. Maintaining item number records on a microcomputer makes it possible to identify growth patterns, identify strengths and weaknesses of the collection, maintain a weeding schedule, provide a profile of receipts for a vendor in a cataloging project, and identify duplication among depositories in one geographic area.

A variety of database management systems exist that would serve the purpose. Selection of a system that is technically supported by the library, institution, or entity in which the depository collection resides is recommended, but not absolutely necessary. In general, the elements to be included in a file structure are format; active/inactive status; selected/not selected; date selected and how selected (survey, class added); agency; category/title; classification stem; and type of publication (monograph, monographic series, serial). Morton has described one project to automate collection development.[18] Mooney has developed an item records management system that uses dBASE and that she has shared with over 70 depositories.[19] A software package specifically designed to help librarians withdraw government documents is entitled "Documents Assistant."[20] Research into and application of these types of technologies to documents collections will be important managerial decisions in the coming years.

NOTES

[1]U.S. Superintendent of Documents, *Instructions to Depository Libraries*, 1988 rev. (Washington, DC: U.S. Government Printing Office), ch. 1, p. 2 of 4.

[2]Catharine J. Reynolds, "How Many Publications In A Linear Foot?" *Documents to the People* 7 (May 1979): 96, 99.

[3]"Distribution of Basic Manuals and Their Updates," *Administrative Notes* 3 (December 1982): 2.

[4]James A. Stewart, "But What Do I Do with All These Maps?" *Illinois Libraries* 68 (May 1986): 347-49.

[5]Julie Jones-Eddy and Ann H. Zwinger, "In-House Preservation of Early U.S. Government Maps," *Government Publications Review* 15 (January/February 1988): 41-47.

[6]Diana Gonzalez Kirby, "Managing Government-sponsored Posters in the Academic Library," *Government Information Quarterly* 6 (1989): 283-94.

[7]Available from TALAS—Division of Technical Library Services, 213 West 35th Street, New York, NY 10001.

[8]Carolyn Horton, *Cleaning and Preserving Binding and Related Materials*, 2d rev. ed. (Chicago: American Library Association, 1969).

[9]*Guide to Microforms in Print* (Westport, CT: Microform Review).

[10]Nora Quinlan, "Strategies for Coping with Government Documents as Rare Books," *Documents to the People* 16 (December 1988): 178-79.

[11]Charles A. Seavey, "Government Graphics: The Development of Illustration in U.S. Federal Publications, 1817-1861," *Government Publications Review* 17 (March/April 1990): 121-42.

[12]Adelaide Hasse, *Report of Explorations Printed in the Documents of the U.S. Government: A Contribution Toward a Bibliography* (Washington, DC: Government Printing Office, 1899; reprinted New York: Burt Franklin, 1969).

[13]L. F. Schmeckebier, *Catalogue and Index of the Publications of the Hayden, King, Powell and Wheeler Surveys*, USGS Bulletin 222 (Washington, DC: Government Printing Office, 1904).

[14]American Library Association, RBMS Ad Hoc Committee for Developing Transfer Guidelines, "Guidelines on the Selection of General Collection Materials for Transfer to Special Collections," *College and Research Libraries News* 46 (July/August 1985): 349-52.

[15]Canadian Government Publishing Centre, *The Depository Services Program* (Ottawa: Supply and Service, 1986), 7.

[16]John S. Wilson, "Weeding the Partial Depository: The Cornerstone of Collection Development," *Documents to the People* 16 (June 1988): 91-94.

[17]Susan Dow, " A Selective Directory of Government Document Dealers, Jobbers and Subscription Agents," *Serials Librarian* 14 (1988): 157-86.

[18]Bruce Morton, "An Items Record Management System: First Step in the Automation of Collection Development in Selective GPO Depository Libraries," *Government Publications Review* 8A (1981): 185-96.

[19]Margaret T. Mooney, "Automating the U.S. Depository Item Numbers File," *Administrative Notes* 7 (November 1986): 2-3; and "Numbers Database: An Experimental Project," *Administrative Notes* 9, no. 7 (May 1988): 14-15.

[20]Katharine Phenix, "Software for Libraries," *Wilson Library Bulletin* 66 (April 1992): 84. This software is available from Kensington Software, 422 East Third Street, Brooklyn, NY 11218-3912; 718-438-8608.

APPENDIX 6.1
DEPOSITORY COLLECTION MAINTENANCE

From *Guidelines for the Depository Library System (Revised 1987) with Minimum Standards for the Depository Library System (1976).* Washington, DC: U.S. Government Printing Office, 1988.

6. Maintenance of the Depository Collection

6.1 Collections should be maintained in as good physical condition as other library materials, including binding when desirable.

6.2 Lost materials should be replaced if possible.

6.3 Unneeded publications should be made available to other libraries in accordance with Chapter 19, Title 44 U.S.C.

6.4 Libraries served by a regional depository may withdraw publications retained for a period of at least five years after securing permission from the regional library for disposal in accordance with the provisions of 44 U.S.C. 1912.

6.5 Depository libraries within executive departments and independent agencies may dispose of unwanted Government publications after first offering them to the Library of Congress and the Archivist of the United States, in accordance with the provisions of 44 U.S.C. 1907.

6.6 The provisions of 44 U.S.C. 1911, disposal of unwanted publications, do not apply to libraries of the highest appellate courts of the states (see 44 U.S.C. 1915).

6.7 Superseded material should be withdrawn according to *Instructions to Depository Libraries* (latest edition).

6.8 Depository publications should be protected from unlawful removal as are other parts of the library's collections.

APPENDIX 6.2
MAPS, CHARTS, AND ATLASES AVAILABLE FOR SELECTION BY DEPOSITORY LIBRARIES

Based on *Administrative Notes*, 10:17 (August 21, 1989): 8-15; revisions from *List of Classes* dated December 1991.

0080-G	Maps and charts (Forest Service)	A 13.28:
0080-H	Posters and maps (Agriculture Dept.)	A 1.32:
0102-B nos.	Soil Survey Reports (Soil Conservation)	A 57.38:
0121-F	Maps and Posters (Soil Conservation)	A 57.68:
0130-J	Maps, charts, qualified areas (Economic Development Adm)	C 46.17:
0140-B	Congressional District Atlas (Census)	C 3.62/5:
0140-B-02	State-county subdivision maps (Census)	C 3.62/6:
0142-H	Maps (Economic Analysis Bureau)	C 59.15:
0146-K	United States maps, GE-50 series	C 3.62/4:
	United States maps, GE-70 series (Census Bureau)	C 3.62/8:
0146-K-01	Maps (Census Bureau)	C 3.62/2:
0146-S	County block maps, CD-ROM (Census)	C 3.62/9:
0191-B-01	Charts and publications catalog 1, United States Atlantic and Gulf Coasts (National Ocean Service)	C 55.418:1/
0191-B-02	Charts and publications catalog 2, United States Pacific Coast (National Ocean Service)	C 55.418:2/
0191-B-03	Charts and publications catalog 3, United States Alaska (National Ocean Service)	C 55.418:3/
0191-B-04	Charts and publications catalog 4, United States Great Lakes (National Ocean Service)	C 55.418:4/
0191-B-11	Maps and charts (National Ocean Service)	C 55.418/6:
0191-B-13	Charts (listed in) ... Catalog 1 (National Ocean Service)	C 55.418/7:
0191-B-14	Charts (listed in) ... Catalog 2 (National Ocean Service)	C 55.418/7:
0191-B-15	Charts (listed in) ... Catalog 3 (National Ocean Service)	C 55.418/7:

Appendix 6.2 □ 97

0191-B-16	Charts (listed in) ... Catalog 4 (National Ocean Service)	C 55.418/7:
0191-B-17	Maps (listed in) Bathymetric Mapping Products Catalog 5 (National Ocean Service)	C 55.418/7:
0191-B-18	Bathymetric Mapping Products Catalog 5 (National Ocean Service)	C 55.418:5/
0192-A-01	U.S. Terminal Procedures (National Ocean Service)	C 55.411:
0192-A-02	Airport Obstruction Charts (National Ocean Service)	C 55.411/3:
0192-A-03	Supplement Alaska (National Ocean Service)	C 55.416:
0192-A-04	Airport/Facility Directory (National Ocean Service)	C 55.416/2:
0192-A-05	Standard Terminal Arrival Charts (National Ocean Service)	C 55.416/3:
0192-A-06	Alaska Terminal Charts (National Ocean Service)	C 55.416/4:
0192-A-07	Standard Instrument Department Charts, Eastern U.S. (National Ocean Service)	C 55.416/5:
	Standard Instrument Department Charts, Western U.S. (National Ocean Service)	C 55.416/6:
0192-A-08	VFR/IFR Planning Chart (National Ocean Service)	C 55.416/7:
	Flight Case Planning Chart	C 55.416/7-2:
0192-A-09	National Atlantic Route Chart (Scale 1:11,000,000) (National Ocean Service)	C 55.416/8:
0192-A-10	North Pacific Oceanic Route Chart (Scale 1:12,000,000)	C 55.416/9:
	North Pacific Oceanic Route Charts (National Ocean Service)	C 55. 416/9-2:
0192-A-11	Sectional Aeronautical Charts (Scale 1:500,000) (National Ocean Service)	C 55.416/10:
0192-A-12	Terminal Area Charts (VFR) (Scale 1:250,000) (National Ocean Service)	C 55.416/11:
0192-A-13	US Gulf Coast VFR Aeronautical Chart (Scale 1:1,000,000) (National Ocean Service)	C 55.416/12:
0192-A-14	VFR Helicopter Chart of Los Angeles (Scale 1:125,000)	C 55.416/12-2:
	New York Helicopter Route Chart (Scale 1:125,000)	C 55.416/12-3:

98 □ Collection Maintenance

	Washington Helicopter Route Chart (Scale 1:125,000)	C 55.416/12-4:
	Chicago Helicopter Route Chart (Scale 1:125,000) (National Ocean Service)	C 55.416/12-5:
0192-A-15	World Aeronautical Charts (Scale 1:1,000,000) (National Ocean Service)	C 55.416/13:
0192-A-16	Enroute Area Charts (US) Low Altitude (National Ocean Service)	C 55.416/14:
0192-A-17	Enroute Low Altitude Charts (Alaska) (National Ocean Service)	C 55.416/15:
0192-A-18	Enroute Area Charts (US) Low Altitude (National Ocean Service)	C 55.416/15-2:
0192-A-19	Enroute High Altitude Charts (US) (National Ocean Service)	C 55.416/16:
0192-A-20	Enroute High Altitude Charts (Alaska) (National Ocean Service)	C 55.416/16-2:
0192-A-22	Pacific Chart Supplement (National Ocean Service)	C 55.427:
0244-A	Maps, Charts, Posters (National Institute of Standards and Technology)	C 13.64:
0250-E-09	Atlases (National Oceanic & Atmospheric Administration)	C 55.22:
0250-F	Maps (National Oceanic & Atmospheric Administration	C 55.22/2:
0273-D-04	Daily weather maps (National Weather Service)	C 55.195:
0273-D-10	Maps and Charts (Environmental Research Laboratories)	C 55.624:
0275-F	Monthly and Seasonal Weather Outlook (National Weather Service)	C 55.109
0275-P	Maps and Charts (National Weather Service)	C 55.122:
0334-C	Boater's Map (Army Corps of Engineers)	D 103.49/2:
0334-C-01	Maps and posters	D 103.49/3:
	Atlases (Army Corps of Engineers)	D 103.49/3-2:
0337-B-05	Navigation charts of various rivers	D 103.66/:
	Cumberland River Navigation Charts	D 103.66/3:
	Tennessee River Navigation Charts	D 103.66/5:
	Upper Mississippi River Navigation Charts (Army Corps of Engineers)	D 103.66/6:

Appendix 6.2 □ 99

0354-A	Maps and Atlases (Military Academy, West Point)	D 109.11:
0378-E-01	ONC—Operational Navigation Charts (Defense Mapping Agency)	D 5.354:
0378-E-02	JNC—Jet Navigation Charts (Defense Mapping Agency)	D 5.354:
0378-E-03	GNC—Global Navigation Charts (Defense Mapping Agency)	D 5.354:
0378-E-04	Series 1105—Area Outline Maps (Defense Mapping Agency)	D 5.355:
0378-E-05	TPC—Tactical Pilotage Charts (Defense Mapping Agency)	D 5.354:
0378-E-06	Public Sale Catalog—Topographic Maps & Publications (Defense Mapping Agency)	D 5.351/3:
0378-E-07	Series 1209—Europe (Defense Mapping Agency)	D 5.355:
0378-E-08	Public Sale Catalog—Aeronautical Charts & Publications (Defense Mapping Agency)	D 5.351/3-2:
0378-E-09	Series 1308—Mid-East Briefing Maps (Defense Mapping Agency)	D 5.355:
0378-E-10	Series 5211—Arabian Peninsula (Defense Mapping Agency)	D 5.355:
0378-E-11	Catalog of Maps, Charts and Related Products; pt. 2, Hydrographic Products volume 1, Nautical Charts & Publications (Defense Mapping Agency)	D 5.351/2:1/
0378-E-21	Charts (contained in) Catalog of Maps	D 5.356:
	Charts, and Related Products, pt. 2, hydrographic products, volume 1, US and Canada (Defense Mapping Agency)	D 5.356:
0378-E-22	Charts (contained in) Catalog of Maps, Charts, and Related Products, volume 2, Central & South America and Antarctica (Defense Mapping Agency)	D 5.356:
0378-E-23	Charts (contained in) Catalog of Maps, charts, and Related Products, volume 3, Western Europe, Iceland, Greenland and the Arctic (Defense Mapping Agency)	D 5.356:
0378-E-24	Charts (contained in) Catalog of Maps, Charts, and Related Products, volume 4, Scandinavia, Baltic & USSR (Defense Mapping Agency)	D 5.356:

100 □ Collection Maintenance

0378-E-25	Charts (contained in) Catalog of Maps, Charts, and Related Products, volume 5, Western Africa and the Mediterranean (Defense Mapping Agency)	D 5.356:
0378-E-26	Charts (contained in) Catalog of Maps, Charts, and Related Products, volume 6 Indian Ocean (Defense Mapping Agency)	D 5.356:
0378-E-27	Charts (contained in) Catalog of Maps, Charts, and Related Products, volume 7, Australia, Indonesia, and New Zealand (Defense Mapping Agency)	D 5.356:
0378-E-28	Charts (contained in) Catalog of Maps, Charts, and Related Products, volume 8, Oceania (Defense Mapping Agency)	D 5.356:
0378-E-29	Charts (contained in) Catalog of Maps, Charts, and Related Products, volume 9, East Asia (Defense Mapping Agency)	D 5.356:
0378-E-30	General Nautical Charts (Defense Mapping Agency)	D 5.356:
	International Chart Series	D 5.356:
0378-E-31	Great Circle Sailing and Polar Charts (Defense Mapping Agency)	D 5.356:
	Great Circle Tracking Charts	D 5.356:
0378-E-32	Omega Plotting Charts (Defense Mapping Agency)	D 5.356:
0378-E-33	Loran C Plotting Charts (Defense Mapping Agency)	D 5.356:
0378-E-34	Display Plotting Charts (Defense Mapping Agency)	D 5.356:
0378-E-35	Series 1144—The World (Scale 1:22,000,000) (Defense Mapping Agency)	D 5.356:
	Series 1145—The World (Scale 1:30,000,000)	
	Series 1150—The World (Scale 1:14,000,000)	
0379-F-04	Series 2201—Africa (Defense Mapping Agency)	D 5.355:
0379-F-05	Series 5103—USSR-Admin Areas (Defense Mapping Agency)	D 5.355:
3079-F-06	Series 5104—USSR and Adjacent Areas (Defense Mapping Agency)	D 5.355:
0379-F-07	Series 5213—SE Asia Briefing Map (Defense Mapping Agency)	D 5.355:
0421-E-09	Maps (Air Force Department)	D 301.76/7:

Appendix 6.2 □ 101

0429-V-05	Maps and Charts (Federal Energy Regulatory Commission)	E 2.15:
0430-K-03	Maps (Western Area Power Administration)	E 6.10:
0431-J-10	Maps and Atlases (Environmental Protection Agency)	EP 1.99:
0438-B	Maps and Charts (Energy Information Administration)	E 3.21:
0486-P-01	Maps (Indian Health Services)	HE 20.9419:
0611-W-nos.	National Wetlands Inventory Maps (Fish and Wildlife Service)	I 49.6/7-2:
0612	Maps and Charts (Fish and Wildlife Service)	I 49.9:
0612-E	Coast Ecological Inventory (Fish and Wildlife Service)	I 49.6/5:
0617	Gazetteers (Defense Mapping Agency)	D 5.319:
0619-G	List of Geological Survey Geologic & Water Supply Reports & Maps (various states) (Geological Survey)	I 19.41/7:
0619-G-01	Maps and posters (Geological Survey)	I 19.79:
0619-G-02	National Mapping Program (Geological Survey)	I 19.80:
0619-G-03	C—Coal Investigations (Geological Survey)	I 19.85:
0619-G-04	GP—Geological Investigations (Geological Survey)	I 19.87:
0619-G-05	GQ—Geological Quadrangle Maps (Geological Survey)	I 19.88:
0619-G-06	HA—Hydrologic Investigations Atlases	I 19.89:
	Hydrologic Unit Map (Geological Survey)	I 19.89/2:
0619-G-07	MR—Mineral Investigations Resource Maps (Geological Survey)	I 19.90:
0619-G-08	I—Miscellaneous Geologic Investigations	I 19.91:
	CP—Circum Pacific Map Series (Geological Survey)	I 19.91/2:
0619-G-09	OC—Oil and Gas Investigation Charts (Geological Survey)	I 19.92:
0619-G-10	OM—Oil and Gas Investigation Maps (Geological Survey)	I 19.93:
0619-G-11	MF—Miscellaneous Field Studies Maps (Geological Survey)	I 19.113:
0619-G-12	SO—Topographic Mapping (Geological Survey)	I 19.95:

102 □ Collection Maintenance

0619-G-13	IS—Index to Intermediate Scale Mapping (Geological Survey)	I 19.96:
0619-G-14	OT—Index to Orthophotoquad Mapping (Geological Survey)	I 19.97:
	DM—Index to USGS/DMA 1:50,000 Scale, 15 minute Quadrangle Mapping	I 19.97/2:
	LU—Index to Land Use and Land Cover Maps and Digital Data	I 19.97/3:
0619-G-16	BLM Surface Management Status 1:100,000 Maps (Land Management Bureau)	I 53.11/4:
	BLM Surface and Minerals Management Status 1:100,000 Scale Maps	I 53.11/4-2:
0619-G-17	22—United States Series of Topographic Maps, Scale 1:250,000 (Geological Survey)	I 19.98:
0619-G-18	24—Alaska 1:250,000 Series (Geological Survey)	I 19.99:
0619-G-19	25—Antarctica Topographic Series Scale 1:50,000	I 19.100:
	25—Antarctica Topographic Series Scale 1:250,000	I 19.100/2:
	25—Antarctica Topographic Series Scale 1:500,000 with contours	I 19.100/3:
	25—Antarctica Topographic Series Scale 1:500,000 without contours	I 19.100/4:
	25—Antarctica Topographic Series Scale 1:1,000,000	I 19.100/5:
	Antarctica Photomap	I 19.100/6:
	AM—Antarctica Geologic Maps	I 19.25/8:
0619-G-21	51—National Park Series (Geological Survey)	I 19.106:
0619-G-22	52—United States 1:1,000,000 Scale Maps (Geological Survey)	I 19.107:
0619-G-24	57—Slope Maps (Geological Survey)	I 19.109:
0619-G-25	58—United States 1:100,000 Scale Series (Intermediate Scale Maps) (Geological Survey)	I 19.110:
0619-G-26	Separate sheets of Selected Thematic and General Reference Maps from the National Atlas (Geological Survey)	I 19.111/a:
0619-G-27	Land Use and Land Cover and Associated Maps (Geological Survey)	I 19.112:

Appendix 6.2 □ 103

0619-G-28	GI—Index to Geologic Mapping of the United States (Geological Survey)	I 19.86:
0619-H-nos.	31—State Map Series (Planimetric, 1:500,000) (Geological Survey)	I 19.102:
0619-M-nos.	7.5' Series (Geological Survey)	I 19.81:
	15' Series (Geological Survey)	I 19.81/2:
	Catalog of Topographic and Other Published Maps	I 19.81/6-2:
0619-M-nos.	Index to Topographic and Other Map Coverage (Geological Survey)	I 19.81/6-3:
0619-M-03	Color Image Maps (Arizona) (Geological Survey)	I 19.81/3:
0619-P-nos.	County Map Series (Geological Survey)	I 19.108:
0624-A-01	National Gazetteer of the United States (Geological Survey)	I 19.16:
0624-C	Flood Prone Areas, various cities (map folders) (Geological Survey)	I 19.70:
0624-E	Newsletter (National Cartographic Information Center)	I 19.71:
0624-E-03	Maps (Heritage Conservation and Recreation Service)	I 70.13:
0627-C	Maps and Atlases (Indian Affairs Bureau)	I 20.47:
0629-B	Maps and Folders (Bureau of Land Management)	I 53.11:
0646-B	National Parks and Landmarks (National Park Service)	I 29.66:
0650	National Monuments and Military Parks (National Park Service)	I 29.21:
0651	National Park Information Circulars	I 29.6:
	National Historic Parks Information Circulars (National Park Service)	I 29.88/6:
0651-A	Maps (National Park Service)	I 29.8:
0651-B	National Seashores, Information Circulars (National Park Service)	I 29.6/2:
0651-B-01	National Lakeshores, Information Circulars (National Park Service)	I 29.6/3:
0651-B-02	National Rivers, Information Circulars (National Park Service)	I 29.6/4:

104 □ Collection Maintenance

0651-B-03	National Scenic Trails, Information Circulars (National Park Service)	I 29.6/5:
0651-B-04	National Historic Site, Information Circulars (National Park Service)	I 29.6/6:
0654	National Recreational Areas, Information Circular (National Park Service)	I 29.39:
0664-C	Maps (Bureau of Reclamation)	I 27.7/4:
0671-A-04	OCS Map Series (Minerals Management Service)	I 72.12/4:
0701-G	Maps and Charts (Federal Railroad Administration)	TD 3.16:
0766-F-03	Maps and Posters (Occupational Safety and Health Administration)	L 35.23:
0811-A	General Publications (Library of Congress, Geography and Map Division)	LC 5.2:
0834-B-01	Maps and Atlases (National Science Foundation)	NS 1.41:
0856-A-01	Maps and Atlases (Central Intelligence Agency)	PrEx 3.10/4:
0862-B	Background Notes, various countries (State Department)	S 1.123:
	Background Notes, Indexes	S 1.123/2:
0864-B-06	Maps and Atlases (State Department)	S 1.33/2:
0876-A	Geographic Bulletins (State Department)	S 1.119/2:
0876-A-02	International Boundary Studies (State Department)	S 1.119/3:
	Geographic Notes (State Department)	S 1.119/4:
0876-A-04	Limits in the Seas (State Department)	S 1.119/5:
0931-G	Maps and Posters (Coast Guard)	TD 5.47:
0982-G-28	Maps (Federal Highway Administration)	TD 2.37:
0987-F	Maps and Atlases (Veterans Administration)	VA 1.70:
1082-D	Maps (Tennessee Valley Authority)	Y 3.T 25:7/

APPENDIX 6.3
POSTER ITEM NUMBERS

Based on *List of Classes* dated December 1991.

80-H	Agriculture Department	A 1.32:
80-H-01	Forest Service	A 13.104:
61-A	Extension Service	A 43.8:
121-F*	Soil Conservation Service	A 57.71:
68-C	Farmers Home Administration	A 84.15:
24-B-05	Agricultural Marketing Service	A 88.38:
74-A-06	Food and Nutrition Service	A 98.16:
30-A-14	Animal & Plant Health Inspection Service	A 101.25:
21-T-06	Food Safety and Quality Service	A 103.18:
74-C-12	Action	AA 1.18:
126-C-02	Commerce Department	C 1.63:
144-A-20	Census Bureau	C 3.270:
244-A	National Institute of Standards and Technology	C 13.64:
250-F*	National Oceanic and Atmospheric Administration	C 55.22/3:
275-T	National Weather Service	C 55.130:
273-D-09	National Environmental Satellite Data & Information Service	C 55.230:
609-C-07	National Marine Fisheries Service	C 55.315:
191-B-11*	National Ocean Service	C 55.418/6-2:
231-B-17	International Trade Administration	C 61.33:
310-K	Defense Department	D 1.56:
312-F	Armed Forces Information Service	D 2.9:
315-F-04	Defense Intelligence Agency	D 5.213:
314-A-10	Defense Logistics Agency	D 7.19/2:
358-C	National Guard Bureau	D 12.14:

106 □ Collection Maintenance

322-H*	Army Department	D 101.35:
334-C-01*	Engineers Corps	D 103.49/3:
351-D	Army Medical Department	D 104.34:
325-S	Publications Relating to Ordinance (Army)	D 105.32:
348-F	Judge Advocate General's Office (Army)	D 108.12:
344-B-01	Military History Center	D 114.13:
370-G	Navy Department	D 201.19:
385-E	Medicine and Surgery Bureau (Navy)	D 206.23:
384-F	Marine Corps	D 214.16/4:
388-B-05	Military Sealift Command	D 216.10:
421-E-01	Air Force Department	D 301.76/3:
421-E-05*	Air Force Department	D 301.76/5:
474-B-02	Energy Department	E 1.70:
455-M	Education Department	ED 1.37:
431-J-12	Environmental Protection Agency	EP 1.48:
216-A-15	Federal Emergency Management Agency	FEM 1.21:
535-A-02	Federal Trade Commission	FT 1.31:
556-C*	Government Printing Office	GP 1.11:
551-A	Superintendent of Documents	GP 3.21/2:
559-E-03	General Services Administration	GS 1.32:
444-K-05	Health and Human Services Department	HE 1.43:
516-K	Social Security Administration	HE 3.22:
485-C	Public Health Service	HE 20.12:
484-D-05	President's Council on Physical Fitness and Sports	HE 20.113:
506-J	National Institutes of Health	HE 20.3020:
507-G-24	National Cancer Institute	HE 20.3175:
507-E-10	National Heart, Lung and Blood Institute	HE 20.3217:

Appendix 6.3 □ 107

497-C-11	National Institute of Dental Health	HE 20.3414:
497-C-14	National Institute of General Medical Sciences	HE 20.3467:
508-S	National Library of Medicine	HE 20.3622:
507-C-12	John E. Fogarty International Center for Advanced Study in the Health Sciences	HE 20.3715:
447-A-22	National Institute on Aging	HE 20.3867:
478-D	Food and Drug Administration	HE 20.4021:
532-E-08	Health Care Delivery and Assistance Bureau	HE 20.5118:
504-E	Centers for Disease Control	HE 20.7014:
497-D-07	Alcohol, Drug Abuse and Mental Health Administration	HE 20.8014:
507-B-39	National Institute of Mental Health	HE 20.8121:
467-A-22	National Institute on Drug Abuse	HE 20.8225:
498-C-09	National Institute on Alcohol Abuse and Alcoholism	HE 20.8310:
507-H-19	Health Resources and Services Administration	HE 20.9012:
486-P	Indian Health Service	HE 20.9415:
512-A-30	Health Care Financing Administration	HE 22.27:
581-E-35	Housing and Urban Development Department	HH 1.98:
603-G-05	Interior Department	I 1.111:
619-G-01	Geological Survey	I 19.79:
627-C	Indian Affairs Bureau	I 20.62:
664-C	Reclamation Bureau	I 27.7/3:
646-S	National Park Service	I 29.20:
611-K	Fish and Wildlife Service	I 49.14:
631-E	Land Management Bureau	I 53.11/3-2:
624-E-04	Heritage Conservation and Recreation Service	I 70.16:
671-A-04*	Minerals Management Service	I 72.16:
722-B	Federal Bureau of Investigation	J 1.14/21:

108 □ Collection Maintenance

725-C	Immigration and Naturalization Service	J 21.12:
968-J	Drug Enforcement Administration	J 24.11:
716-B-01	Office of Attorney General	J 33.9:
745-A-02	Labor Department	L 1.80:
766-F-03	Occupational Safety and Health Administration	L 35.23:
777-B-01	Wage and Hour Division	L 36.210:
637-N	Mine Safety and Health Administration	L 38.14/2:
785-A*	Library of Congress	LC 1.51:
806-G-02	Asian Division	LC 17.10:
806-A-16	National Library Service for the Blind and Physically Handicapped	LC 19.18:
815-K	Processing Services (Library of Congress)	LC 30.29:
290-K-07	Merit Systems Protection Board	MS 1.12:
290-K-08	Special Counsel Office	MS 2.9:
830-H-06*	National Aeronautics and Space Administration	NAS 1.43:
837-H	United States Postal Service	P 1.26:
74-E-03	Peace Corps	PE 1.12:
299-A	Personnel Management Office	PM 1.35:
854-H	Management and Budget Office	Prex 2.32:
864-B-06*	State Department	S 1.41:
900-C-20	International Development Agency	S 18.60:
901-A-03	Small Business Administration	SBA 1.33/2:
910-Y	Smithsonian Institution	SI 1.38:
917-A	National Gallery of Art	SI 8.10:
925-H	Treasury Department	T 1.32:
950-J	Customs Service	T 17.21:
955-E	Internal Revenue Service	T 22.41:

966-A	Mint Bureau	T 28.21:
974-A	Secret Service	T 34.10/2:
928-E	Financial Management Service	T 63.122:
971-A-02	Savings Bond Division	T 66.8:
971-H	Alcohol, Tobacco and Firearms Bureau	T 70.21:
982-G-38	Federal Highway Administration	TD 2.59/2:
982-D-25	National Highway Traffic Safety Administration	TD 8.31:
985-N	Veterans Administration	VA 1.16:
1062-C-09	Consumer Product Safety Commission	Y 3.C76/3:14/
1063-K-03	U.S. Institute of Peace	Y 3.P31:3/
1082-K	Tennessee Valley Authority	Y 3.T25:8/

*Includes more than posters (i.e., maps, photos).

APPENDIX 6.4
ARCHIVAL AND PRESERVATION SUPPLY DEALERS

Archival Products
Conservation Resources International
12040 South Lakes Drive
Reston, VA 22091
1-703-648-9166

Hollinger Corporation
P.O. Box 8367
Fredericksburg, VA 22404
1-800-634-0491

Talas—Division of Technical Library Services
213 West 35th Street
New York City, NY 10001
1-212-736-7744

University Products
517 Main Street
P.O. Box 101
Holyoke, MA 01041-0101
1-800-762-1165

7

Technology in Document Collections

Debora Cheney
Head of Documents/Maps Section
The Pennsylvania State University

The purpose of depository libraries is to make U.S. government publications easily accessible to the general public and to ensure their continued availability in the future.[1]

Probably no other single trend threatens the principle of freedom of access to government publications as much as the current trend to convert print publications to microformats and electronic formats. This trend, spurred by political, economic, and technological forces during the 1980s, threatens to make information less accessible to the public. Unless plans are made soon to archive this information, much of it may be lost forever.

Why does a conversion from paper format to microforms or electronic formats result in less access to more information? Four reasons explain this phenomenon. As microforms and electronic formats become more prevalent in depository libraries, a pattern of "cost-shifting"[2] from the government to the library (or the user) is making it increasingly difficult for libraries to make this information available. The technology itself often serves as a barrier to the information it contains, because users must learn software protocols to access the information. Title 44 of the U.S. Code lacks clear language requiring these materials to be distributed through the depository library program. Finally, unless document librarians want to contribute to the barriers between the public and government information available in these new formats, they now must be prepared to serve as an interface between the patron and sources such as microfiche, floppy disks, CD-ROMs, electronic bulletin boards (EBBs) and on-line databases. This role requires document librarians to possess increasingly more skill and knowledge of a wide range of technology. The depository librarian's role is complicated by the limited technical support available, the need for information product standardization, and the haphazard way in which materials are obtained for depository distribution.

To understand why microformats and electronic formats threaten the principle of free access to information, and to understand the many challenges the change to these formats presents to document librarians, we need to understand why this change has occurred. This chapter provides an overview of the issues and problems facing U.S. document librarians as they make microformats and electronic-formatted sources available to the public. Although the focus is on U.S. documents, the issues discussed also apply to state and international documents.

MICROFORMATS IN GOVERNMENT DOCUMENT COLLECTIONS

As early as 1977, the Government Printing Office (GPO) distributed some microfiche to depository libraries. However, 1981 could more rightly be cited as the beginning of the movement away from print publications and toward microfiche. Since then, the receipt of microfiche in depository collections has grown exponentially, and now more than half of all GPO publications are issued on microfiche.[3] Today, microfiche is the preferred format for all types of publications distributed by the GPO.

Although 1981 marked a new era, depository libraries were no strangers to microform collections. Before 1981, commercial publishers, such as Congressional Information Service (CIS), Readex, Scholarly Resources, and University Publications of America, had been the traditional providers of microformat collections. Many depository libraries purchased these collections because they allowed libraries to fill gaps in their collections (e.g., with Readex's and CIS's non-depository collections), to save space, to preserve sources, and to make publications available more quickly, especially congressional and statistical publications. Microfiche worked well for documents that were primarily textual in nature. It provided an archival medium and produced space savings for libraries. These publishers also provided indexes to the sources available in their microformat collections. As these indexes provided access to a specific microformat collection, they usually surpassed the access available for documents through the *Monthly Catalog*.[4]

A series of cost-cutting laws and government directives in the 1980s[5] served as a catalyst for the GPO to begin justifying the increased use of microfiche. Currently the microfiche distribution program has reached a status quo. The GPO has issued guidelines (SOD-13)[6] that provide criteria for determining which documents can be converted to microfiche without consulting with the library community, as well as a list of depository item numbers that can be converted to microfiche.[7] Libraries may now select individual item numbers in either paper or microfiche format.[8] This allows each depository library to select the format, based on its own needs and those of its users, as well as the specific publication being offered (for example, microfiche is an excellent way to replace frequently updated titles). It also allows the GPO to realize some cost savings in distributing these materials.

Microfiche distribution has, however, some decided disadvantages for depository libraries. First, libraries do not always receive the format they selected for an item number. If print supplies are insufficient, the GPO distributes microfiche copies to some libraries without warning and without the option to claim a paper copy. Second, the GPO has not yet perfected its method of contracting out the production of microfiche from paper copies and has been plagued by microfiche of poor reproduction quality. When contractors default on the microfiche production contracts, many depository libraries are left without recourse to obtain these publications until the matter is solved by the GPO. The most notable example of this problem was the 1987 microfiche default that suddenly left libraries without titles they had expected to receive.[9] This backlog is targeted for elimination by the end of fiscal year 1992. Third, depository libraries are unable to determine how many microfiche they will receive with an item number. This makes it difficult to predict storage and access needs. Fourth, microfiche that come with headers not including the Superintendent of Documents (SuDocs) number make additional work for depository libraries, which must determine some way to add these numbers. Fifth, libraries must make a decision where the large volume of microfiche will be housed within the library building—for example, within the documents section of the library (if one exists) or in the microforms area.[10] Sixth, the microfiche format makes it difficult for depository libraries to catch problems such as incorrect headers (when the header does not describe the title on the microfiche or the title on the microfiche has been classed in the wrong SuDoc number).

Despite these disadvantages, the GPO depository microfiche program has resulted in depository libraries receiving previously unavailable materials. For instance, some agencies now provide the GPO with microfiche to be distributed to depository libraries—microfiche of titles not included in the depository program as paper items. The GPO has also been able to obtain microfiche copies of titles that were previously available only by subscription (e.g., the Security and Exchange Commission's *Docket* and *Digest*). Some agencies that once operated their own depository programs now rely upon the GPO to distribute much of their material, rather than maintaining another, separate depository system (e.g., National Aeronautics and Space Administration and Department of Energy). Private publishers are allowed to distribute fiche directly to depository libraries for some titles, thus ensuring that the libraries receive these materials as quickly as possible (e.g., the Equal Employment Opportunity Commission's *Decisions*).[11] The result is a system that works with some advantages and disadvantages to the document collection. Any depository librarian must consider a variety of issues as microformats are added to the collection.

Providing Access to Microformats: A Primer

Inevitably, documents collections face many challenges in providing patron access to microformats (see figure 7.1), and they must do so within an environment of user resistance to microformats. A recent study at Rutgers University showed that the "overwhelming majority of respondents claimed never to have used any of the specialized government publications microformatted collections" available at Rutgers's Alexander Library.[12] Although GPO microfiche were used slightly more at this library than the microformat collections the library had purchased from private publishers, overall use of all government publications microform collections was much lower than the use of print publications. The specific usage pattern, of course, could be unique to this library, but the general trend probably would hold in most document collections unless the library has taken (or plans to take) special care to ensure that all microforms are readily accessible.

Microforms have never been popular. Users tend to limit their searches to print publications, unless they absolutely must (because of their information needs) use a microformat. Some of this continuing dissatisfaction is a holdover from the first years this technology was made available, when the equipment used to view these materials was both cumbersome and difficult to use. Although equipment has greatly improved recently, not all libraries are able to afford the latest and best technology or enough of it to ensure that patrons will not have to use outdated equipment. Even with appropriate equipment, dissatisfaction continues for several reasons. Frequently materials are microformatted at a reduction ratio that makes it extremely difficult to view the original document, at the level of detail necessary, without a lens of greater magnification. The quality of reproduction also affects the patron's ability to make use of a microformatted source. Unfortunately, materials not suited for microformats continue to be converted to them anyway.[13] Finally, the lack of standards for producing microformats and the lack of consistency in what information is included in each header affect every library's ability to process effectively, catalog, and retrieve these materials without additional effort.

Document librarians must consider this resistance and develop strategies to address these problems in accessing microformats. First, the question of the different microformats—microfiche, microfilm, and opaque cards—all of which have different housing requirements, must be considered. At the most basic level, these needs are driven by each format's different size and shape, but they are also affected by the film type. For example, most microfiche distributed by the GPO are diazo microfiche. On the other hand, microfiche purchased from commercial publishers are silver halide microfiche. These two types cannot be housed in the same microfiche cabinets, making it impossible to interfile these collections. Complicating this scenario is the opaque card, a format no longer being produced, but still a presence in many document collections. Their size (approximately 6 by 9 inches) prevents them from being interfiled with microfiche or microfilm. The result is a variety of microformatted collections, all of which contain government information sources, but none of which can be interfiled to assist the patron in locating them.[14]

Second, the physical surroundings of a microformats area require special attention, if a library hopes to preserve its investment in its microformat documents collections. Libraries must address a variety of issues related to how these materials are cared for and stored. Temperature, humidity, lighting levels, shelving, cabinets and containers, care, weight loads, sufficient electrical wiring, equipment to view each microformat available in the library,[15] equipment or facilities to print from each microformat available in the library, and facilities to reproduce microfiche (fiche-to-fiche) all must be dealt with in each library.[16]

Third, the level of service the library is able to provide and the access library users have to these collections will influence how heavily the microforms collection is used. Libraries need to consider cataloging and processing, staffing levels, staff education, access, and location issues. From the user's perspective, these decisions probably are some of the most important the library will make and they directly affect how heavily these collections are used. As the analysis of Rutgers's Alexander Library showed, frequently a documents collections' facilities for viewing and printing microforms contributes to the low level of use.[17]

Libraries have a substantial investment in government microforms collections. These collections contribute to and influence a library's total collection development policy. This investment should be maintained while balancing the "public nature" of these materials and every citizen's right to access government information.

Fig. 7.1 Providing access to microformats: A checklist.

Different Microformats Have Different Needs
- different film types cannot be housed together
- different microformats (fiche, film, opaque cards) will require different shelving arrangements

Physical Surroundings Require Special Attention
- Temperature and relative humidity levels
- Lighting levels
- Shelving
- Cabinets and containers (envelopes, boxes, reels) appropriate for each microformat and for preservation of these materials
- Care (cleaning, handling, etc.)
- Weight loads
- Electrical wiring for any necessary equipment
- Equipment to view each type of microformat available in the collection
  --does this equipment provide a variety of reduction ratios?
  --is the equipment easy to use?
- Equipment or facilities to print each type of microformat available in the collection
  --will there be a charge for copying?
  --will the equipment make good-quality copies?
- Facilities to reproduce microfiche (fiche-to-fiche)

Service and Access Needs
- Cataloging and Processing
  --will microformats be cataloged and how?
  --how will microfiche be marked with property stamps and call numbers (when not included on headers)?
  --will microfiche be stored with or without envelopes?
- Staffing Levels
  --who will file and refile these materials?
  --who will be responsible for maintaining the equipment and supplies for readers and reader-printers?
  --who will provide assistance with materials and equipment?
  --who will be responsible for instructing and assisting patrons in the use of these materials?
- Education
  --will instruction be provided in the content and availability of these materials?
  --how will this instruction be provided (bibliographic instruction, user aids, at the reference desk, etc.)?
- Access
  --how will users access the collection (self service, by request)?
  --will these materials circulate?
  --will portable microfiche readers be available for loan?
  --are there adequate signs?
  --is the collection organized in a way that is obvious to the user?
- Location
  --will the collection be located near paper format documents?
  --will the collection be located near indexes that provide access to the collection?

ELECTRONIC FORMATS IN GOVERNMENT DOCUMENT COLLECTIONS

In 1988, the GPO introduced additional nonbook formats to depository libraries. By the end of 1991, the GPO had made 75 unique titles available on CD-ROM (totaling 120 CD-ROM disks) and created access to the Department of Commerce's *Economic Bulletin Board*, the Federal Depository Library Program Bulletin Board (FDLP/BB), and the Hermes Project containing U.S. Supreme Court opinions. This dramatic change in format is an example of the challenges depository libraries already face and a harbinger of many other new challenges.

Although government agencies have used electronic formats to store information for many years, the 1980s brought a change in the way and the extent to which they used electronic media. Their use of electronic formats grew in part out of the use of electronic technology within the federal government for everything from typesetting to data collection and analysis. However, it was also spurred by the Reagan administration's attempts to privatize many of the federal government's information-related activities and to reduce the government's role in publishing print materials. The same series of laws and directives that forced the GPO to distribute more titles on microfiche also forced agencies increasingly to use electronic formats for storage and retrieval of their information.[18] At the same time, laws and directives were encouraging agencies to seek more cost-effective means to distribute information previously distributed in paper. As the 1980s came to a close, document librarians realized that more government-produced information was available *only* in electronic formats and that agencies were not making these sources available to depository libraries through the Depository Library Program (DLP).

Electronic sources have several advantages for both library users and agencies: they are more compact; they can be cheaper to produce, when produced in large volume; they can make information available more quickly; they have a high storage capacity; they can provide improved searching capabilities (e.g., key-word and boolean searching); and they have a high degree of user acceptance. However, they also have many disadvantages for libraries and their users. It can be costly to produce or buy good retrieval software and user interfaces; it is expensive to train staff and users to use these sources; and it is a drain on library budgets to provide equipment and printing capabilities. The quality of the user interface and retrieval software can limit the use of sources available in electronic formats and may, in effect, become a barrier to information access. Users also must have the appropriate hardware and software or they will not be able to make use of information stored on electronic formats.[19]

In addition, the archival nature of these sources is, at best, tenuous. For example, although the exact life span of a CD-ROM is unknown, most experts agree that it does not match the shelf life of microfiche. The archival nature of on-line electronic bulletin boards is even more questionable. Unless the contents of an EBB are regularly copied to a computer file and stored for archival purposes, the data that enter an EBB can be lost forever. However, the cost (for staff time, telecommunications, charges, and storage costs), not to mention the technical difficulties of downloading large amounts of data over a telephone, makes this virtually impossible for depository libraries.[20] However, no guidelines currently exist requiring agencies to archive the information on their EBBs. Electronic formats, then, can have an impact on the availability of information in the present and in the future.

The Realities of Electronic Resource Distribution

The formats of two publications—the *Congressional Record* and the *Department of State Bulletin*—illustrate the impact such a change can have on the availability of information in depository libraries. In the first example, the GPO cut back the production of the final edition of the 1985 *Congressional Record* to a single format, paper, because of a budget crisis, although the *Record* had previously been offered in both paper and microfiche. Thus, libraries that had selected the microfiche format were left without this important resource, and only 60 regional depository libraries and selected libraries in states without a regional library received a print version of the final edition of the *Congressional Record*. Once the budget crisis was over, however, the GPO did not authorize a microfiche version of the *Congressional Record*, because it was then evaluating its *Congressional Record* on CD-ROM pilot project. This product was finally shipped to libraries in December 1990. Depository libraries were dissatisfied with the user interface for this product and have voiced their unwillingness to have the CD-ROM version replace either the print or the microfiche versions. Until a more acceptable user interface can be developed for the CD-ROM version, most depository libraries will not have access to the final edition of the *Congressional Record* either in paper or in microfiche. Unless the user interface is greatly improved, the CD-ROM version cannot be considered an equivalent replacement for the print or microfiche versions.

In a second example, the Department of State sought to discontinue the *Department of State Bulletin* and replace it with an on-line database. After various user groups, including libraries, stated their dissatisfaction with this plan, the *Bulletin*, renamed the *Dispatch*, was continued. However, the *Dispatch* contains only part of the information typically covered in the old *Bulletin*; the complete text of what had been covered in the *Bulletin* now appears only in an on-line database. Depository libraries must make special arrangements to access this database and to receive reduced rates. Thus, depository libraries must pay to receive all the information they once received free. Both examples raise a number of questions about whether information once available in print (or microform) will continue to be made available to depository libraries, if their format changes to an electronic format.

Two additional developments further threaten the availability of government information in depository libraries. First, the private sector is now providing access to a great deal of government information. This occurs when the government sells information it has collected or when it contracts with companies to provide a service previously provided by the government (e.g., the Security and Exchange Commission's EDGAR system).[21] These providers then charge fees to users who need information originally collected by government agencies.[22]

Second, as electronic technology becomes more prevalent, libraries are also being asked to take on more of the costs of making this information available to the public. For instance, libraries are now required to purchase hardware and software, train staff, and pay for telecommunications and access charges to on-line databases and EBBs. They are also prohibited from charging fees to use government information.[23] As the cost of being a depository library climbs, more libraries may be forced to reevaluate their decision to be a depository library and whether to make these sources available in their libraries in the future.[24]

Although the number of electronic sources available through the depository program has increased since 1988, only a portion of the government-funded electronic sources are distributed or made available to depository libraries. For example, government agencies offer more than 60 bulletin boards,[25] but only 2 are available to depository libraries as GPO pilot projects: the Department of Commerce's *Economic Bulletin Board* and the FDLP/BB. Generally, most agencies do not attempt to distribute or make electronic sources available to the public through the Depository Library Program (DLP). This results, in part, from a need to modernize Title 44 of the U.S. Code.[26]

However, a variety of other problems also affect the availability of electronic formats through the DLP. Examples of these problems include the facts that production of CD-ROMs is not centralized in the GPO; not all agencies view the DLP as the best way or even a desirable way to disseminate electronic information; the GPO plays a passive role in obtaining these sources from agencies (many have argued that the GPO is "outside the loop" in obtaining and disseminating these new formats)[27]; and some agencies do not attempt to distribute these sources because funding cutbacks have affected not only their ability to distribute the source itself, but also to provide staff and user support for the materials. Furthermore, many believe agencies use the electronic format of information as a way to avoid making information available to the public via the Depository Library Program.[28] Thus, because Title 44 does not specifically include electronic sources in the DLP and does not give the GPO the authority to centralize their production and distribution, a growing number of fugitive sources are escaping distribution through the DLP.

Title 44 may lie at the root of the problem of fugitive documents, but several issues must be addressed to accommodate electronic sources that *are* distributed via the DLP. These issues are similar to many problems encountered when microformats were first distributed. Guidelines are needed to limit which titles and types of sources should be converted to electronic formats and which electronic format (CD-ROM, on-line database, bulletin board, floppy disk) is appropriate.[29] Some titles should continue to be made available in more than one format (possibly all three formats—paper, microform, and electronic). Libraries need to know how information will be supplied if their library does not receive a CD-ROM or floppy disk distributed through the Depository Library Program.[30]

However, there are also problems unique to electronic sources. Since 1988, the GPO has made some headway in identifying these problems and has begun to find its role in solving them. It has done this through two means: a series of pilot projects used to "test the feasibility of and practicality of disseminating government publications to Depository Libraries in electronic formats"[31] and an information-gathering survey dubbed the "Technology Tea."

The Pilot Projects

From 1988 to 1991, the GPO conducted several pilot projects for the Joint Committee on Printing. The total analysis of these projects was scheduled to be completed by mid-1992. Each project provided depository libraries and the GPO with insights into the problems that disseminating electronic information could produce. Each project allowed selected libraries to gain access to electronic sources that had previously been unavailable. These projects included CD-ROM sources (*Census Test Disk no. 2*[32]; the EPA's *Toxic Release Inventory* CD-ROM; the *Congressional Record* on CD-ROM), as well as on-line and bulletin board sources (the Bureau of Commerce's *Economic Bulletin Board*, the DOE ITIS database project, and the Hermes database).

The pilot projects provided document librarians with an opportunity to grapple with many of the problems caused by electronic sources. At each step, document librarians became increasingly aware that the access to these materials must be extremely user-friendly, or the electronic format itself would effectively threaten the principle of free access to government information. To accomplish this, standards are needed to govern the way data files are formatted and organized and for the user interface that makes such data accessible.[33] In addition, depository librarians soon realized that someone, either the GPO or the agencies supplying these electronic sources, must be responsible for providing a great deal more assistance and customer support. To fill that gap, document librarians now use their own electronic discussion list—GovDoc-L—to communicate directly with each other and to share problems and solutions. GovDoc-L contains many messages related to electronic sources; in the absence of technical support from the GPO or the agency supplying the electronic source, it is a valuable source of information and help for problems of every kind related to documents.[34] Another source of information about electronic sources is the "Electronic Corner" column included in each issue of *Administrative Notes* (revived November 15, 1990). Together these sources provide much of the informal communication necessary to ensure that electronic sources are available in all depository libraries as quickly as possible.

The Technology Tea

During the Fall 1990 meeting of the Depository Library Council, the GPO invited attendees to provide "constructive, realistic, and achievable comments" for a survey titled "The Electronic Acquisition and Dissemination Survey" (later dubbed the "Technology Tea" because of the time of day the meeting was first held). This survey provided 10 scenarios that reflected actual dissemination decisions that Library Program Services (LPS) had faced. After the survey was published in *Administrative Notes*,[35] 300 additional librarians responded to the 10 scenarios in the survey. Much of the practical feedback contributed to the survey was a result of experience gained through the pilot projects.

The Technology Tea communicated to depository libraries the variety of problems the GPO faces when electronic sources are distributed through the DLP, and it gathered information from depository libraries on how the GPO should and could assist these libraries in the acquisition and dissemination of these materials. The GPO learned that depository libraries are unwilling to sacrifice information for format. Depository librarians want the GPO not only to take an active role in ensuring that electronic sources are distributed, but also to provide leadership in creating standards so that these sources can be used more easily and effectively. Nonetheless, as libraries make these sources available to their users, they will have to consider a number of issues.

Providing Access to Electronic Formats: A Primer

The GPO distributed the first "E" shipping list to libraries in October 1990. By creating a separate shipping list designation, the GPO recognized the importance of electronic sources and their distinct format. Despite this recognition, the sheer number and variety of electronic sources and the speed at which they suddenly appeared presented several difficulties for depository libraries. Most libraries did not have personnel trained to use these sources or the necessary hardware, as demonstrated by a 1988 depository library survey that showed that only 40 percent had CD-ROM equipment. By 1991, this number had increased to 74 percent.[36] Thus, one of the first decisions each library needs to make is whether to select item numbers for electronic sources and try to make CD-ROMs, on-line databases, and bulletin boards accessible within the library.

Having made that decision, each depository library faces a number of challenges as it prepares to provide access to electronic sources (see figure 7.2). These challenges fall into the same categories as those for microformats. First, different electronic sources require different hardware and software. To date, the GPO has made publications available to libraries on CD-ROMs; floppy disks (both 5.25-inch and 3.5-inch); on-line databases; and EBBs. In addition, these materials not only come in different physical formats, but they also contain different types of information: textual data (e.g., the *Congressional Record* on CD-ROM), numeric data (e.g., some files on the Commerce Department's *Economic Bulletin Board*), graphics (e.g., the *1:1,000,000-Scale DLG Data, Hydrography/ Transportation* CD-ROM), and a mix of information types (e.g., the National Trade Data Bank (NTDB) CD-ROM, which contains files with text data and files with numeric data) and coded data that can be used only with a software interface (e.g., the Tiger CD-ROMs). All these formats require a computer to access their information, and each also requires additional hardware (modem, CD-ROM reader) and software. The GPO's "Recommended Minimum Technical Guidelines" advises that the library have five different types of software available (operating system software, database management software, spreadsheet software, word processing software, and communication software); a computer with both 3.5-and 5.25-inch floppy disk drives and a VGA or Super VGA monitor; a CD-ROM drive; a printer; and a modem.[37]

Second, the physical surroundings for these sources require special attention. The number of workstations, type of electrical wiring, telecommunications wiring and access, the capability to print and download data and text, and the shelving and storage of these materials all must be planned with care.

Third, electronic-formatted sources have a wide variety of service and access needs. To ensure that users find these materials, each depository library needs to decide how to catalog and process these materials. Once they have made the materials available, depository librarians will be confronted by a variety of problems caused by the lack of standardization in formats, user interfaces, and installation instructions. For example, depository librarians must become familiar with many software packages and sources if they are to help patrons use or locate data. However, some electronic sources are not accompanied by a software interface at all, but are simply a computer file (either on-line, on a floppy disk, or on a CD-ROM) containing either text or numeric data. This requires the depository librarian to become knowledgeable about additional commercial software packages (e.g., word processing, database management, spreadsheet, and geographic information systems (GIS) software) if they are to provide their patrons with access to the information contained on the electronic source. Each library will have to decide how much support it can provide for these software packages.

In addition, the lack of standardization or technical support makes installing these sources and making them available to the public an additional challenge. Each agency provides instructions for installation in a different way, varying from a "Readme" file on the floppy disk or CD-ROM, a documentation (.doc) file on the disk or CD-ROM, or, occasionally, accompanying print documentation. Frequently, different sources have different configuration requirements (contained in the config.sys file), making it difficult to operate them on the same computer workstation or local area network (LAN). Some CD-ROMs will not run on a LAN at all. Sometimes, even when help screens or tutorials are provided, they are less than truly helpful.[38]

On-line sources can be even more challenging; if no on-line help is provided, it is often unclear where to find documentation for databases and electronic bulletin boards. Often software to be used with an electronic resource is available from a source other than the GPO or agency. For example, the EXTRACT software to be used with the Bureau of Census CD-ROMs is available from three different sources.[39] Public domain software and shareware software can also be used with some electronic sources and is available from a variety of sources. Thus, document librarians may spend a great deal of time locating software packages and printing out the documentation and installation instructions, with little or no help from the GPO or the agency that provided the information, before they are even able to make the source available to the public.

One of the most important service needs is to provide training for the library staff who will assist patrons in using electronic sources. Each library must decide who will be responsible for helping patrons use and access these sources and provide appropriate training. Training typically requires two levels: knowledge about the data or information included on the CD-ROM or floppy disk, and an understanding of the software packages that will be used to access that data. This training is available from a variety of sources, but varies in quality and content. Possibilities include:

- training from the agencies providing the information (these courses typically deal more with the data provided and the software interface they have provided, if any);

- state GODORT meetings;

- IASSIST Conferences;[40]

- ICPSR courses (these courses can be very useful for information about the content of specific datafiles);[41]

- state data centers;

- training offered by the software vender (for example, GIS software vendors often provide training for their software); and

- classes offered at local educational institutions or within the library [especially for courses on DOS, Lotus 1-2-3, dBase, or Statistical Package for the Social Sciences (SPSS)].

At the most basic level, however, all public service staff should be able to answer questions about the availability of these sources and how and where they can be accessed, as well as providing information about their content.

Additionally, libraries need to consider educational, access, and locational questions. Each of these is similar to the issues raised by microformats. Ultimately, each library will be forced to decide whether it can provide the same level of service for all electronic sources. How each library addresses service and access needs within the library will determine to what extent library users are able to use these sources successfully and the extent to which the format itself becomes a barrier to information.

Fig. 7.2. Providing access to electronic formats: A checklist.

Different Formats Have Different Needs
- GPO's "Recommended Minimum Technical Guidelines"

Physical Surroundings Require Special Attention
- Number of workstations based on number of users and number of titles
    - --does the workstation have space to write, for user manuals?
    - --are workstations located in an area conducive to quiet study?
- Electrical wiring
- Telecommunications wiring and access
- Capability to print and/or download
    - --will downloading be encouraged or required?
    - --where will patrons obtain floppy disks?
- Storage (shelving or cabinets)

Service and Access Needs
- Cataloging and processing
    - --will these materials be cataloged?
    - --where will these procedures take place?
- Staffing levels
    - --who will be responsible for helping patrons use these materials?
    - --how will staff be trained?
    - --will different levels of training be required and provided?
    - --who will be responsible for installing and troubleshooting?
- Access
    - --how will users access these sources (self-service, by request, etc.) and will it vary depending on the format (on-line databases vs. CD-ROMs)?
    - --will these materials be allowed to circulate?
    - --will the library provide commercial software packages to access these materials and what level of support will they provide for this software?
    - --will all sources receive the same level of staff support?
    - --how will user manuals and documentation be printed out and updated, etc.?
- Education
    - --will instruction be provided in the content and availability of these materials?
    - --how will this instruction be provided (bibliographic instruction, user aids, at the reference desk, by appointment, etc.)?
- Location
    - --will these materials be located near paper and microformat documents?
    - --will these materials be located with similar materials available from other sources (CD-ROMS from commercial publishers)?

CONCLUSION

"The public has a right to information contained in government documents which have been published at public expense, the Government has an obligation to ensure availability of, and access to, these documents at no cost. These documents are a permanent source of Federal information."[42] As increasingly more information is "published" in nonbook formats, document librarians play an even more important role in fulfilling these goals of the DLP. Yet, these goals are threatened by the increased cost to libraries (and individuals) of making these sources available to the public; by the technology itself; by the need for clear language in Title 44 that specifically includes nonprint sources in the DLP; and by the way government agencies view the role of libraries in disseminating electronic information.[43]

Many believe that all government-funded information systems should be available to the general public through the DLP. This would include sources such as the Department of Justice's JURIS system, the House of Representatives' LEGIS system, and the Library of Congress's SCORPIO system. GPO's strategic planning report, *GPO/2001, A Vision for a New Millennium*, is preparing for the gradual development and implementation of electronic dissemination capabilities at the GPO.[44] Many large research libraries are beginning to use their on-line catalogs and university networks to bring heavily used government information, such as census data, to their users. As we face these challenges, some believe, depository libraries will need to change "from being collection oriented to [being] access oriented."[45] That change is right around the corner.

NOTES

[1] Depository Library Council to the Public Printer, *Guidelines for the Depository Library System (Revised 1987) with Minimum Standards for the Depository Library System (1976)* (Washington, DC: U.S. Government Printing Office, 1988): 1.

[2] Ridley R. Kessler, Jr., "White Paper on Depository Program Expenses for Libraries and Users," *Documents to the People* 20 (March 1992): 27-30.

[3] In 1978, 4,045 titles (a total of 1,544,755 microfiche) were converted to microfiche; in 1989, 28,770 titles (a total of 13,672,308 microfiche) were converted to microfiche. From "Number of Publications Distributed to Depository Libraries (per Fiscal Year)," *Administrative Notes* 11 (April 25, 1990): 16.

[4] Louise Snowhill, "Privatization and the Availability of Federal Information in Microform: The Reagan Years," *Microform Review* 18 (Fall 1989): 206.

[5] Ibid. 203-5.

[6] "Format of Publications Distributed to Depository Libraries (SOD 13)," *Administrative Notes* 8, no. 21 (December 1987): 21-23.

[7] "Depository Items Subject to Microfiche Conversion," *Administrative Notes* 7 (May 1986): 27-34.

[8]"Appendix B: Instruction for Depository Libraries' Selection Update" in *Instructions to Depository Libraries, Revised 1988* (Washington, DC: U.S. Government Printing Office, 1988): 3-6.

[9]John Chapman, et al., "The U.S. Government Printing Office Responds to Criticism of Its Microfiche Procurement Practices: Who Says GPO Does Not Give a Damn?" *Government Publications Review* 16 (July/August 1989): 345-51.

[10]"Microform Storage Should Be Located Convenient to the Documents Area—Space Standard 8-9," in U.S. Government Printing Office, Depository Library Council to the Public Printer, *Guidelines for the Depository Library System (Revised 1987) with Minimum Standards for the Depository Library System (1976)* (Washington, DC: U.S. Government Printing Office, 1988): 7.

[11]Snowhill, "Privatization," 206. However, each of these arrangements can be temporary. For example, the EEOC has been unable to fund the distribution of these microfiche directly to depository libraries. The GPO is now distributing the EEOC *Decisions*. "EEOC Case Decisions," *Administrative Notes* 11 (November 15, 1990): 2.

[12]Patricia Reeling, Mary Fetzer, and Daniel O'Connor, "Use of Government Publications in an Academic Setting," *Government Publications Review* 18 (September/October 1991): 500.

[13]Microforms are best for "applications requiring compact high-quality storage and retrieval of both text and graphics with economical low-volume publishing and where rapid random searching and browsing are not priorities." Herbert B. Landau, "Microform vs. CD-ROM: Is There a Difference?," *Library Journal* 115 (October 1, 1990): 59.

[14]"Chapter 12: Microfiche," in *Instructions to Depository Libraries, Revised 1988* (Washington, DC: U.S. Government Printing Office): 1-3.

[15]Nancy Patricia O'Brien, "Micro-Opaque Copiers: Is There a Resolution?," *Government Publications Review* 16 (July/August 1989): 377-86.

[16]For additional information about the care and maintenance of microforms, consult Ralph J. Folcarelli, *The Microform Connection: A Basic Guide for Libraries* (New York: R. R. Bowker, 1982).

[17]Reeling, Fetzer, and O'Connor, "Use of Government Publications," 500-1.

[18]Snowhill, "Privatization," 203-5.

[19]The GODORT Government Information Technology Committee (GITCO) has adopted "Seven Electronic Information Goals"—education/transparency, usability, affordability, transferability, longevity, accessibility, and agency support—that should guide agencies as they "propose and develop electronic information storage products." Reported in *Documents to the People* 19 (December 1991): 241.

[20]Jim Jacobs, "U.S. Government Computer Bulletin Boards: A Modest Proposal for Reform," *Government Publications Review* 17 (September/October 1990): 394.

[21]James McGrane, "The Edgar Challenge, Automating the U.S. Security and Exchange Commission's Internal Review Processes, Filing, and Information Dissemination Systems: A Development Note," *Government Publications Review* 18 (March/April 1991): 163-69.

[22]Daniel Gross, "Byting the Hand That Feeds Them: Information Vendors Are Robbing the Government Blind," *Washington Monthly* 23 (November 1991): 37-41.

[23]"Spring 1991 Depository Library Council Meeting: Summary," *Administrative Notes* 12 (July 15, 1991): 15.

[24]The costs associated with being a depository library are even more overwhelming for regional depository libraries, especially with regard to electronic sources. See Barbara Hale and Sandra McAninch, "The Plight of U.S. Government Regional Depository Libraries in the 1980s: Life in a Pressure Cooker," *Government Publications Review* 16 (July/August 1989): 387-95.

[25]For a list of EBBs, see Florence Olsen, "Bulletin Boards Give Users the Line on Federal Info," *Administrative Notes* 12 (June 30, 1991): 20-23.

[26]The General Counsel's opinion regarding "GPO Dissemination of Federal Agency Publications in Electronic Format" concludes that the GPO "is authorized to distribute Federal agency publications in electronic format to depository libraries." Unfortunately, not all agencies abide by this opinion. *Administrative Notes* 10 (July 31, 1989): 5-7.

[27]"Spring 1991 Depository Library Council Meeting: Summary," *Administrative Notes* 12 (July 15, 1991): 24.

[28]For a discussion of this, see Leo T. Sorokin, "The Computerization of Government Information: Does It Circumvent Public Access Under the Freedom of Information Act and the Depository Library Program?," *Columbia Journal of Law and Social Problems* 24 (1991): 267-98.

[29]CD-ROMs are best for applications "where many copies are needed and where compact document storage and retrieval must be married with computer searching and retrieval CD-ROMs. It may not be appropriate for applications where archival quality and economic graphic image display are primary concerns." From Landau, "Microform Differences," 59.

[30]For a more thorough discussion of these issues, see the "Discussion Papers" prepared for the Fall 1991 Depository Library Council Meeting. *Administrative Notes* 13 (January 31, 1992): 28-60.

[31]"Information Technology Program (ITP) Update," *Administrative Notes* 12 (April 15, 1991): 6.

[32]Steven W. Staninger, "Using the U.S. Bureau of the Census CD-ROM Test Disc 2: A Note," *Government Publications Review* 18 (March/April 1991): 171-74.

[33]The Special Interest Group on CD-ROM Applications & Technology (SIGCAT) and the GODORT Government Information Technology Committee (GITCO) have been active in working to provide guidelines for standards. See also a report by the CD-ROM Consistent Interface Committee, *CD-ROM Consistent Interface Guidelines: Final Report*, August 1991.

[34]"GovDoc-L: On-line Discussion of Government Documents Issues," *Administrative Notes* 11 (November 15, 1990):15-18; and Diane K. Kovacs, "GovDoc-L: An On-line Intellectual Community of Documents Librarians and Other Individuals Concerned with Access to Government Information," *Government Publications Review* 17 (September/October 1990): 411-20.

[35]"Electronics Acquisitions and Dissemination Issues Survey," *Administrative Notes* 11 (December 30, 1990): 1-6.

[36]"Spring 1991 Depository Library Council Meeting: Summary," *Administrative Notes* 12 (July 15, 1991): 21.

[37]"Recommended Minimum Technical Guidelines for Federal Depository Libraries," *Administrative Notes* 12 (August 31, 1991): 1-3.

[38]For example, a help message from the Chronic Disease Prevention CD-ROM instructs "the displayable view screen is displayed when a view is selected from the select displayable view menu." From a GovDoc-L message from J. Mike Davis, "Subject: Chronic Disease Prevention CD-ROM," March 2, 1992.

[39]Usually the EXTRACT software is provided on a CD-ROM, but it is also available from the Bureau of Census EBB and the Center for Electronic Data Analysis. "Electronic Corner," *Administrative Notes* 12 (March 30, 1991): 2-3; and *Administrative Notes* 12 (December 31, 1991): 10-11.

[40]The International Association for Social Science Information Services and Technology (IASSIST) is an international association of individuals who are engaged in the acquisition, processing, maintenance, and distribution of machine-readable text and/or numeric social science data.

[41]ICPSR is the InterUniversity Consortium on Political and Social Research. The organization, located at the University of Michigan, encourages the use and distribution of machine-readable data archives.

[42]"Guidelines for the Provision of Government Publications for Depository Library Distribution," *Administrative Notes* 11 (July 31, 1990): 5.

128 □ Technology in Document Collections

[43]For a discussion and overview of how one agency views the role of libraries in linking government information to users, see Elizabeth Stephenson, "Data Archivists: The Intermediaries the Census Bureau Forgot, a Review Essay of the 'Role of Intermediaries in the Interpretation and Dissemination of Census Data Now and in the Future,'" *Government Publications Review* 17 (September 1990): 441-47.

[44]U.S. Government Printing Office, *GPO/2001, Vision for a New Millennium* (Washington, DC: U.S. Government Printing Office, 1991).

[45]"Spring 1991 Depository Library Council Meeting: Summary," *Administrative Notes* 12 (July 15, 1991): 26.

8

Circulation

Susan Tulis
Head, Documents Department, Arthur J. Morris Law Library
University of Virginia Law School

The topic of circulating documents has not been discussed at length in the literature of documents librarianship. In fact, it has barely been commented upon through the years. There are two primary reasons for this. First, issues concerning bibliographic control consume most access discussions. Second, local circulation practices for both general and special collections in individual libraries are a major factor in any decision concerning documents. This chapter discusses the legal basis for circulating documents and issues that must be faced when managing a documents collection.

TO CIRCULATE OR NOT TO CIRCULATE

The first question that has to be answered is: "Are you going to circulate your documents?" Whether you circulate your documents depends upon three things:

- the rules and requirements of your depository arrangements;

- your library's general circulation policy; and

- whether you have an integrated or separate collection.

If the collection is separate, there may be a different circulation policy than if the collection is integrated. It may be different not only in terms of whether the materials circulate, but also in terms of the loan period, the library location from which they circulate, and the type of circulation system used.

In the case of U.S. federal documents, there is no legal guidance to help you in formulating your circulation policy. Title 44, section 1911, of the U.S. Code states that "depository libraries shall make Government publications available for the free use of the general public...." This requirement has been interpreted through the years in one of two ways: that the federal depository libraries should circulate their documents; or that the libraries should not circulate documents because they must be on the shelves and available at all times.[1] As a result of this unclear requirement, not all federal depository libraries allow their documents to circulate. However, according to the 1989 Government Printing Office's Biennial Survey of Depository Libraries, 91 percent of the 1,371 federal depository libraries responded affirmatively to this question and circulate some of their materials.[2] What is not known is the total percentage of the documents collection that does circulate. For instance, congressional hearings might circulate, while serial titles, such as the *EPA Journal*, might not. With the appearance of microfiche titles, and more recently electronic resources, this issue has quickly become even more complex. However, it should be noted that "neither the [Depository Library] Act nor the Congressional hearings that preceded its enactment states anything categorically about the circulation or non-circulation of the deposited documents."[3] The GPO, in its *Instructions to Depository Libraries*, defines *free access* to mean "that any member of the general public can physically handle and use a Government document at the library without impediment."[4] The instructions further state that:

> If documents circulate as do other materials in your library, so much the better. (Those libraries wishing to keep their depository collections intact may find it convenient to purchase extra copies of Government publications through the Government Printing Office's Sales Program for use in circulation.)

Section 9-3 of the "Guidelines for the Depository Library System" finishes the debate with this statement: "The library should have the option of establishing its own circulation policies for use of depository materials outside the library."[5]

For international and state documents collections, the requirements, when any exist, are equally confusing. There are depository arrangements among various international governmental organizations (IGOs) and selected libraries. Such a depository arrangement is established through a formal signed agreement between a library and an IGO. The terms of the agreement usually require that the library, in exchange for receiving the publications, make these materials available to the public. A recent survey of IGO depository libraries found that:

> Of the seventy-two respondents, forty-five (62.5%) reported no barriers to public access, while the remaining twenty-seven respondents (37.5%) indicated some form of restriction to public access. Seven reported the collection to be noncirculating, six answered that stacks were closed to the public, and nine indicated that there were closed stacks and that the collection was noncirculating.[6]

Similarly, state depository libraries have various rules and regulations that vary from state to state. To determine what those are in your state, it is suggested that you consult Margaret Lane's classic source *State Publications and Depository Libraries*.[7]

In deciding whether to circulate your documents, you also should be aware of the problems that frequently arise when materials are circulated. Materials may be lost or damaged and they may be impossible to replace, as many government documents go out of print very rapidly. If materials are charged out to one person for an extended period of time, all others are denied access to them. Intensive use of materials may require that the library bind documents, an expensive practice for any collection.

If You Decide to Circulate ...
Questions to Consider

If your materials are to circulate, three questions must be addressed:

- Who may borrow?

- What materials may be borrowed?

- How may materials be borrowed?

Each of these questions should be viewed in light of your library's overall circulation policy.

Who constitutes your primary borrowing group, given your library? It probably will be students and faculty in an academic setting, the "public" in public libraries, and lawyers and judges in court libraries. A key issue is what to do about secondary client groups or nonaffiliated borrowers. What borrowing privileges do they have? Should they be the same as or different from those of your primary clientele? It is best to keep your documents collection policies in line with those governing your library's main collection. Nonetheless, it is important to keep in mind that all federal depository libraries are required to serve the needs of the people within their congressional districts, even if these are not the primary users of the collection. It is also essential to remember that a library can lose its depository status if this "public" is denied access to the depository collection.

Are you going to let everything in the documents collection circulate? Who is going to make that decision? When will that decision be made in the technical processing routine? How are you going to indicate which materials do not circulate? It is possible that specific materials will never circulate, and restrictions may be placed on the circulation of other government documents. Some frequently cited noncirculating materials are: documents with reference value (such as statistical abstracts, organizational materials, indexes, and telephone directories); serial set volumes; recent Supreme Court slip opinions; unbound periodicals; the *Congressional Record*; the *Federal Register*; the U.S. Code; United Nations *Official Records*; maps; and high-use items.

Now that government information is appearing in formats other than just ink on paper, a decision must be made about the circulation of these media. Do CD-ROMs have to be used in the library? Will you let an original microfiche circulate, or will you make a duplicate for circulation purposes? What about floppy disks? Will you make a working copy that is available for use and circulation, and store the original as a master?

The policies and procedures for borrowing documents should in large part mesh with your library's overall circulation policy. However, if variations are possible, these are the types of questions that must be considered.

What time limits are you going to place on the circulation of documents? A week, a month, a semester? Do faculty have a longer circulation period than students? Who gets fined for overdue materials? How much should the fine be? Should bound periodicals have a different loan period than monographs? Where do the materials get checked out: in the documents department or at the main circulation desk? If it is at the documents department, you can count on a significant staffing cost.

What type of circulation system is going to be used? Will it be a manual card-based system or an automated system? If it is a manual system, are you going to have a single card file arranged by document title or class number, or multiple files arranged by date due, patron name, and document information? Will patrons have to write in their names and other pertinent information on a card (which means dealing with illegible slips or incomplete information)? How will you handle renewals, overdue notices and charges, billing, telephone renewals, and interlibrary loans in a manual system? What mechanism will you use to indicate when the book is due back? Are you going to glue in a book pocket, a date-due slip, or attach/insert a date-due slip with each circulation?

Many of these questions also arise with an automated circulation system. In an automated environment, the questions of barcoding and item records need attention. When do you barcode materials—when they are processed or as they circulate? Where do you put the barcode, especially on items like microfiche or CD-ROMs, if they do circulate? Some libraries put the barcodes on the microfiche envelope; one library also puts the last six to seven identifying digits of the barcode on the fiche header. Do you even need to barcode to circulate the materials? The majority of the automated systems in use today (e.g., NOTIS, Innovative Interfaces Inc., VTLS, CLSI, LS 2000) have a circulation component to them. Documents are being circulated through these systems, although some handle the Superintendent of Documents classification numbers better than others.

A decision that has to be made with all of these systems concerns the item records. Are you going to create unlinked item records, create short bibliographic records to attach to the item records, or only attach item records to a complete bibliographic record? Will you leave unlinked item records in the system forever, assuming that the title might circulate again, or delete them after a certain period of time? If the title is not in the OPAC, will you decide to add it to the catalog if it circulates once, twice, or x number of times? Who will create the unlinked records or short bibliographic records? Should it be documents staff or the circulation staff? Obviously, many of these questions have already been answered for the rest of the library collection, and it is best if the documents collections can just follow suit.

Circulation Management Data

One of the more difficult tasks for any library manager is to justify to the administration the cost of staffing and maintaining a collection. Gathering use data is particularly essential for a documents collection, as it is frequently viewed as a "free" collection and therefore not as "essential" as one for which the library has paid. Use data will help in justifying your staff and the costs incurred in automating your processing and circulation activities.

Whether one circulates materials or not, sample in-house use statistics should be kept to demonstrate usage. If the collection also circulates, one should gather (at the least) total usage data sorted by document source (e.g., federal, state, IGO). Additional data sorted by type of user (public, student, faculty) also helps in such justifications. If an automated circulation system is in operation, usage by issuing agency can be helpful in justifying purchases relevant to specific collections (e.g., CIS congressional backfile microfiche collections) and in honing document collection development policies and item selections.

NOTES

[1] Bernadine A. Hoduski, "The Federal Depository Library System: What Is Its Basic Job?" *Drexel Library Quarterly* 10 (January/April 1974): 107.

[2] Conversation between the author and GPO staff concerning data retrieved from Biennial Survey data, August 1992.

[3] Philip A. Yannarella and Rao Aluri, "Circulation of Federal Documents in Academic Depository Libraries," *Government Publications Review* 3 (Spring 1976): 44.

[4] U.S. Government Printing Office, *Instructions to Depository Libraries* (Washington, DC: U.S. Government Printing Office, 1988).

[5] "Guidelines for the Depository Library System (revised 1987)" in *Instructions to Depository Libraries* (Washington, DC: U.S. Government Printing Office, 1988).

[6] Willis F. Cunningham, "IGO Depository Collections in U.S. Libraries: A Directory and Analysis," *Government Publications Review* 18 (July/August 1991): 373-74.

[7] Margaret T. Lane, *State Publications and Depository Libraries: A Reference Handbook* (Westport, CT: Greenwood Press, 1981), 181.

9

Staff Training and Development

Jack Sulzer
Head of General Reference
The Pennsylvania State University

This chapter covers issues related to training and developing staff to work with government information resources. One should think of it as a checklist of items to know, become familiar with, and remember when developing a training program for a documents collection. It is designed primarily for the new documents manager. As such, it is a practical guide to the "nuts and bolts" of staff training and development. It does not include detailed instructions for teaching each job in a documents collection, but rather emphasizes general concepts that should be part of a training program. Elements of a good training manual will be covered, but one is advised to write and compile a manual that is most suitable to the specific needs of one's own documents department.

THE NATURE OF TRAINING AND THE ENVIRONMENT

Good training is a matter of good teaching. This means that the trainers, as teachers, must have a thorough knowledge of the jobs they are training someone to do. They must be well organized and present the job knowledge in a systematic and understandable way. Although good trainers are not necessarily star teachers, they all enjoy working with people and can communicate well. They often can do the jobs they are training others to do. However, that is not a prerequisite for a documents manager to train new employees. A thoughtful trainer can assign someone else who does know a particular job well to do specific task training.

Training is an economic and ongoing process. It is economic because it must be efficient and timely. Its purpose is to teach individuals to do a job productively and efficiently and help them to take their place on the staff as quickly as possible. Training also must be ongoing to develop a staff that continually improves its skills and its capability to adapt to job changes and new tasks.

The requirements and limits of any training program will be determined by the type of library in which the documents collection exists and whether the collection is centralized or integrated with the rest of the library's collection. The budget, type, and size of the library will influence the number of staff working in the documents collection, the range of activities for which employees are responsible, and the levels of public service and technical processing the training must support. For example, a centralized documents collection in a major academic library may require a large staff with a variety of skills to do the amount of processing, collection maintenance, and public service required by faculty, students, and other library staff. The academic library may have a pool of students to draw upon as part-time library workers and a work/study grant program to help finance these positions. Conversely, a documents collection in a medium-sized public library may be integrated with the rest of the collection, require no special maintenance or processing, and service a much narrower range of user needs. The public library may have to rely completely on volunteers and a small full-time staff.

The nature of each library's environment will decide the type and extent of any training program designed. It is crucial to consider the library's situation before putting any time and effort into training staff—this is the key to the economy of training. Extensive training for a sophomore undergraduate who will be working 10 to 15 hours a week and is likely to be on the job for two to three years may be worthwhile. However, it is usually not a good investment to spend too much time and effort on the single job a volunteer might do for six hours a week.

Training needs are also determined by the levels of employees (e.g., full-time/nonprofessional, part-time/nonstudent, student) and the categories of the jobs to be done. Job categories can be broken down into four major groups:

1. collection maintenance (including shelving and filing routines, shelf reading, weeding, and shifting);

2. equipment maintenance (including setup, servicing, cleaning, and troubleshooting for microform readers, photocopiers, reader/printers, microcomputers and their component printers, CD drives, etc.);

3. technical processing (or opening and processing depository shipments, check-in, cataloging, etc.); and

4. public service (including circulation and reserve functions, as well as reference assistance).

Depending upon the size of the collection, the clientele, and the environment of the library, training people in some or all areas will be necessary.

SELECTING EMPLOYEES

Training begins with hiring. When selecting someone for a job in the documents collection, whether for a part-time or full-time nonprofessional position, the manager must decide whether a particular candidate is right for the job. Any training program will have its greatest impact when used to instruct people who want the job, understand what it requires, and are interested in learning how to do it. No training program, no matter how well designed, will produce a good employee from a candidate with little understanding of the position who was hired precipitously.

Job Descriptions

How does the manager choose the right person for the job and be assured that the candidate understands the performance expectations involved with a job? Job descriptions are one useful management tool that can be used in advertising a job properly, in laying the groundwork for productive interviews, and in choosing the right candidate. The fundamental elements of any complete job description are outlined in figure 9.1.

Fig. 9.1. Parts of a job description.

---

* Proper title of the position.

* Position description (a brief description).

* Responsibilities (a lengthier, more detailed list of duties and assignments that is fairly specific, but no longer than a paragraph or two).

* Minimum qualifications (covering minimum qualifications <u>expected</u> of all candidates for the position, plus additional qualities and experience that are desirable or preferred).

* Additional information about the position (e.g., schedule, pay method and/or wage, benefits, etc.).

A job description should be written, kept on file, and updated regularly for each position in the documents unit. This should be done even for part-time jobs. An accurate job description serves three initial purposes. It provides the manager with a documented description of the duties of the position; it gives the personnel officer of the library information useful in screening prospective candidates; and, when shared with candidates, it helps them to decide whether they are interested in the job and prepared for the interview.

Time spent in developing good job descriptions is well spent. It will bring qualified candidates to the interviews and set up the first important question of any interview after the introductions are covered: "Did you read the job description and do you have any questions about the position at this point?"

Interviews

A successful interview gives the manager the information needed to form an opinion about whether a person is suited for the job. Notice that the word *opinion* is used here. Hiring, in large part, is a subjective process, even when done in accordance with the basic employment rules of the library and affirmative action/equal employment opportunity guidelines. Good interview practices do not guarantee that the right person will always be hired. However, if the manager follows good interviewing practices consistently, it will usually save headaches later in actual training and supervising.

There are many sources on interviewing techniques and developing good interviewing skills. The manager may want to consult some of these by reading in personnel or library literature for practical applications. With or without this research, there are a few fundamentals that, when mastered, will prove invaluable in hiring.

Before the interview, the manager should review a candidate's application or résumé. Any questions about background and experience specific to the candidate should be noted. References should always be checked, though there are different schools of thought on whether this should be done before or after the interview. Judge what is appropriate and best for your situation.

The length of a personal interview will be determined by the realities of the calendar and the clock. It should be long enough to allow the participants to become comfortable and have an informative discussion. Generally this will be between 30 minutes and an hour, depending on the position.

The interviewer should be looking for specific qualities in the applicant that are appropriate to the job (see figure 9.2), and should avoid asking questions that can be answered with "yes" or "no." Also refrain from asking seemingly open-ended questions that imply the preferred answer (e.g., "How do you feel about working in a library?") A better question would be, "Why do you want this job?" It is important to get the candidate talking. Ask short, pointed questions and respond to the answers with follow-up questions, but do not do all the talking (see figure 9.3). The interviewer should take some time to explain the job and respond to any questions the candidate might have. Throughout the conversation, it is very important to make sure the candidate understands what the job is, what is required, and what is expected in job performance.

College and university work/study programs present special challenges when hiring suitable staff. Frequently the documents manager's choice of employees is limited and the interview process outlined is much less effective, as there is little control over which students are assigned to work in the library. Here is another area in which a well-written job description is essential. The person assigning the work/study students should know exactly what is required in the position and the manager's expectations. Maintaining an ongoing and good relationship with the student aid officer and the library's personnel officer may pay dividends in getting high-quality work/study students for the job.

Fig. 9.2. Qualities to look for in an applicant.[1]

* **Library Experience:** Familiarity with libraries either as a student or an employee.

* **Communication Skills:** It is difficult to train a person who does not ask questions or respond to them well.

* **Responsibility:** A person leaves the impression of responsibility through promptness for the interview, courtesy with the interviewer, interest in the job, and general enthusiastic attitude. It is indicated by an understanding of the requirements of the position.

* **Interest:** Specific questions from the applicant about details of the job will indicate interest. An interest in current events, political science, or history and social sciences will often result in good performance at the documents reference desk.

* **Enthusiasm:** Indicated by curiosity about the documents department and government information, as well as a desire for library work. A candidate's overall attitude in the interview helps in evaluating this trait.

* **Longevity:** Ask questions that show whether the applicant will stay with the job for a reasonable period of time and is worth training.

* **Flexibility:** Include the ability to meet the scheduling requirements of the job and ability to respond to changes in work schedules.

Fig. 9.3. Sample interview questions.[2]

* Why did you decide to apply for a job in the library?

* What in your prior experience applies to this job, as you understand it?

* How do you deal with people in pressured situations?

* What public service experience do you have?...that you think applies?

* Will you be able to work evenings and weekends?

* What aspect of any job you have held did you enjoy most? The least? Why?

* How politically aware do you consider yourself?

* How are you at handling detail? How well organized do you consider yourself?

* How would you handle this [hypothetical] situation?

After the interview, a tour of the documents collection is often appropriate, but it should be short and introductory. A tour helps the candidate decide whether he or she wishes to work in that setting and gives the interviewer further opportunity to talk and observe the candidate's responses.

What has this got to do with training? Interviews and reference checks are time-consuming, but it is better to put the time into an effective hiring process than to select an inappropriate person for the job. In addition, if time is spent developing a logical training routine, it is important not to waste it on a high rate of staff turnover because of poor hiring practices.

STAGES OF A TRAINING PROGRAM

Three general phases constitute a training program. The degree of effort and the length of time spent in each stage will depend upon the position's responsibilities and upon the experience level a new employee brings. All three stages of training are equally important in the development and maintenance of a capable documents staff.

The first stage is initial orientation and training. This phase starts on the first day of the job and includes getting the new employees on the payroll; setting up work schedules; orienting them to the documents collection; introducing them to other staff; and beginning special instruction in the routines of the job. A training manual is of great use during this initial training and can act as a checklist to guarantee that all parts of the job are covered. This is usually the most time-intensive phase for the manager in developing a well-trained staff. Depending upon the level of the position and the nature of the particular job, this stage can take anywhere from six hours to six months, and may include a probationary period.

The second area of the training program covers staff development and retraining. Again, this process depends upon the position and changes in the nature of the work. This is an important area for training, because its goals are to maintain an efficient staff and attain effective staffing patterns. This area includes training in new or changed job routines, continuing staff education in additional aspects of library work, and public service training. The documents manager uses this phase to develop a knowledgeable and versatile staff with the flexibility to meet the challenges of changing conditions. The importance of this cannot be overemphasized for the documents collection—an area of the library experiencing rapid changes in information technology.

The third area is staff evaluation. This is an ongoing process and is every bit as critical as the initial basic instruction. Regular evaluation of staff performance not only is important in determining who keeps the job or who merits a raise, but also is a useful tool in evaluating an employee's understanding of the job, discovering if additional instruction is necessary, and helping to set personal goals for developing job skills.

Contents of a Training Manual

A training manual can be as simple as a few guide sheets handed out to new staff members or as extensive as a study guide or staff handbook. In any presentation, it should provide staff with basic information about their employment (e.g., library job policies and rules, wages and pay schedules, rights and benefits, job descriptions, evaluations). It should include detailed instructions and procedures for each job done in the documents unit. Finally, it should give some guidance for dealing with situations outside the routine.

The format of a manual should allow easy updating. Each section should be discrete, so as to allow revisions without affecting other sections. This offers the additional advantage to the manager of having individual sections as possible training handouts for new employees in specific jobs. A manual does not have to be written from the ground up. It is more often a matter of compiling and formatting information that already exists in some documented form. The basic content of job descriptions and specific routine procedures for jobs can be written by the people doing the jobs and then edited by the manager for the manual. Library policies and procedures, rules of conduct, and the like can usually be easily compiled from various library administrative documents. Information about classification schemes and shelving order can be adapted from published sources or the shelving manuals of the circulation department. For example, a clear and concise explanation of the Superintendent of Documents classification scheme can be found in Elizabeth Pokorny and Suzanne Miller's *U.S. Public Documents, A Practical Guide for Non-Professionals in Academic and Public Libraries*.[3]

An extensive outline for a training manual is presented in appendix 9-1. It is intended as a guide to the various elements that a documents training manual might contain. The local situation and the jobs covered will determine how extensive and detailed the manual needs to be and the order of priority in which the contents are arranged.

In such a manual, the *Introduction* should be a brief description of the documents collection. It should explain how the documents unit is organized and the publications and types of materials it collects. It should answer these types of basic questions: Does the section do its own processing and cataloging? Does it provide its own reference service? Do documents circulate from that unit? What types of positions are there and what do they involve? *General Rules of Conduct* are the library's policies and rules for its staff and any special rules the documents unit has. In short, what is the minimum expected of each staff member? *Job Descriptions* should be a copy of the information discussed in the interview, and *Duty Routines* should detail specific activities, in their priority order of performance, for each position from the time of arrival at work until departure. *Classification Schemes* used and *Shelving and Filing Rules* depend entirely on the publications collected, their formats, whether they are integrated with the rest of the library's collection, and how they are processed. For each classification system used, the manual should provide the rules of order and contain illustrations with examples of the different class numbers in proper sequence.[4] The *Shelflists and Catalogs* and *OPACs* sections should emphasize the importance of these bibliographic sources as records of holdings and for access to the collection. For instance, if one has an OPAC that can shelflist on document classification numbers, one should note the importance of this tool to shelvers as a reference point in deciding proper shelf order. *Automated Products and Services* should discuss briefly the various systems that the library has for technical processing of documents, acquisitions, and reference service. The *Documents Reference Indexes* section should list the primary bibliographic sources used in reference service, with a brief annotation explaining coverage and primary use. Any available user guides designed for library patrons could be included here or appended to the manual. *Circulation Rules and Procedures* will depend upon whether materials circulate directly from the documents unit, and should provide guidance for staff in dealing with difficult circulation situations. *Shelving and Filing Exercises* should consist of brief instructions for exercises, question sheets, examples, and materials for the exercises appended to the manual. For example, a shelving exercise might include a question-and-answer sheet on the organization of the SuDoc class scheme, plus a set of brightly colored, SuDoc numbered cards so that the trainee can place them in the proper locations in the stacks or microfiche cabinets. The *Equipment Maintenance and Service* section should explain the cleaning and service routines for hardware in the section and discuss procedures for trouble-shooting, replacing toner in photocopiers, light bulbs in microform readers, rebooting computers, etc. This section also should tell where complete operating and service manuals for each piece of equipment are filed and include a list of telephone numbers to call for service and repair.

Despite the detail often put in manuals, it is important to remember that the training manual should not stand alone. It cannot do the training for the manager. Rather, it must be considered a tool for the very personal, labor-intensive business of training. To be a useful tool, it must be part of a complete training program.

INITIAL TRAINING PROCEDURES

The initial training process is based on a prescribed set of routine procedures to ensure thorough training and to cover the same information for all staff members. It is important to schedule carefully the training of new staff, so that they are not overwhelmed with details about the job and they have time to assimilate, understand, and practice skills. A general outline of procedures for basic orientation and training of all staff in the documents unit is illustrated in appendix 9-2. The outline emphasizes the fact that training is a labor-intensive process that requires the manager to be well organized and directly involved as an instructor and mentor.

Careful scheduling of the training process is as important to the manager as it is to the new employee. Training usually vies with the manager's other public service or technical processing duties; consequently, the training procedures must be organized so this aspect of the manager's job has equal standing with other responsibilities. Proper training is an investment in staff resources that should not be short-changed because of pressure to be on the reference desk or to finish a cataloging backlog. Whether proceeding according to an outline, or from a pre-scheduled calendar of activities, the best training process is based on some form of checklist that will ensure that each step in the process is completed with each new staff member.

The three broad areas for most documents training relate to the specific jobs that are done in the unit: collection maintenance, technical processing, and reference service. The elements of basic training in collection maintenance are self-evident, as shown in appendixes 9-1 and 9-2 of this chapter. Training in technical processing is beyond the scope of this chapter and is highly dependent upon a library's individual decision on how to process documents. The chapters on collection development (chapter 2), acquisitions (chapter 3), and bibliographic processing (chapter 5) contain training elements that could be applied to the manual framework provided here. Pokorny and Miller's *U.S. Public Documents* also provides an excellent overview of documents processing at the paraprofessional level. Nevertheless, training for reference service is a general area in which there are some basic rules and procedures that can be outlined and applied in all libraries.

TRAINING FOR THE PUBLIC SERVICE DESK: THE FUNDAMENTALS

As pointed out in chapter 10, "the reference desk is the place that determines, more than any other, the public's view of the Documents Department." Good performance at the reference desk is a question of attitude, mastery of reference fundamentals, and, to a large extent, educational background and innate ability. The rewards of a careful hiring process and good basic technical training are obvious when staff are assigned to the reference desk.

Levels of staffing and types of reference service are discussed in chapter 10. No matter how the manager chooses to staff the desk or define the level of reference service provided, each staff member must have a fundamental core of public service knowledge and be trained in service priorities and standards.

Core of Knowledge

Because many questions asked at reference desks deal with library services and policies, it is important for all desk staff to be familiar with the library floor plan, hours of operation, circulation rules, and location of services. Besides a thorough knowledge of the library's OPAC, all staff members at the documents desk should know the items listed in figure 9.4, particularly the reference sources that pertain to documents. This is hardly a comprehensive list, but it represents fundamental information that every staff member should know and be prepared to provide. One may choose to add to or delete from this checklist according to specific library needs. This type of information should be available at the desk in a Desk Service Manual for quick referral.

Technical Knowledge of Departmental Routines

Besides this basic knowledge about the library, staff should understand how their knowledge of collection maintenance responsibilities and technical processing can be applied to reference service. One main advantage that staff of a centralized documents collection have is an understanding of the depth and breadth of the collection—an awareness that comes naturally from acquiring, processing, cataloging, shelving, filing, and maintaining the materials. For example, shelvers who will be covering the desk need to understand not only how the SuDoc scheme is organized for filing purposes, but also that the scheme helps in answering reference questions. Knowledge from each job can have similar applications and value in public service. If they are well trained and feel comfortable at handling their non-public service assignments, staff transferred to the desk will have overcome a basic hurdle in providing reference service.

Service Priorities

Staff also should know the unit's reference priorities. A busy service unit means a great deal of stress for all those "on desk." As it is impossible to control the ebb and flow of business at the desk, the staff must know in what order they are to handle user requests, answer the telephone, and fix equipment for patrons. This may seem simplistic to a trained professional reference librarian, but it is entirely another matter for nonprofessional staff who are trying to answer a barrage of various reference questions while attempting to fix a jammed photocopier or printer. For example, staff may be instructed that people standing at the desk take precedence over those on the telephone. When there are several people waiting for service, it may be appropriate to poll those waiting, answer the quick questions, and politely ask those with more complex queries to wait to be considered in turn. It is always appropriate to ask someone to come back, call back, or to be called back with an answer. Most library users do not mind this if they are given the proper attention and are treated courteously. Establishing these priorities, communicating them to the staff, and ensuring that they are followed is essential for quality reference service.

Fig. 9.4. Core of knowledge.

- Administrative office locations (including immediate supervisor)
- Handicapped entrance locations and services
- Restroom locations
- Public phones
- Circulation rules and procedures
- Microform collections locations
- Copiers, change machines, etc.
- Classroom locations
- Computer labs
- Group study areas
- CD-ROMs locations and subject coverage
- Hours of the library and specific library services, such as mediated data-base searching or photoduplication
- Hours and locations of special collections
- Reserve reading and reserve policies
- Emergency building evacuation procedures
- Reference service priorities
- Standards of reference desk etiquette
- Basic documents catalogs and index locations
- Locations of all series and types of documents in the collection
- Locations and use of "ready reference" or quick reference documents sources

Desk Etiquette

Service priorities lead directly to standards of conduct on the desk. Remember, the library's image, and that of the documents unit, depends almost entirely upon how library users and colleagues in other departments are treated by the documents staff. Some basic ideals for achieving courtesy in the workplace and providing a comfortable environment for library users are outlined in figure 9.5. Perhaps it should include the item "Be able to leap tall buildings in a single bound," but these are ideals. Training and managing staff to aspire to these ideals will create the proper atmosphere at the desk. In no other situation is it as important for the manager to set an example. At this point the manager moves beyond being a trainer and becomes a coach or mentor.

Dealing with Patrons

No matter how well these priorities and guidelines are followed, someone is going to get angry sometime. Staff will require guidance in handling difficult situations and difficult people. In training staff to deal with these problems, managers need to emphasize that there is a diversity of clientele and a variety of unforeseeable situations that may arise. Different situations will require different techniques. In this aspect of training, it is probably best to seek professional help. The library's personnel or human resources officer may be able to offer some special training, or might suggest classes or workshops that will provide staff with some guidance in dealing with angry or difficult people and diffusing explosive situations. This is an important part of the reference skills package that all staff should have.

REFERENCE TRAINING: BEYOND THE FUNDAMENTALS

Reference service training can be divided into four general phases that run concurrently. *Phase one* is the extension of basic training. This should not begin until the new staff have learned the basic skills of their routine assignments. At this point, training for reference service consists of instruction in the fundamentals covered earlier in this chapter, plus the basics of telephone skills, doing reference interviews, and providing referrals to professionals or other areas of the library. Telephone reference will depend upon the policies and standards set by the individual documents unit. However, the same standards of courtesy and etiquette apply as when dealing with a patron in person—in fact, tone of voice and courteous manners are even more critical. Teaching someone to do a reference interview is also a matter of basic practice. At the least, all staff should know that many patrons are seeking more information than their initial question suggests. Staff should be taught to engage patrons in conversation so they will reveal their real questions. An excellent source for training in this area is Elaine Zaremba Jennerich and Edward J. Jennerich's *The Reference Interview as a Creative Art*.[5]

Fig. 9.5. Desk etiquette.

Courtesy in the Workplace

* Be on time for desk hours
* Take only work to the desk that can be interrupted
* Attend to unanswered questions from the previous shift immediately
* Support colleagues at the desk
* Be desk oriented and help at busy times when off desk duty
* Keep telephones open for service related calls
* Be personable, be open and supportive, be positive, and be willing to ask colleagues for help

Courtesy to Patrons

* Welcome patrons with a smile
* Respect ALL patrons and their queries
* Be aware of patrons in the desk area and offer assistance
* Be approachable and not "uninterruptable"
* Be sensitive to non-verbal cues to patrons such as tone of voice, facial expressions, posture, gestures, and eye contact

Phase two of reference training involves assistance from the rest of the staff in the documents unit. Each desk assistant who is expected to perform reference service beyond the quick "ready reference" category should receive some basic instruction in the reference tools for each collection and special subject resources within the area. The librarian responsible for each unit in the collection (federal, state/local, international, etc.) should do this instruction. Of course, this takes time and requires sensible scheduling, not only because of the number of persons involved, but also because the trainee must be given time to study and assimilate this large amount of information.

It is important that as many staff as possible be involved in this phase, for two reasons. First, it is a developmental opportunity for senior staff to review their own knowledge and participate in the advancement of the departmental team. Second, during this phase new staff learn about their colleagues' expertise and develop a sense for referrals. For the trainee, it also highlights the variety of skills and knowledge needed to provide good overall reference service and demonstrates the need for teamwork.

Phase three of reference training should overlap the first two stages. During this time, the new staff member should have an opportunity to study and do exercises. The exercises may consist of completing pathfinders on basic reference questions, doing library workbook exercises, studying and using flyers, brochures, and guide sheets on automated resources prepared for patron use, etc. This semi-independent study is most effective if scheduled when the trainee is learning about the individual collections, services, and reference tools in the unit. As the exercises and study segments are completed, the manager should review each one with the staff, address misunderstandings, and answer questions. For help in this area, the ALA/GODORT Education Committee has started an exchange of instructional handouts and guide sheets used in documents departments around the country. This collection of handouts includes guide sheets intended not only for patron use, but also for training staff in using many documents sources. For example, the training set has a quick reference guide to NOTIS, international and foreign statistics, updating the census, federal regulations, the *Monthly Catalog*, and the census of governments. A list of the handouts and the guide sheets themselves are available on disk, in IBM or Apple format, from the current chair of the Education Committee.[6]

Phase four, the last leg of initial training, consists of observation at the reference desk. During this stage, the trainee should be scheduled on desk with fellow staff members. This gives the trainee the opportunity to "tag along" with those working at the desk and to see colleagues in action. It also provides an opportunity to jump in when the trainee feels comfortable, without being under the pressure of answering all questions. This is the most difficult part of training to control, because at a busy desk anybody within patron view winds up dancing in the fire. But that, too, is a good experience. The trainee is still in a situation where he or she has colleagues close by for assistance, while developing confidence in his or her own abilities.

ONGOING STAFF DEVELOPMENT AND TRAINING

Once staff are considered "trained," it is time to begin further staff development, especially in the area of reference service. A development program is important to maintain the effectiveness of the staff and to keep jobs from becoming routine, boring, and a breeding ground for morale problems. There are many facets to continuous training and staff development. It will suffice to mention a few to give some idea of what can be done to develop a consistent, ongoing program of training and staff development.

Regular assignments should be used as a basis for developing public service abilities. In this sense, rotating assignments and training staff in different jobs enhances their skill at the desk. Enlisting the aid of staff in training new members of the unit or retraining their colleagues to new assignments can also be fruitful. Staff can be assigned to update or develop new user guides, processing manuals, or training manuals. All these activities require staff to use what they have been taught and learn new things on their own. They also provide an opportunity for creativity and help to reaffirm the sense of "team" that is so important in running a reference unit.

Other ideas that have proven successful are in-depth tours of other library operations; field trips to government agencies; and participation in local campus seminars, personal development classes, and local library conferences. Another practice that is economical, effective, and even fun is in-service reference seminars on special topics and sources. Staff from other sections of the library could be asked to present a lecture on resources in their collections related to government information. A documents staff member might do the same for another reference section. This practice not only expands knowledge of overall library resources, but also can result in better referrals. An offshoot of this idea is the "One Minute Librarian" or "One Minute Workshop." These are very brief presentations done as part of regular staff meetings. As a "One Minute Librarian," any staff member may do a quick show-and-tell on a new reference source or one that has been long forgotten and newly discovered. The "One Minute Workshop" consists of a brief discussion of the various ways in which a difficult question received by a staff member could have been handled. This not only builds staff knowledge, but also encourages the staff to trust one another and work as a team.

Finally, real fun is also a staff development tool. Socializing develops esprit de corps and helps build trust. Social occasions also acquaint staff members whose schedules do not mesh. Throwing a party is a good way to make new staff feel welcome. Parties are the best reward, aside from a raise, for a job well done, and are good stress relievers when the pressure builds at busy times of the year.

EVALUATING PERFORMANCE

Performance evaluation is not often considered as part of a staff training program. However, if ongoing training and staff development are important to the institution, then appraising staff performance must be included as a development tool. A performance evaluation is the primary means of formal communication between the documents manager and the staff member. This process provides two valuable services. First, staff have an opportunity to give their manager feedback on supervision style and ability. This can help the supervisor to refine the training program. Second, although most staff continually seek feedback from their supervisor regarding their performance, they may not be attuned to the messages that their manager is sending, or they may choose to ignore negative feedback. The performance appraisal, in its most positive form, is intended to overcome these inadequacies of human communication.

In a library setting, staff evaluations should be a developmental and motivational tool rather than a disciplinary threat. A good evaluation system is based on the manager's and employee's trust in the process. This means that abuse by either party cannot be allowed. Performance evaluations should be fair and based on data and facts. However, it is difficult to quantify even the most routine processing jobs in the documents unit and almost impossible to do at the documents reference desk. Nor should quantifiable measures form the entire basis for performance evaluation, particularly in reference situations. Much of the evaluation in this area is based on the manager's judgment about the quality of work done.

How, then, is a performance appraisal process made "fair," so that it is an effective motivational and developmental tool that can be used effectively in the training process? Understanding and negotiation are the keys. Performance expectations and guidelines for the library and the unit must be written, specific, and clear. The manager must be sure that the employee understands performance expectations. This understanding is based on a written, detailed job description covering all expected duties.

General areas in which staff should be evaluated are promptness, attitude, attention to detail, judgment, timeliness in job completion, accuracy, quality of work, and initiative. Additional elements can be added depending upon the local situation and staff levels. However, each element should be accompanied by a definition outlining performance expectations. The library may already have a standard form that can be adapted for the documents unit. Here is another area in which valuable professional help from the library's personnel officer can be sought.

Performance evaluations should be scheduled regularly. It is usually best for the employee to receive written comments from the manager before an interview takes place. The employee also should have the option of submitting a written response, and should be encouraged to do so for the record. An employee's signature on any evaluation should show understanding of, but not necessarily agreement with, the evaluation. The evaluation interview should be scheduled to allow time for the manager and the employee to comment, criticize, and respond to the written evaluation and any comments made during the interview. The interview should end with an oral summary of the discussion and agreement upon goals for the next scheduled evaluation. The results of this summary should be written and shared with the employee and the library's personnel office.

The developmental aspect of performance evaluation comes in setting the performance goals for the employee. Again, the key is negotiation and understanding. The manager should not set performance goals without the employee's clear understanding of, and agreement with, those expectations. Unless goals are set to correct a deficiency, it is best to allow the employee to establish personal goals. It is the manager's job to ensure that objectives outlined are reasonable and measurable and that the employee understands how these goals meet the needs of the unit. Through these discussions, regular evaluations, and ongoing training, the manager can develop a quality documents unit.

NOTES

[1] Adapted from a supervisor's manual prepared by Michele Starr, Documents Services Assistant, Documents/Maps Section, The Pennsylvania State University Libraries, 1989.

[2] Ibid.

[3] Elizabeth Pokorny and Suzanne Miller, *U.S. Public Documents, A Practical Guide for Non-Professionals in Academic and Public Libraries* (Englewood, CO: Libraries Unlimited, 1989).

[4] Other sources of information on primary classification schemes that may be used in the documents collection can be found in Lois Mai Chan, *Immroth's Guide to the Library of Congress Classification*, 4th ed. (Englewood, CO: Libraries Unlimited, 1990); and in John P. Comaroni, et al., *Manual on the Use of the Dewey Decimal Classification: Edition 19* (Albany, NY: Forest Press, 1982). In addition, examples of state and local documents classification schemes that are adaptable to any documents collection can be found in: Russell Castonguay's *A Comparative Guide to Classification Schemes for Local Government Documents Collections* (Westport, CT: Greenwood Press, 1984); Caroline Shillaher, *A Library Classification for City and Regional Planning* (Cambridge, MA: Harvard University Press, 1973); and John H. Sulzer, *Revised Classification Scheme for Pennsylvania State Publications* (Harrisburg, PA: The State Library of Pennsylvania, 1987).

[5] Elaine Zaremba Jennerich and Edward J. Jennerich, *The Reference Interview as a Creative Art* (Littleton, CO: Libraries Unlimited, 1987).

[6] A list of current GODORT officers, with mailing and E-mail addresses and telephone numbers, can be found in each issue of *Documents to the People*.

APPENDIX 9.1
DOCUMENTS STAFF TRAINING MANUAL TABLE OF CONTENTS

Source: Adapted from the *Documents/Maps Section Training Manual* of The Pennsylvania State University Libraries, compiled and revised since 1978 by Jack Sulzer, Diane McManus, Christine Whittington, Patricia Scott, and Michele Starr.

I. Introduction

    A. The Documents Section in the Library Organizational Structure relative to other public service units

    B. Depository status

        1. Federal

        2. State

        3. Local

        4. International/IGO

        5. Foreign

    C. Documents processing

    D. Documents circulation

    E. Documents staff organization

II. General Rules of Conduct

    A. Courtesy

    B. Following instructions

    C. Schedules

    D. Breaks

    E. Talking

    F. Pay Periods

    G. Eating and drinking

    H. Grievances

III. Responsibilities and Duty Routines

    A. Job descriptions

        1. Student assistants

        2. Reference desk assistants (Student/Nonstudent part-time)

        3. Part-time clerks

        4. Clerks (full-time)

    B. Duty routines

        1. Student assistants

        2. Reference desk assistants

        3. Clerks (part-time)

        4. Clerks (full-time)

IV. Classification Systems

    A. Library of Congress

    B. Superintendent of Documents

    C. State documents

    D. Local documents

    E. International documents

    F. Special systems

        1. RAND

        2. NTIS

        3. ERIC

V. Shelving and Filing Rules

    A. Documents

    B. Microforms

    C. Transmittals

- VI. Shelflists and Catalogs
- VII. Online Public Access Catalog (OPAC)
- VIII. Automated Products and Services
  - A. On-line databases
  - B. CD-ROMs
- IX. Circulation Rules and Procedures
  - A. Charges
  - B. Overdues
  - C. Reserves
- X. Documents Reference Indexes
  - A. Use and location
- XI. Shelving and Filing Exercises
  - A. Documents
  - B. Microforms
  - C. Transmittals
- XII. Equipment Service and Maintenance
  - A. Microform readers
  - B. Reader/Printers
  - C. Photocopiers
  - D. Micro-computers
  - E. CD-ROM equipment
  - F. PCs

Appendices

    User guide sheets and brochures
    Equipment manuals and instructions
    Reference Service Workbook*
    Service desk standards
    Reference exercises
    Technical Processing Manual*
    Depository shipments processing
    Check-in
    Cataloging/OPAC input

*Note: These may be wholly separate manuals, depending upon the size of the documents operation.

APPENDIX 9.2
OUTLINE OF TRAINING PROCEDURE

Source: Adapted from the *Documents/Maps Section Training Manual* of The Pennsylvania State University Libraries, compiled and revised since 1978 by Jack Sulzer, Diane McManus, Christine Whittington, Patricia Scott, and Michele Starr.

I. General Orientation

   A. Register with Personnel (fill out W-4 forms and pick up time cards)

   B. Tour the library

      1. extensive, detailed tour for nonstudent desk aides

      2. general orientation to library sections and services for student desk assistants

      3. no tour for non-desk student assistants

   C. Set up work schedule

   D. Issue copies of appropriate sections of Training Manual (provide time on the job for reading)

II. Introduction to the Documents Section

   A. Review training manual readings, answer questions

   B. Tour the Documents Section

      1. introduce each staff member, explain their duties and areas of responsibility

      2. show locations of each collection of publications

      3. begin explaining various classification schemes

      4. point out areas of responsibility for shelvers

      5. indicate work stations

         a. bulletin board

         b. closet or lockers

         c. time card and schedule postings

         d. supplies

      6. cover equipment locations

III. Classification Systems (explain basics while touring)

   A. Library of Congress

   B. Superintendent of Documents

   C. State/Local

   D. International/IGO

   E. Foreign

   F. Special collections

IV. Special Collections and Items

   A. Special collections

      1. special markings

      2. special locations

   B. Dangers of misshelved materials

   C. Use of book trucks

   D. Shelving "dummies"

   E. Circulation procedures (noncirculating items)

V. Begin Exercises (as appropriate for staff position)

   A. Shelving and filing (for each collection of publications)

   B. Using documents indexes

   C. Searching the OPAC (complete on-line catalog workbook)

   D. Using CD-ROMs (following user guide sheets)

   E. Locating special materials

VI. Complete Exercise Process

   A. Correct and review exercises

   B. Further explanation in problem areas

   C. Retest in problem areas

VII. Desk Routine (for reference desk aides and student desk assistants)

    A. Conduct on desk

    B. Location and use of desk materials

        1. telephone (use and etiquette)

        2. emergency numbers

        3. supplies

        4. campus directories

        5. local and library maps and location sheets

        6. library handbooks

        7. keys

        8. library brochures and handbooks

    C. Circulation procedures

    D. Schedules for desk, shelvers, other library areas

    E. Log book

    F. Tough question answer box

    G. Desk reference collection

        1. ready reference sources

        2. manuals

        3. bibliographies

    H. Open/Closing routines

10

Providing Reference Service to Document Collections

Diane Garner
Head of Documents and Non-Book Formats Department
Harvard College Library
Harvard University

This chapter is aimed at the person in charge of organizing and managing a documents reference desk. It is not a textbook on how to do documents reference. There are several fine documents reference handbooks listed in appendix 10.1 that will serve that purpose well. Nor is it a manual on how to train staff to do reference work. For that the reader is referred to the discussion in chapter 9 on staff training. The purpose of this chapter is to consider some ideas about the nature of documents reference work, to discuss some issues the manager faces in running a documents reference service, and to offer some practical advice from experienced documents librarians.

NATURE OF DOCUMENTS REFERENCE

Documents reference is not fundamentally different from other kinds of reference service. Questions are asked by the patron and clarified and negotiated by the librarian. The librarian then finds an answer or shows the patron how to find an answer or devise a search strategy. Documents reference is narrower and better defined than general reference and broader and less well-defined than subject specialties like music or engineering. Documents are defined by their source—government agencies. Whereas general reference includes in its repertory information on any subject from any source, documents reference includes information from a government body on any subject for which a government body publishes information. (And, of course, a documents reference collection also will have reference works from nongovernment sources that support reference work with government sources, such as a dictionary of economic terms used in government statistics or a commercial telephone book of government offices.) Because governments are interested in a wide array of subjects, documents reference also covers a wide array of subjects and overlaps with general reference and many subject specialties. However, the context will be determined by the agency's mission and the government's purpose in publishing the information. *Public affairs*, broadly defined, form the core of the reference repertory in a typical full-service documents collection.

No one person can be expert in all aspects of all governments and their activities, but a basic knowledge of how governments work and an abiding interest in public life are indispensable for anyone who serves on a documents reference desk. When hiring staff to work on a reference desk, the manager should look for individuals who are interested in public affairs, read newspapers, and keep up with what is going on in the world. Curiosity and concern for public life can be encouraged by making newspapers and news magazines available to staff on the reference desk. When it is feasible, radio and television live coverage of events—confirmation hearings, press conferences, and the like—might be made available in the workplace.

Staff should also be encouraged to develop connections with the world outside the library. A staff member with ties to local or state government can be a great asset; contacts in an agency aid both reference and collection development. The national and international community of documents librarians is another resource that should be cultivated. Although the demand for professional development may seem at times to detract from reference desk responsibilities, professional involvement can also enrich and deepen the staff's reference abilities. For example, the person who keeps up with the discussions at meetings, on electronic mail, and in the press about the 1990 Census products is able to give more informed and authoritative service. The person who goes even further and publishes on a reference subject not only develops an expertise for the department, but also becomes a magnet for more information, as professional colleagues elsewhere turn to him or her.

The Library Context

The reference services offered at a documents reference desk are influenced by the nature of the documents collection and its place within the library setting. Documents collections may exist in many different kinds of libraries—large, public, or university research libraries; medium-sized public libraries and small and medium-sized college and university libraries; and school libraries, law libraries, corporate and other special libraries. In a small library, it is likely that the documents collection will be integrated into the general library collection and that documents reference will form a part of the general reference function. The larger the library and the more general its mission, the more likely it will be to have a separate documents department. Even in such an environment, documents are frequently combined with other units, such as maps or microforms. Whether separate or integrated, documents must be seen as a part of the whole continuum of reference services.

The needs of the users should be the first consideration. What is needed in the library of an educational institution will be different from what is demanded in a corporate library. What is appropriate in a small public library may not be adequate in a large research library. The manager must also consider what resources are available, both in the workforce and in the collection. A university research library with a large reference staff, a comprehensive documents collection, and the means to acquire many collateral resources will be able to offer a much greater range of services than a small public library with a limited staff and even more limited budget. A separate documents department may be able to give more in-depth and specialized service than a general reference department, but it also may have to duplicate some services of a general reference department. Having separate reference desks for general reference, subject specialties, and documents will require a greater degree of coordination and a greater number of resources than having all reference services concentrated in one area.

Networking

Whatever the setting—whether the library is large or small, public or private; whether its purpose is to serve a high school, a university, or a corporation; whether it is a separate department or integrated with another reference department—the manager must be aware of the full range of information that is available both within and outside the library. No documents reference service, however large or comprehensive, will be able to answer all the questions that come its way. The user may be better served by resources that are not part of a documents collection. Or it could simply be that other resources will extend and complete the information available in the documents department. Conversely, the documents department may have information vital to other areas of the library.

One of the manager's responsibilities will be to facilitate an exchange of information between the documents reference service and other reference services. "Fear and loathing" of documents is a disease that affects not a few general reference librarians. The way to get them beyond that fear is to expose them to what documents librarians know is a fascinating array of information. Exchanges of personnel at the desk for a few hours a week have succeeded, in some places, in broadening the perspective and the skills in the staff on both sides of the exchange. Four hours a week is probably the minimum with which anyone can hope to become competent in a reasonable time. Such exchanges also require a considerable amount of training. They are probably worth the time and the effort only if the library has a stable staff. (Exchanges also give some flexibility in scheduling the desk during emergencies, in that there are more people to call on.) Other than full-scale exchanges, one might consider offering joint seminars with other units on topics of general interest, such as finding statistics. These have the double reward of educating staff about sources and of fostering cooperation between units.

Finally, the manager should not lose sight of the help available from the broader community of documents librarians. Although the setting may determine what is available locally, it should not impose unnecessary limitations. Compiling and keeping current telephone numbers of other libraries, government agencies, legislative offices, and other useful organizations should be a priority. If the library has access to the Internet, the listserv GovDoc-L puts help from hundreds of documents librarians nationwide and worldwide at one's fingertips.

160 □ Providing Reference Service to Document Collections

A TAXONOMY OF DOCUMENTS REFERENCE

Separate documents collections are usually organized by level of government—local, state, regional, national (U.S. and foreign), and international. Most of the reference tools available also follow the same pattern. Therefore, we tend to approach a reference question by asking whether it is a "local, state, or federal" question. This is perfectly legitimate, but it does not go far enough in providing an intellectual framework with which to approach reference work. As illustrated in figure 10.1, with a knowledge of reference principles and a working knowledge of government, one can organize the attack.

Fig. 10.1. Approaches to Documents Reference.

- We might begin by asking if the request is for a known item (exact or inexact)--
  - e.g., a person, an author, a telephone number, a title, a limited piece of data or a general subject--
    information about a program, statistics on ..., publications on ...

- Is the request for a particular kind of product?
  - e.g., a series of statistics
    a legislative hearing
    a technical report

- What government agency is likely to have produced the information?
  - e.g., Census Bureau
    Centers for Disease Control
    Congress
    Supreme Court

There are many ways of looking at a question, not all of them mutually exclusive. It is important for good reference service that staff be aware of the multifaceted approach to questions and that they be given the necessary tools to use their reference skills. In fact, the tools available determine how to approach a question. If the *Monthly Catalog* is the only index available, the search strategy will be simpler (but the search more difficult) than if CIS's *Index to Congressional Publications* or the *American Statistics Index* are also available.

Documents collections may include information from or about all levels of government and about almost any subject. Although it is not possible here to go into great detail about the questions that come up at a reference desk, a brief survey of the kinds of questions that arise for different levels of government might be useful.

Local Government

In most libraries, the local government collection is limited to publications of nearby towns and cities. The information most frequently requested reflects local concerns with budgets, taxes, land use and planning, and local ordinances. The *Index to Current Urban Documents* may be useful for collections that attempt to offer access to a wide range of localities, but for practical purposes access to local government information usually requires a knowledgeable and resourceful staff, as there are few reference tools. Local newspapers are indispensable for coverage of local government. Personal contacts with city hall and with agencies such as the planning commission or the board of education will alert the staff about publications and inform them about the wealth of information that may be available in unpublished format. Frequently, users with a need for local information have to be referred directly to the agency.

Regional Organizations

A library's collection of publications of regional organizations probably will be limited to the organizations that affect the local area. Regional organizations are created by agreements on regional cooperation for such things as mass transportation, economic development, environmental protection, shared waterways, and the like. They may exist within a state or between states and sometimes even between countries. Learning of their existence, let alone finding their documents, may be difficult.

State Government

State government publications, though not as numerous as federal publications, usually cover the same range of governmental activities. People look for directory information about state government and government officials, state court opinions, copies of bills, statutes and reports of state legislatures, the state budget, and regulations and reports of administrative agencies (particularly statistics). There is no comprehensive access tool for state publications, but many printed and electronic sources cover some part of the universe of state publications. The *Monthly Checklist of State Publications* from the Library of Congress lists publications from every state, but it is very selective. LEXIS and WESTLAW are fairly comprehensive guides to many of the legal publications of all 50 states. The OCLC database contains bibliographic records for many state publications. The *Statistical Reference Index (SRI)* is an excellent indexing and abstracting service for selected statistical publication series of each state. Some state libraries may make catalogs or lists of publications in their own state. In the end, the library's own bibliographic records may be the best approach. Given the lack of other access points, it is particularly important for state documents to be included in the library's on-line or manual card catalog.

U.S. Federal Government

Federal documents account for most of the reference questions and the largest part of the collection in the typical U.S. documents library. They also have the best access tools: the *Monthly Catalog of U.S. Government Publications*, *CIS Index to Congressional Publications*, and *American Statistics Index*, to name but a few. The range of information in federal publications is vast. If one were to try to name only a few areas of particular importance to the reference desk, they would have to include the budget, the Census, statistics, legislative publications, statutes, and court reports. In some libraries, technical reports and patents might also be important. At a minimum, staff who work with federal documents need to know how a bill becomes law and the documentation that results from the process; how to navigate their way through the decennial censuses; how to find federal court cases; how to find statutes; how to find basic and popular statistical series; and how to use the *Monthly Catalog*.

Many reference handbooks have been written for federal publications. For older documents, Schmeckebier's *Government Publications and Their Use* or Boyd and Rips's *United States Government Publications* have information that is not easily available anywhere else. Joe Morehead's classic *Introduction to United States Public Documents* has been a standard textbook for library school courses in government documents and remains a valuable tool for the reference desk. Judith Schiek Robinson's *Tapping the Government Grapevine* is especially useful for more current government information.

Non-U.S. National Documents

Collections of foreign national (or subnational) documents are likely to be found only in large research libraries. Acquiring them and giving reference service requires a considerable outlay of resources, both in money and in staff time and effort. The developed nations—Canada, Western European countries, Japan, Australia, and New Zealand—all produce extensive government publications. Access to them varies from country to country, with English-language countries generally having greater bibliographic access to government publications. They cover the same wide array of subjects as do U.S. federal publications. Questions may range from requests for a government report to a legislative proceeding to census data to laws. There is no substitute for understanding the governmental structure and processes of each country and for having a knowledge of their publication patterns.

Official publications of Third World countries are another matter. They are often irregular in publication schedule and difficult to obtain. Reference requests tend to concentrate on development plans, official gazettes, legislative proceedings and statistics, and especially national censuses (partly because these are the kinds of information most readily available). For most libraries, referral to a large research library is the only way to connect patrons with the information they need. Two publications sponsored by the American Library Association's Government Documents Round Table (GODORT) are useful for identifying publications and library collections of foreign government publications: the *Guide to Official Publications of Foreign Countries* and the *Directory of Government Document Collections and Librarians*.

International Documents

International intergovernmental organizations (IGOs) are formed by sovereign nations for various purposes—to keep the peace, to promote development, to provide relief, to aid against enemies. There are worldwide IGOs (e.g., the United Nations) with a very broad mission and regional IGOs with a limited mission (e.g., Arab Monetary Fund). A knowledge of the organization is especially necessary for effective reference service with IGO documents, because of the paucity of bibliographic access and because, like other areas of documents, IGO reference is tied to the work of the IGO. There are hundreds of IGOs, but only a handful produce enough documentation to be of interest to most libraries. The United Nations is the best known among them, and a good deal of IGO reference in libraries is for model U.N. groups. The European Communities is a close second in use. Many IGO publications, such as those of the World Bank or the Organisation for Economic Cooperation and Development, are treated like books and are integrated into the rest of the library's collection along subject lines. Hence, the reference work involved with their publications is limited primarily to catalog assistance.

Most IGOs distinguish between "publications" and "documents." Publications are promoted and sold, often through commercial channels. These frequently merit the same level of bibliographic treatment as books in the national databases. Documents are more likely to be free, deposited, or available only on standing order. Documents are not well indexed unless an index is produced by the agency itself.

For a subject approach to a whole range of IGOs, the best index is the *Index to International Statistics*. As its title suggests, it restricts itself to IGO publications that contain a significant proportion of statistics. The larger IGOs produce catalogs (and sometimes indexes) of their own publications. Many IGOs have computerized databases of their documentation, and some of these are available to libraries, either directly through national library databases such as RLIN, or through the mediation of the agency's library.

Questions may arise about the organization itself, about its member countries, or about activities under its auspices (e.g., the legislative process in the European Communities, or a country's position on an international political question, or a refugee program in a troubled area of the world). Statistics compiled by international organizations are particularly in demand. For a more thorough discussion of IGO reference, see Mary Fetzer's chapter on "Reference and Information Work" in *International Information: Documents, Publications, and Information Systems of International Governmental Organizations*.

MANAGING A DOCUMENTS REFERENCE DESK

Managing a reference desk effectively means using the available resources of people, materials, services, and facilities to satisfy the needs of users. This requires information on users' needs, an appreciation of the unit's capacity to meet users' demands, and leadership to motivate staff. Some practical considerations are discussed here, including the compilation of statistics to track users' needs, the staffing patterns of the desk, the pressures that new technologies may put on a reference desk, and the tools needed at a documents reference desk.

Staffing the Documents Desk

The reference desk is the place that determines, more than any other, the public's view of the documents department. If patrons get prompt, pleasant, and helpful service, the department will have a good reputation as a public service unit. It is important, therefore, that staff have a positive attitude about serving on the reference desk and that being "on call" and available be their primary responsibility when they are assigned to the desk. The decisions about staffing a documents department reference desk are not significantly different from decisions about staffing any reference desk.

Levels of Reference Service

The most basic and frequent level of service is usually called "ready reference," dealing with the simple questions that can be answered easily from a few sources. All levels of staff who serve on the reference desk should be capable of this level of service. More complex or obscure questions call for extended reference service and may require a staff with more experience and training. In some situations, particularly in libraries in educational institutions, reference service may become an educational function, teaching how to find answers rather than finding answers for patrons. Occasionally patrons may have to consult the resident "expert," and in these cases it is a good idea to provide for reference by appointment. This may be with someone on the documents staff who specializes in the documents of a given country or agency, or it may be with someone who specializes in a certain subject area, such as law. In some libraries, reference by appointment is the norm for all but the simplest of ready reference.

Mixture of Staff

Some libraries decide that only professional librarians can give adequate reference service. Others are willing and able to hire and train nonprofessional staff to do reference work. What is appropriate in a given library will depend on the clientele and their needs and expectations. If, as in most libraries, the reference desk meets a wide variety of needs, then some combination of professionals and nonprofessionals will be the most efficient and cost-effective means of staffing the desk.

Models for Scheduling

Accurate statistics about desk activity are helpful in determining how the desk should be staffed. Too many people on desk at a quiet time might encourage bad habits, such as wasting time, doing nothing, or gossiping in a public area. More serious is the possibility of creating a wrong impression that the department is not working up to capacity. Administrators have a special knack for wandering through a department at the least busy moments, just when you are trying to convince them that you need more staff. Flexibility and the capability to add, change, or subtract staff on short notice are useful.

A number of questions arise when managing and staffing a documents reference desk. Who makes the schedule? How often is it done? What combinations of staff should be applied? A good manager should accommodate preferences of the staff as much as possible. Some managers like to reserve the power and the blame for the schedule to themselves. It can get to be an onerous task, though, especially if it has to be made weekly and requires a lot of juggling of complex schedules. It also can be a lightning rod for staff complaint, especially when they feel the pressures of other duties. Dissatisfaction can be deflected somewhat if there are specific staffing guidelines that everyone understands. It is possible to use automated desk scheduling programs, but it is difficult to program all the variations in the use of staff time that might arise, and it is equally difficult to apply a program written for another library setting.

Statistics: To Keep or Not to Keep

Data about reference desk activity can be a useful tool in several ways. Statistics can make a stronger argument to administration to hire staff. Statistics can give a clearer picture of the real needs of the reference desk. Knowing when the desk will be busy, what kinds of questions are being asked, and what services or equipment are being used can help the manager plan for adequate staffing and services.

Too often, statistics are kept because they have always been done that way. Like any other practice, the taking of statistics should be examined from time to time. Do they tell you anything you need to know? Do they tell you everything you need to know? What data are required by the library administration? Are those data sufficient for the needs of the documents department? Some activities, such as use of an on-line database, can be counted automatically by a system. Others must be tallied manually. The accuracy of manually gathered data must be viewed with some skepticism, if for no other reason than the fact that a staff busy answering questions will tend to forget to keep track of the number of questions. Even so, the numbers will still be an indication of the level of activity. A more serious consideration is that having to keep statistics on a regular basis is a distraction from the real work of the desk, which is reference. Do statistics have to be kept at all times, or will sampling at certain times of the year provide enough information?

Typically, documents reference desks keep data about the number of queries in certain categories, such as telephone or in person and short or extended reference. You also may need information for more specific purposes, such as the use of a CD-ROM product. It is important that everyone understand and agree on the meaning of the categories, at least to the extent that is possible. When the categories are vague or ambiguous, the data gathered will not be very reliable. Consider, for example, categories that attempt to measure queries on jurisdictional lines—queries about local, state, and federal government. If what you want to measure is the use of a part of the collection, then it must be well understood that it was where the answer came from and not the question that determines the category. If the answer to a question about a state was found in a federal publication, then it was a "federal" question, even though it was about a state. The manager should question whether such data serve any useful purpose.

166 ☐ Providing Reference Service to Document Collections

Nonbook Media at the Reference Desk

In recent years, electronic media have profoundly altered reference service. In the 1970s, microformats seemed like a major hurdle as a reference tool, but libraries quickly adapted to tools such as the *Publications Reference File (PRF)*. Electronic media offer even greater challenges. The manager must consider what products and services to offer, whether to pass on costs for commercial services, and where and in what manner to offer the services. Putting popular services at the reference desk makes them more visible and more accessible to potential users. The staff at a busy reference service desk may not be able to handle electronic reference, in which case it might be necessary to provide a separate area supervised by extra staff. If that is not feasible, electronic reference by appointment may be the answer.

Given the dynamic nature of electronic publishing, a list such as this one is quickly outdated (figure 10.2). This figure lists examples of what exists as of this writing.

Fig. 10.2. Electronic documents reference sources 1992.

Bibliographic tools
    Statistical Masterfile (CD-ROM)
    Congressional Masterfile (CD-ROM)
    UN Index (CD-ROM)
    Monthly Catalog (Several CD-ROM products)

Statistical reference tools
    County and City Data Book (CD-ROM)
    County Business Patterns (CD-ROM)
    1990 Census (CD-ROMS)
    Economic Bulletin Board (On-line)

Text reference
    National Trade Data Bank (CD-ROM)
    GPO's Hermes Bulletin Board (Supreme Court Opinions) (On-line)
    Legislate (On-line)
    Washington Alert (On-line)
    Lexis/Nexis (On-line)

Frequently Asked Questions

It is a truism in reference that 80 percent of the questions asked can be answered by 20 percent of the reference collection. An informal poll of documents librarians across the country was conducted on GovDoc-L to determine the most frequently asked questions. Figure 10.3 outlines the questions most frequently cited by the librarians who responded to the poll.

Fig. 10.3. Most frequently asked about topics.

State and federal regulations
State and federal statutes
Economic statistics, e.g., Consumer Price Index
Population data, Census and Current Population Surveys
Names and addresses of Congressional and state legislators
Data about foreign countries
Foreign diplomatic representatives
Crime statistics
Statistics about local areas
A known hearing
Bills on a subject by a known sponsor and status
Federal programs
Tax forms
Government jobs
A document requested by title

The Desk Reference Collection

An efficient reference desk should have a collection of the most frequently used sources for the convenience of staff answering in-person and telephone questions (figure 10.4). Although having a collection at the desk cannot guarantee that the source you need will always be available, it does provide some security for the most vital part of the collection. The desk reference collection should be frequently reviewed by the staff that work on the desk to keep it useful—annually at a minimum. Arriving at a consensus about the criteria for what belongs in the desk collection should not be difficult as long as the staff who use it are consulted. Usually there is not a great deal of room for a large collection at the desk. Even if space is not a problem, a collection of more than a dozen shelves defeats the purpose of having a ready reference that can be remembered and used often.

Fig. 10.4. A suggested reference desk collection (in most cases the latest editions or recent issues).

United States Government Manual	Background Notes, U. S. Department of State
Congressional Directory	Treaties in Force
[Your State] Government Directory, also known as a Bluebook	The Diplomatic List
	Encyclopedia of International Organizations
Telephone books, federal, state and local	Directory of Foreign Document Collections
Local government directory	Issues Before the General Assembly
Statistical Abstract of the United States	Guide to Official Publications of Foreign Countries
Historical Statistics of the United States	
[Your state] statistical abstract	The Budget of the United States
County and City Data Book	[Your state] budget
State and Metropolitan Area Data Book	Catalog of Federal Domestic Assistance
Occupational Outlook Handbook	Politics in America/Almanac of American Politics
Handbook of Labor Statistics	
Economic Indicators	Andriot's Guide to U.S. Government Publications
Digest of Education Statistics	
Uniform Crime Reports	Publications Reference File (GPO)
Sourcebook of Criminal Justice Statistics	Information USA
U.S. Industrial Outlook	Federal Data Base Finder
UN Statistical Yearbook	CQ's Guide to Congress
UN Demographic Yearbook	CQ's Guide to the Supreme Court
Latest Census volumes for your state	CQ's Guide to the Presidency
World Factbook	CQ Weekly Report/National Journal
An almanac, such as the World Almanac	Book of the States
Statesman's Yearbook	Subject Compilations of State Laws
Chiefs of State and Cabinet Members of Foreign Governments	Complete Guide to Citing Government Documents

ACCESS TOOLS FOR THE DOCUMENTS COLLECTION

Along with these basic reference sources, there are indexes, catalogs, and other access tools that are essential for documents reference. They should be kept as close to the reference desk as practical. Putting them behind the desk makes them convenient for staff use, but removes them from easy public access for self-service. Shelving them away from the desk works only if they are not consulted often by the staff and if users do not need staff assistance. The usual solution is to put them within sight of the desk on tables with center shelves and plenty of work space (figure 10.5). Short user guides can be placed beside the indexes for self-service. These user guides may be developed by staff. For some commercial products, such as those from the Congressional Information Service, user guides are available from the publisher.

These access tools may include a card catalog, the library's on-line catalog, electronic catalogs such as the *Monthly Catalog* CD-ROM, the documents shelflist, other on-line databases, or printed indexes. The access tools will vary depending on the documents collection and the library's budget. At a bare minimum, a documents library should have the *Monthly Catalog of U.S. Government Publications* and, if the library has United Nations documents, the *U.N. Index*. Beyond the sources listed in figure 10.5, there are numerous useful products that cover special subjects, such as *Energy Resource Abstracts*, or special collections, such as *Major Studies and Issue Briefs of the Congressional Research Service Cumulative Index*.

Fig. 10.5. A suggested index collection.

Monthly Catalog of U.S. Government Publications (CD-ROM, printed, on-line)
Cumulative Title Index to U.S. Public Documents
Cumulative subject indexes to the Monthly Catalog
UN Index (printed, CD-ROM, access to UNBIS via RLIN)
CIS Index to Congressional Publications
Serial Set Index
Congressional Masterfile CD-ROM
American Statistics Index
Statistical Reference Index
Index to International Statistics
Statistical Masterfile CD-ROM
Monthly Checklist of State Publications
Your State's Publication list
Index to Current Urban Documents
Canadian Government Publications
HMSO Monthly Catalogue
Publication catalogs of international agencies
Government Reports Announcements and Index
Patent Index
CASSIS (the Patent CD-ROM index)
Indexes to FBIS reports
Transdex Index (to JPRS reports)
PAIS Index

SOME PRACTICAL AIDS

Over time, busy reference staffs have developed ways to make their jobs easier. These include anticipating and preparing in advance for questions they know will be asked, preparing handouts, and passing the word along from one to another about "hot" questions and possible sources. A *notebook*, kept at the desk, is a convenient way for staff to pass along questions, answers, and comments about the business at the desk. It is a good idea to be sure comments are dated and signed and that everyone understand what the notebook is for (not personal comments or pornography—it's surprising what gets written near midnight on the reference desk).

Many reference desks maintain *reference files* of frequently asked or especially difficult questions. Besides asking staff to add cards to the file as they run across difficult questions, the notebook can be culled periodically for good questions and answers for training new staff. These reference files should be updated from time to time, as answers and sources change over time.

In libraries serving educational institutions—academic, school, or public libraries—it is a good idea to acquire copies of *class assignments* when those assignments involve research in documents. Staff can be prepared to show students where to look. For large classes, this also may be the salvation of the collection. Copies of documents in heavy demand can be made; books can be placed on reserve or in secure areas.

Bibliographic instruction, as discussed in chapter 11, is another preventive way of dealing with the pressures on the reference desk, by teaching users en masse instead of one at a time. When groups appear to be asking the same set of questions repeatedly, it might be worthwhile to inquire if it is a class project and to contact the teacher to offer library instruction.

Because documents reference often concentrates on public affairs, a *current events file* or *newspaper clippings* can be very useful. Immediately after an election, for example, the only place to find election results that people want immediately is in the newspaper.

For more complex questions and for electronic media, a *step-by-step guide* (also known as a *cheat sheet* or *recipe*) on how to find the answer or how to access the data can allow patrons to do it themselves and free the staff for other questions. More general guides, such as pathfinders or bibliographies, can also be useful. *Automated log-ons* for on-line databases can make the difference between an on-line service that is never used for reference and one that staff turn to often. If the log-on is completely automated, including the password, on-line services can be opened to end users for self-service. Security is a consideration, but passwords can be masked and the workstation locked up when it is not supervised. The user-friendliness of the database and training of end users is another issue for which libraries and vendors are finding solutions. Although these guides save a lot of time in the end, they are fairly time-consuming to prepare, and one should look to cooperative ventures. ALA/GODORT's Education Committee has an exchange of handouts, on paper and on floppy disk. Users of GovDoc-L frequently announce that they have created user guides that they are willing to share. The GPO's *Administrative Notes* has a Readers' Exchange, "The Electronic Corner," where depository librarians are invited to share their solutions to the problems presented by installing, understanding, and promoting the influx of government electronic products available to U.S. GPO depository libraries.

APPENDIX 10.1
RECOMMENDED READING FOR DOCUMENTS REFERENCE

Local Documents

Nakata, Yuri, Susan J. Smith, and William B. Ernst. *Organizing a Local Government Documents Collection.* Chicago: American Library Association, 1979.

Regional Documents

Sulzer, Jack, and Roberta Palen. *Guide to the Publications of Interstate Agencies and Authorities.* Chicago: American Library Association, 1986.

State Documents

Fisher, Mary L. *Guide to State Legislative and Administrative Materials.* AAL publications series; no. 15. 4th ed. Littleton, CO: Sponsored by the American Association of Law Libraries, published by F. B. Rothman, 1988.

Lane, Margaret T. *Selecting and Organizing State Government Publications.* Chicago: American Library Association, 1987.

U.S. Documents

Boyd, Anne Morris, and Rae Elizabeth Rips. *United States Government Publications.* 3d ed. New York: H. W. Wilson, 1949.

Herman, Edward. *Locating United States Government Information: A Guide to Sources.* Buffalo, NY: H. W. Wilson, 1983.

Kinder, Robin, ed. *Government Documents and Reference Services.* New York: Haworth, 1991.

Morehead, Joe, and Mary Fetzer. *Introduction to United States Government Information Sources.* 4th ed. Littleton, CO: Libraries Unlimited, 1992.

Robinson, Judith Schiek. *Tapping the Government Grapevine: The User-Friendly Guide to U.S. Government Information Sources.* Phoenix: Oryx Press, 1988.

Schmeckebier, Laurence Frederick. *Government Publications and Their Use.* 2d rev. ed. Washington, DC: Brookings Institution, 1969.

Sears, Jean L., and Marilyn Moody. *Using Government Publications.* Phoenix: Oryx Press, 1985-1986.

Foreign Documents

Guide to Official Publications of Foreign Countries. Bethesda, MD: Congressional Information Service, 1990.

Harrington, Michael. *The Guide to Government Publications in Australia.* Canberra: Australian Government Publishing Service, 1990.

Johansson, Eve, ed. *Official Publications of Western Europe.* London: Mansell, 1984-1988.

Rodgers, Frank. *A Guide to British Government Publications.* New York: H. W. Wilson, 1980.

Richard, Stephen. *Directory of British Official Publications: A Guide to Sources.* 2d ed. London; New York: Mansell, 1984.

Turner, Carol A. *Directory of Foreign Document Collections.* New York: UNIPUB, 1985.

International Documents

Hajnal, Peter, ed. *International Information: Documents, Publications, and Information Systems of International Governmental Organizations.* Englewood, CO: Libraries Unlimited, 1988.

Jeffries, John. *A Guide to the Official Publications of the European Communities.* 2d ed. London: Mansell; New York: Distributed in the United States and Canada by H. W. Wilson, 1981.

11

Outreach, Promotion, and Bibliographic Instruction

Susan Anthes
Associate Director for Public Services
University of Colorado

Although depository laws ensure the availability of government information to citizens, only a few Americans are aware of these depository arrangements and use the resources available. Fortunately, government documents librarians are generally advocates for their collections and place a high value on both publicizing and encouraging the use of their collections. They believe in the right of all citizens to have access to government information and that use of this information will enable people to make better public and private decisions.

Informal promotion of government documents and the information in them relates to many topics covered in this book. Bibliographic processing, classification, access issues, collection development, and reference work all affect the ability of a library to promote its collections to the public. The success of these outreach efforts depends on several factors, including the accessibility of collections through public card or electronic catalogs; the amount and type of material held; and the quality and quantity of reference assistance.

This chapter discusses more proactive steps that documents librarians can take to encourage use of their collections. More formal promotion and outreach efforts develop awareness and stimulate the use of government publications as viable information sources. Specific characteristics of government documents, such as their broad spectrum of subjects, many formats, levels of readability, and lack of copyright make them especially useful, timely, and significant for particular audiences.

OUTREACH PROGRAMS

Administrators, librarians, and staff working with government information want their collections to reach appropriate users. One way of achieving this end is to develop an outreach program. Such a program will identify a specific audience and stimulate a need for information that the collection contains. Once the informational need has been established, some form of instruction for the collection should be prepared. Teaching the necessary skills to access information is a significant outreach effort to library patrons. Even with the best possible reference assistance, it is important to teach patrons to find bibliographic information on documents and to locate the physical documents themselves. A complete outreach program should also focus on the critical evaluation of the usefulness of particular kinds of government-produced information.

Outreach program goals for a government documents collection will vary according to the type and size of library collection available. A small public library with only a few city and state items will have different objectives, and thus different programs, than a full regional depository located in a major research library. However, the goals of any outreach program are the same. Hernon identified four goals that may be applied to all types of promotional efforts.[1]

The first goal is to increase user awareness of government information and its potential uses. Until users know about the wide variety of materials published by various governments and their agencies, they cannot begin to seek out the information. A business person may know, for example, about government contracts, but might not know about a publication such as *Commerce Business Daily*.

The second goal is to increase familiarity with government information collections so that they can be used effectively and appropriately. Many sophisticated library patrons never investigate the resources in government documents collections. This may be because of a poor physical location for the collection; lack of bibliographic access through conventional catalogs; or simply because the collection has never been highlighted or pointed out.

Goal three, particularly for academic or school libraries, is to offer bibliographic instruction on government documents. Often when users find helpful information in a documents collection, they are inspired to search for additional information. Bibliographic instruction, either in a formal classroom setting or on a personal, one-on-one basis, provides awareness of government information resources.

The fourth and final goal is to expand the delivery of government information to all types of users. The ultimate goal of the depository laws, documents collections, and any outreach efforts is to see that users (taxpayers and citizens) know about, can access, and effectively use information that governments have collected and published.

Promotion and Outreach

Several kinds of programs will be effective in reaching potential government publications consumers. Obviously, the more a program is tailored to specific patron needs, the more helpful it will be. Some special libraries will be able to identify specific users, design a program just for them, and initiate such users into the world of government information. Other libraries will need a broader approach, offering several types of outreach programs for their various patrons.

Developing Outreach Programs

Libraries can take several steps to determine how to design their outreach programs (figure 11.1). The first step is to decide what the library wishes to accomplish through such a program. What kind of information should be promoted? It is best to decide which specific collections or services should be highlighted. Small business owners, for example, should be aware of publications offering them assistance, such as grant and contract opportunities; local economic development data; state and federal regulations; and the availability of other small business programs. Local citizens and community action groups may wish to take advantage of environmental protection information and toxic release data. In an election year, people are always concerned about the voting records of their local, state, and national representatives. Or the library may provide copies of tax forms to the public, which also serves to draw patrons into the government documents collection. Each of these examples provides the library an opportunity to promote a particular collection or service to a targeted user group.

Fig. 11.1. Implementing an outreach program.

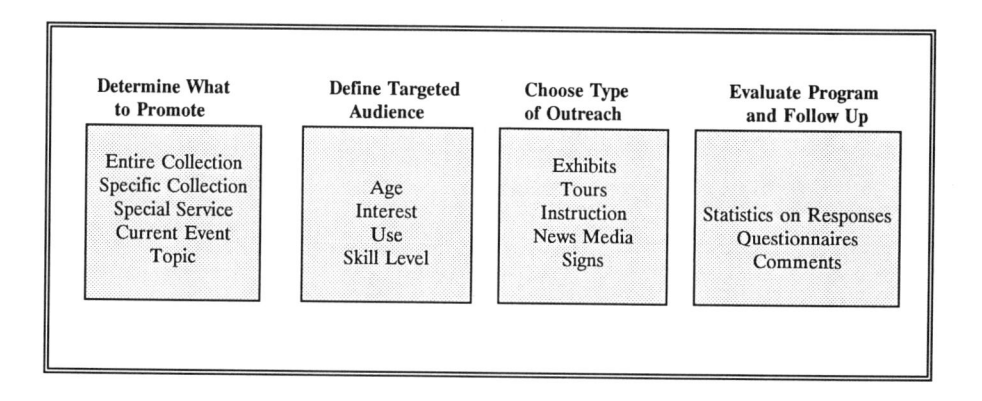

Determine What to Promote	Define Targeted Audience	Choose Type of Outreach	Evaluate Program and Follow Up
Entire Collection Specific Collection Special Service Current Event Topic	Age Interest Use Skill Level	Exhibits Tours Instruction News Media Signs	Statistics on Responses Questionnaires Comments

In formulating an outreach plan, it is helpful to consider how people gather information when they have a perceived need—in particular, how they hear about government information. People often rely on personal contacts and discussions to meet their information needs. Newspaper accounts, television reports, and press releases about new government information, reports, or studies all make people aware of government publications. Class presentations, browsing in a library, or working with reference tools such as indexes and bibliographies also may alert people to government publications. Often government agencies publish promotional bits of information, such as news releases, that refer to more complete sources of statistics. Perhaps the newest way for people to hear about government information is through the growing number of electronic bulletin boards and electronic reference sources. These services are heavily used by those with a specific identifiable interest area. Participating in these electronic communication forums will help government documents librarians to see how users learn about sources of information. They can also contribute information about government publications directly to other bulletin board participants.

The second step in promoting government documents use is to identify the clientele most likely to benefit from the collection. Government publications may be important to a broad range of users, including elementary school children; students at all other educational levels; business persons; professionals; and scholars in government, science, and the social sciences. An outreach program would do well to take account of the age, interest, and library skill levels of its target audience. It should also assess the nature of user needs. Does the selected audience require a brief summary of information or in-depth reports? Are statistics valuable? Would narratives be a better approach? This type of analysis, though difficult, produces a more effective promotion program by refining the exact interests of a particular audience.

Once the audience and its needs are known, an outreach program can be designed. Any successful outreach program will require a commitment of staff and fiscal resources. Therefore, an assessment of needed resources should be completed and their availability confirmed before any program is undertaken.

Types of Outreach and Promotion

Outreach efforts take many forms. By using several types of promotion, libraries can reach different audiences. Some typical outreach efforts conducted by libraries to promote their collections and services are discussed here. One should not, however, feel limited to traditional methods. There are many creative ideas in public relations texts about outreach efforts for all types of organizations. Some not specifically designed for libraries could be adapted successfully by government publications libraries.

Classes for interested users are one simple way to start promotional efforts. Although classes, seminars, tours, workshops, and lectures are sometimes considered appropriate only for school and academic libraries, they are equally valuable in other settings. Workshops offering "hands-on" experience in finding and using government information (e.g., genealogy workshops for local history/genealogical societies) should be considered for adult learners who respond well to an active learning environment. Tours of the government documents collection, given at appropriate times, allow librarians to meet motivated patrons personally, and give users an overview of services and materials offered. Handouts describing the government publications library or specific finding tools are often all people need to get started using documents. Handouts should be well designed and written, avoiding library parlance, and placed near the indexes or collection described. Recently, there have been efforts on the part of state and national (GODORT) organizations to provide a clearing house for samples of effective handouts or bibliographies. Interested librarians should contact these organizations for assistance.

Signs to draw attention to important parts of the collection or important services should not be overlooked as promotional tools. It may seem that no one reads signs, but some users, particularly those reluctant to ask for help or join a class, find signs especially useful. Signs can be used to direct attention to new publications of interest, services offered, special tools, and electronic access.

Selective housing arrangements for GPO or other depository materials could be used to place key, selected sources or parts of the collection in other libraries where interest in them is concentrated. For example, ERIC fiche could be housed in a school media or curriculum library; health and NLM materials in a medical or hospital library; and maps in a map or geography collection. This also will broaden awareness of documents collections, not only among users, but also among fellow library staff members.

Another way to reach a specific audience is through media coverage in community newspapers, student newspapers, or a variety of other local sources. A newsletter or current awareness service can be sent to regular users as well as new audiences. Sometimes it is more effective to use newsletters published by other organizations. For example, putting information about new city or state documents in the local League of Women Voters' newsletter may reach those who need to access government publications. Establishing good working relationships with publishers of such sources may provide considerable opportunities for collection exposure. It may be possible, through these acquaintances, to be invited to speak to a local group, such as the Better Business Bureau or a local inventors' society, about the collections and services available in the documents department.

Displays within the government publications library or elsewhere in the library are an effective way of generating interest in specific publications and subjects. Correlating a display with current events, whether local, state, or national, is particularly effective. The very nature of government publishing is ideal for these types of displays. New publications that may be unusual or unexpected can arouse interest. Mounting displays can exploit the talents of artistic staff members or the experience of a library display and exhibits committee. When possible, it is also important to make exhibit material available for closer scrutiny or circulation by interested patrons. Displays in locations outside the library, such as the student or community center, and posters in local schools, expand awareness of government publications and draw new users into the library.

Word-of-mouth advertising is an important and free advertising medium. The personal touch given through in-depth reference service is a good way to advertise the collection. People who receive excellent help will remember and will encourage others to use the services provided.

New technologies offer ways to update and improve outreach programs. New computer capabilities such as hypermedia allow patrons to experience "tours" on-line, where they can interactively question the computer program and go to parts of the program that interest them. Thus, patrons are not obligated to sit through long presentations to get specific questions answered. Hypermedia allows for creativity and individually tailored programs, including graphics such as maps integrated with text describing sources. Computer-assisted instruction (CAI) offers additional means for reaching users at the time of their need. Programs such as these can be set up and left running in a department; they require little or no staff intervention once the equipment and program are designed and in place. A word of caution is appropriate when discussing CAI or hypermedia programs: Look for a system that is flexible, can accommodate the rapidly changing field of government information, and can be easily modified for your library situation. Participation in electronic bulletin boards, loading databases on local or wide area networks, and creating or providing new on-line services will also enhance awareness of a collection.

Although it is often true that there are few resources, staff, and little money to do promotional work, and that the GPO offers little in the way of assistance,[2] some of the ideas discussed here can be accomplished with few additional resources. Continuous improvement and updating in signs, class material, tours, and media coverage is important. Promotional efforts should be coordinated with a library public relations or outreach office, if such a department exists. Another way to improve promotional efforts includes working through the library's staff development program to educate the rest of the library staff and professionals about unique government materials. Good referral networks can be enhanced by presentations to teachers, business people, and officials, and are very effective in promoting collection use. Such work requires tireless enthusiasm and a willingness to insinuate documents into every workshop, sign, article, or reference exchange occurring in the library.

Evaluation

If you decide to undertake a promotional campaign, it is essential to evaluate its results. Evaluating promotional efforts not only tells you how well a program worked, but also helps you design the next outreach project more successfully. Improving and refining outreach strategies should be a continuing activity of every promotional effort. Standard assessment tools, such as evaluation forms, questionnaires, and comment sheets, may be used with most outreach programs.

BIBLIOGRAPHIC INSTRUCTION

Classes, tours, workshops, and seminars have been mentioned as effective means of promoting a government documents collection for all types of users. Most bibliographic instruction in government publications is offered at college and university libraries. A typical bibliographic instruction session on government publications involves a librarian offering a one-to two-hour session on accessing government information. The class may or may not have a related assignment, and may contain a range of students, from those who know (and care) nothing about libraries to enthusiastic users. It is, however, safe to assume that few class members know much about document collections and their potential value. There is a vast field of literature available on bibliographic instruction, and readers are referred to that body of information for current research and ideas in the field. Most of this literature has applications to teaching government publications.

A good way to introduce material is to discuss why documents are useful and important, emphasizing specifically how the publications presented can help that particular audience. It is not hard for most documents librarians to be enthusiastic about their subject. Letting that enthusiasm show in a presentation tells an audience that this is a valuable subject that can help them in many ways. However, perhaps because of this enthusiasm, there is a tendency to cover every aspect of documents and every tool used to access and identify information. This overkill may lead to rushed presentations and a severe case of information overload for students. It is far better to give a class an idea of the types of information available and a sense that they can come back for more information when they are ready or need more specific help. Showing the class members a few truly significant items will enable them to focus on the possibilities the collection offers for them. It will not discourage them with the thought that the material and access to it are so complex that they will never be able to use it.

Enthusiasm for the subject helps presentations to be lively, funny, interesting, and informative. Examples of relevant materials and important reference sources should be emphasized so that the class knows that such material exists and is retrievable. Amusing and unusual documents, such as comic books, Army recipe cards, and strange research reports, can be used to illustrate various points. To hold the attention of participants, the presentation should refer to a class assignment or a particular information need. Small group, in-class activities, such as using indexes, answering questions from census material, and working with computer or CD-ROM sources involves students actively in the presentation and encourages experiential learning. All of these activities will make classes interesting and more memorable.

Documents collections are sometimes perceived to be "different" or "difficult" as compared to other library collections. Therefore, working within the context of other library bibliographic instruction programs may help to remove such perceptions. If possible, team-teach with a colleague. It is strongly suggested that all library instruction be based in a research strategy, rather than adopting a simple "show-and-tell" approach.[3] Although it may be useful to show examples to whet appetites for documents, demonstrations should be done in the context of a methodology for approaching information needs or research questions.

Research Strategy

A good research strategy gives the user a starting point for a search and a logical way to proceed through that search until the information is found, or all possible avenues have been explored. Most students will need only a small part of an extensive search strategy, but will feel more comfortable with an outline of possible options. A handout with a strategy outlined (see figure 11.2) gives students a way to proceed when they are ready to begin research. A bibliography will highlight specific steps or tools for the class and its assignment.

The first step in any research strategy is to carefully define research topics, identifying several ideas or components of the topic, if possible. Listing terms and possible variations for subject headings will give students a sense of the importance of vocabulary control in completing a research paper. At this point, the documents librarian can explain "free text" versus "controlled vocabulary" subject access and the significance of boolean operators for searching. A research strategy for government publications may include background sources, such as the *United States Government Manual*, the *Congressional Directory*, and other handbooks, guidebooks, and directories for state, international, and regional information. Encyclopedias and dictionaries are also useful background sources and may be pointed out to students.

The next step is to introduce students to the *Monthly Catalog* in paper, CD-ROM, or on-line format as the equivalent of the card catalog or public access

180 ☐ Outreach, Promotion, and Bibliographic Instruction

Fig. 11.2. Research strategy.

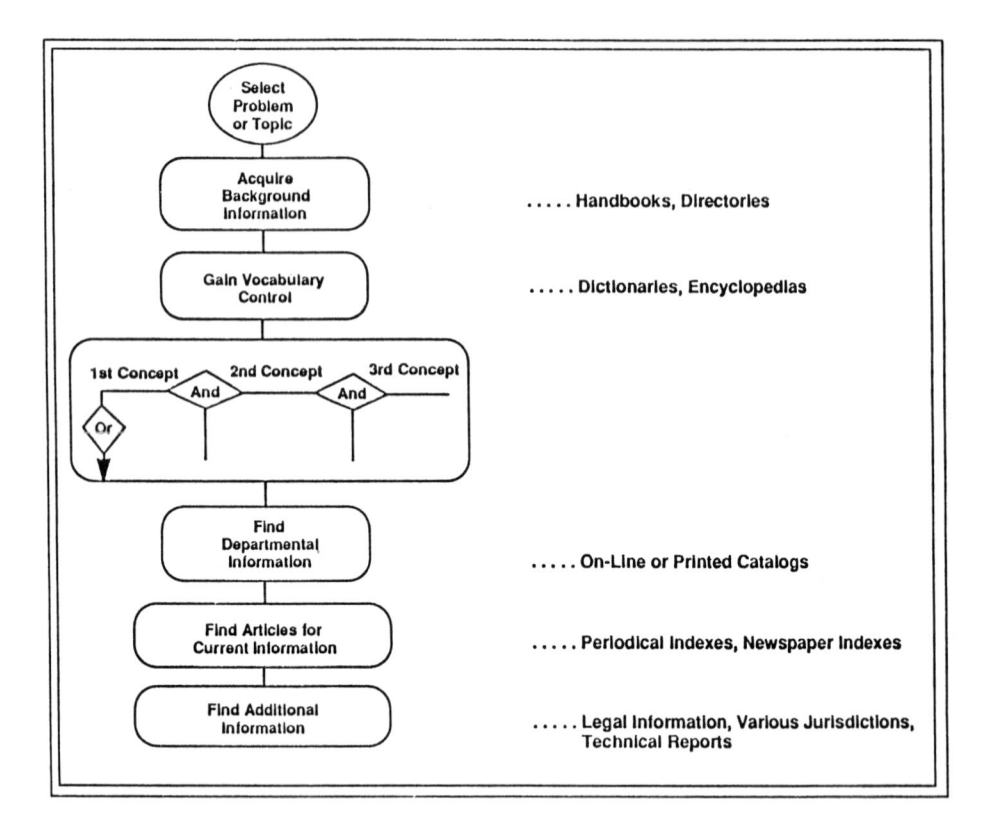

```
Select Problem or Topic
        ↓
Acquire Background Information  ..... Handbooks, Directories
        ↓
Gain Vocabulary Control  ..... Dictionaries, Encyclopedias
        ↓
1st Concept — And — 2nd Concept — And — 3rd Concept
   Or
        ↓
Find Departmental Information  ..... On-Line or Printed Catalogs
        ↓
Find Articles for Current Information  ..... Periodical Indexes, Newspaper Indexes
        ↓
Find Additional Information  ..... Legal Information, Various Jurisdictions, Technical Reports
```

catalog for the rest of the library. The *Monthly Catalog* provides information on U.S. federal government departmental and congressional publications. Catalogs or indexes providing similar information for state and international sources should be identified. At this point, it will be necessary to explain whatever classification, filing, and shelving arrangements the particular library uses.

Specific tools that access departmental publications should be considered. Publications such as CIS's *Index to Congressional Publications* and its *American Statistics Index* for statistical sources provide good access to specific types of material. From here, the search strategy may cover periodical indexes, such as *PAIS*, and other current awareness publications. Research or technical reports from NTIS or ERIC may follow, along with an explanation of the different types of government information formats.

Another consideration in formulating a search strategy for government information is discovering publications from different jurisdictions. A strategy, if appropriate, could be arranged by local, state, regional, national, foreign, and international sources. It is also possible to formulate a strategy based on electronic information. Electronic access tools should be listed when available, as they are often the first choice of users now. These tools are very popular, but not every library has the full range of government information in electronic format.

However, the formats of information and the jurisdictions covered are not as important for students as the general concepts of what is published and how to access, evaluate, and use it.

Concentrating a presentation on key concepts is more effective and less confusing than including everything. The most important point for students to learn is that governments publish valuable information that is freely accessible to them. A second important point to emphasize is that the government documents staff will help them retrieve information when they need it. Students also should be taught the difference between background sources or secondary sources and primary material. They should understand what a catalog or index does and the concept of subject cataloging. Students will then be able to ask for an index on a particular subject or type of document. These concepts follow and reinforce any previous bibliographic instruction.

Another important point students need to consider is the nature of government information. Students should be aware that they need not accept information uncritically just because it is published by a government. A useful and interesting class activity is to critically analyze a particular document to see its biases, the politics behind its publication, the authority of the authors, etc. This aspect of bibliographic instruction is often overlooked, but can be most illuminating for students.[4]

Finally, some studies have been published in library literature about the emotional reactions and needs of students.[5] It is reported that students are often fearful of libraries, afraid of "looking stupid," or afraid that they will fail in their efforts in the library. Anything an instructor can do to lessen these reactions will produce better informed and more capable students. When dealing with government documents, acknowledging that such feelings frequently exist in all library users may be helpful in reaching some students.

NEW TECHNOLOGIES

As more documents collections are included in on-line catalogs, outreach is automatic and may cause a huge influx of patrons to the documents library. Bibliographic instruction, handouts, and signs must become vital parts of any program to teach users to access the information they have now uncovered in the catalog. Electronic formats will generate even more questions and more demands for teaching. Nonbibliographic databases are now available from governmental sources; ways to inform patrons that they are available and how to evaluate and access their information must be developed. Documents librarians will have to become knowledgeable about software, networking, and other new technological developments.

New information technology raises issues concerning access and availability of government information. New technology may improve access to some data, but it may limit access to only those who can pay for electronic equipment and telecommunications resources. As more documents appear only in electronic format, this raises questions about promotion and use of those materials. Is the intent of depository laws being met if citizens must have computers, modems, software, and the expertise to use them before they are able to get government information? What of smaller libraries that cannot afford to buy such equipment? It appears that the format of information may limit access itself in the short term.

CONCLUSIONS

A search of the literature on managing government publications collections reveals that little has been published about promotion, outreach, and bibliographic instruction of these collections. Jackson,[6] Harleston,[7] and Nakata[8] do not address the question at all. Nonetheless, there is an underlying assumption in these books that promoting these collections is a responsibility of documents librarians. Working to expand the user group is an ongoing and never-ending job. Constantly changing documents and tools to access them will keep documents librarians continually involved with promotion and instruction efforts.

As shown in this chapter, there are many ways to promote a collection of government information. The methods chosen should reflect thoughtful consideration of several factors, such as the material to be promoted, how much use the collection can support, and what audience should be targeted. Such analysis will help the librarian design the best promotional program for a collection. Throughout this process, it should be remembered that librarians and their staff are the most effective means to enhance collections. Personal service and attention will attract new users and bring back old ones time and again.

NOTES

[1]Peter Hernon, *Public Access to Government Information: Issues and Strategies* (Norwood, NJ: Abbey Press, 1984), 130.

[2]Ibid. 138-9.

[3]Deborah Fink, *Process and Politics in Library Research: A Model for Course Design* (Chicago: American Library Association, 1989), 73.

[4]Ibid. 181.

[5]Carol Collier Kuhlthau, "Developing a Model of the Library Search Process: Cognitive and Affective Aspects," *RQ* 28 (Winter 1988): 232-42.

[6]Ellen Jackson, *A Manual for the Administration of the Federal Documents Collection in Libraries* (Chicago: American Library Association, 1955).

[7]Rebekah Harleston, *Administration of Government Documents Collections* (Littleton, CO: Libraries Unlimited, 1974).

[8]Yuri Nakata, *From Press to People: Collecting and Using U.S. Government Publications* (Chicago: American Library Association, 1979).

12

The Politics of Documents Librarianship

Ridley Kessler
Regional Librarian of North Carolina
University of North Carolina

and

Jack Sulzer
Head of General Reference
The Pennsylvania State University

To deal effectively with a government that produces and distributes a large body of information, documents librarians must do two things. First, it is essential that they develop a good understanding and basic knowledge of the government's information structure. This includes knowing the agencies that publish the information; how the information is produced and distributed; the agencies that manage the government's information functions; and the government bodies that develop and control information policies. The second thing documents librarians must do is develop an awareness of the issues surrounding government information activities. Knowledge of the key information issues, who the stakeholders and the decision makers are, and current government activities will make the difference between an effective documents librarian and one with limited professional ability.

This chapter covers the fundamental knowledge that every government information librarian should have about information-producing and policy-making bodies of our government. This is the core of knowledge required to survive. As such, it is only a first step, an initial guidepost toward becoming a professional. Our hope is, however, that it will act not only as a primer, but also as a pathfinder that will serve the student and new librarian as an outline and reference for the future.

This chapter is limited to a discussion of the federal government of the United States. Nonetheless, many of the issues discussed also apply to state and international documents librarianship. What follows is a description of the U.S. Government Printing Office, its history, purpose, and organization; the role of Congress in information issues; the responsibilities of the regional depository libraries; the mission of the Depository Library Council; and the role of federal agencies.

Finally, this chapter deals with relations between librarians and the government. It outlines a working knowledge of information issues presently being debated by libraries and the decision makers in Congress and the federal agencies.

THE GOVERNMENT PRINTING OFFICE

Since its inception in June of 1860 by Joint Resolution 25, the Government Printing Office has been "authorized and directed to have executed the printing and binding authorized by the Senate and House of Representatives, the executive and judicial departments...."[1] The mission of the GPO has changed little over the last 132 years. It is still responsible for the printing and binding for Congress, the Executive Office, and the executive departments and independent agencies. Title 44, section 501, of the U.S. Code, the statute now governing public printing, states that the only exceptions to printing outside the GPO must be granted specially by the Joint Committee on Printing (JCP). The JCP decides whether government printing should be done by another federal agency or by private contract.

The Public Printer, who heads the GPO, oversees a huge printing and distribution operation with a work force of approximately 5,000 people.[2] According to the 1990 Government Printing Office *Annual Report*, the GPO printed 1.9 billion publications for the government. This is too large a job for the GPO to do in-house, and in 1990 only 24 percent of the publishing revenue received came from the Central Printing Plant or from the six regional printing plants the GPO operates. Seventy-six percent of the GPO's printing revenue is contracted out to private commercial printers, who now do the bulk of all government printing.[3]

Printing and production of government information is just one part of the Government Printing Office's mission. More important to librarians are its document dissemination activities. The first law concerning public access was passed on December 27, 1813, during the Thirteenth Congress. Joint Resolution 1 empowered Congress to distribute the *Journals* of both houses to colleges and universities in each state. This law stated that distribution would begin with the Thirteenth Congress and continue with all future congresses.[4] This resolution was the first recognition of government's obligation to provide public access to the information it produced. Subsequent resolutions and laws passed in the 1840s, 1850s, and 1860s increased the numbers of documents to be disseminated, authorized congressional designation of depositories, and created the Office of Superintendent of Public Documents.

On January 12, 1895, the Richardson Bill was passed into law.[5] Generally known as the "Printing Act of 1895," this major statute codified all of the laws dealing with the printing and distribution of public documents. It is now the heart and soul of Title 44. It gathered all functions of government printing, distribution, and sale of information under the bureaucratic umbrella of the Government Printing Office. The Superintendent of Documents was put under the authority of the Public Printer and placed in charge of all distribution, including the depository system and sales. The Printing Act of 1895 also mandated the establishment of the first official bibliographic sources for government information, later known as the *Monthly Catalog*, the *Documents Catalog*, and the *Documents Index*.

Today the Public Printer is appointed by the president and confirmed by the Senate. The Deputy Public Printer is the chief administrative officer of the GPO, and the operational units of Customer Services, Production Services, and Procurement Services report directly to this office. (See figure 12.1.) The Chief Financial Officer is in charge of budget, accounting, and financial planning, and oversees all personnel and labor matters. The Superintendent of Documents, who reports directly to the Public Printer, is most directly concerned with the Depository Library Program (DLP) and government documents librarians.

Fig. 12.1. GPO Organization.

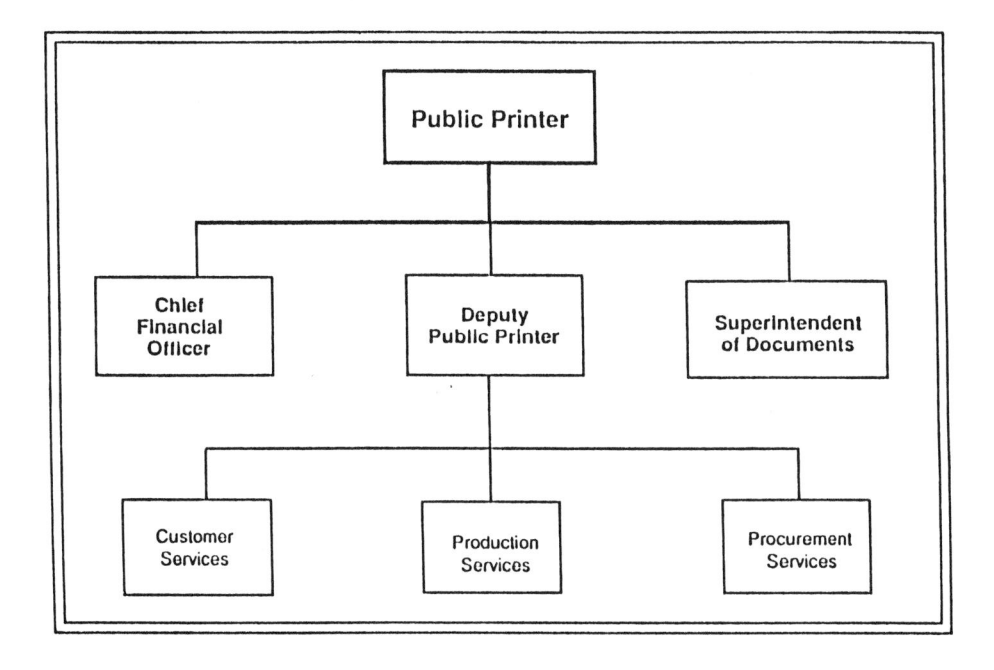

```
                    ┌──────────────────┐
                    │  Public Printer  │
                    └──────────────────┘
                             │
          ┌──────────────────┼──────────────────┐
          │                  │                  │
    ┌───────────┐      ┌───────────┐      ┌──────────────┐
    │   Chief   │      │  Deputy   │      │Superintendent│
    │ Financial │      │  Public   │      │ of Documents │
    │  Officer  │      │  Printer  │      │              │
    └───────────┘      └───────────┘      └──────────────┘
                             │
          ┌──────────────────┼──────────────────┐
          │                  │                  │
    ┌───────────┐      ┌────────────┐     ┌─────────────┐
    │  Customer │      │ Production │     │ Procurement │
    │  Services │      │  Services  │     │  Services   │
    └───────────┘      └────────────┘     └─────────────┘
```

THE SUPERINTENDENT OF DOCUMENTS

The Superintendent of Documents is responsible for the distribution and sales of government publications. This position oversees two major departments, the Documents Sales Service and the Library Programs Service (LPS) (figure 12.2). The Documents Sales Service is responsible for the sale of government publications by mail, telephone, or through the 23 GPO bookstores throughout the nation. The Superintendent of Documents is authorized by law to sell publications at cost plus 50 percent. In 1990, the GPO Sales Service sold 28.5 million documents from an inventory of approximately 16,000 titles.[6] In the last few years, the GPO has also begun offering magnetic tape and diskette formats to the public. There is a ready market for these electronic products and sales doubled from 1989 to 1990.

Sales Service

The Sales Service oversees two other major distribution programs. One is the Statutory and Agency Distribution Program. This program authorizes the Sales Service to distribute documents for other government agencies, at their

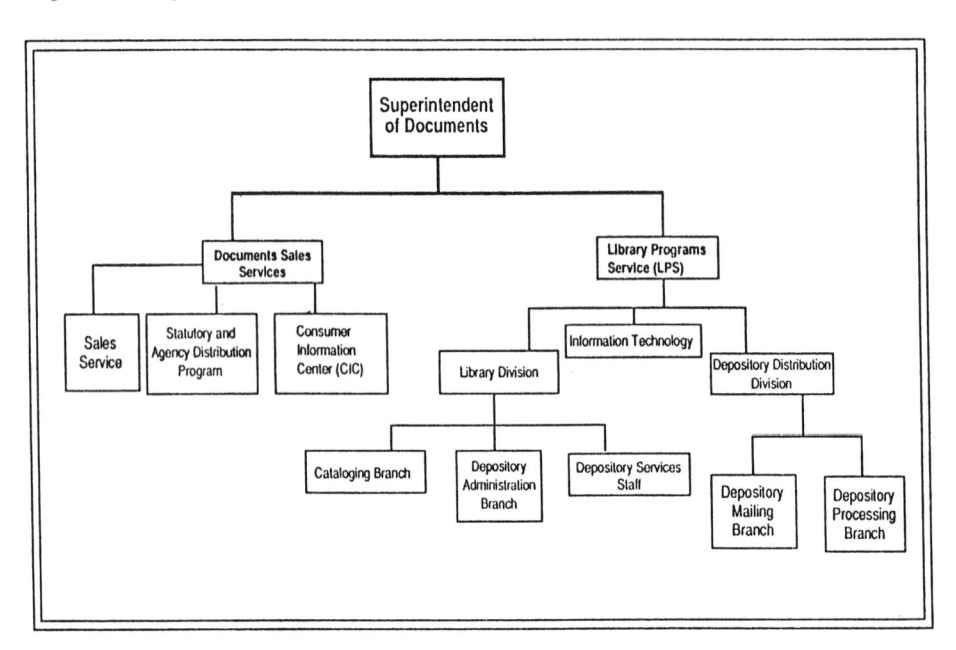

Fig. 12.2. Superintendent of Documents organization.

```
                        Superintendent
                        of Documents
        ┌───────────────────┴───────────────────┐
   Documents Sales                         Library Programs
      Services                              Service (LPS)
  ┌───────┼────────┐                  ┌──────────┼──────────┐
 Sales  Statutory and  Consumer    Information Technology   Depository Distribution
Service Agency Distribution Information                           Division
         Program    Center (CIC)  Library Division
                          ┌──────────────┼──────────────┐
                     Cataloging Branch  Depository    Depository Services   Depository    Depository
                                        Administration     Staff            Mailing       Processing
                                          Branch                            Branch         Branch
```

request, and to be reimbursed for any expenses incurred. In fiscal year 1990, 38.4 million publications were mailed out for other government agencies, and the GPO received $4,907,000 in reimbursements from those agencies.[7] The Statutory and Agency Distribution Program also authorizes the Sales Service to distribute documents free of charge to designated recipients. According to the 1990 *GPO Annual Report*, 4.8 million documents were distributed under this statutory requirement.[8]

The second program in the Sales Service is the Consumer Information Center (CIC). The Sales Service fulfills orders for the CIC at the Government Printing Office's distribution facility in Pueblo, Colorado. The CIC, which is a part of the General Services Administration, distributes for 40 government agencies free and low-cost publications dealing with consumer interests. These publications cover a wide range of subjects for consumers, such as the environment, health, nutrition, and money management. The GPO is reimbursed for distributing this information by the CIC. In October of 1990, when the Center celebrated its 20th anniversary, it had distributed more than 230 million publications.[9] The CIC issues a quarterly free *Consumer Information Catalog* listing all its available publications.

The Library Programs Service

The Library Programs Service (LPS) is the other major division of the Superintendent of Documents' Office, and is the most important link between the depository community and the Government Printing Office. This unit is responsible for all bibliographic control of government publications, exchange of documents between the United States and foreign governments, location of publications in electronic formats to distribute through the depository system, and management of the approximately 1,400 libraries that make up the Depository Library Program. All these functions are divided among two sections of the LPS, the Library Division and the Depository Distribution Division. These divisions report directly to the Director of LPS.

Library Division

The Library Division is the section most visible to librarians because it is the branch that deals directly with depositories. The chief of the Library Division oversees the Depository Services Staff, the Cataloging Branch, and the Depository Administration Branch.

The Cataloging Branch (CB) is responsible for cataloging all government publications and electronic information that comes to the GPO. It maintains the cataloging records database and produces the machine-readable cataloging data that are used by the Library of Congress for MARC tapes. All the documents cataloged at the GPO follow the *Anglo-American Cataloging Rules (AACR II)*. The CB is also responsible for creating and printing the *Monthly Catalog of United States Government Publications*.

The Depository Administration Branch is the GPO's acquisition unit and is responsible for acquiring and classifying all documents distributed by the system. It also contracts for and procures microfiche for the GPO. This unit assigns classification numbers to all documents, maintains the Superintendent of Documents (SuDoc) Classification System, and publishes *An Explanation of the Superintendent of Documents Classification System*,[10] along with the *GPO Classification Manual: A Practical Guide to the Superintendent of Documents Classification System*.[11] Besides these duties, the Depository Administration prepares all of the shipping lists that accompany depository shipments, oversees depository library selection profiles, and manages the item number file. It creates and publishes the *List of Classes of United States Government Publications Available for Selection by Depository Libraries*,[12] and the record of those publications available for deposit, including titles, item numbers, and classification numbers. This branch also operates and maintains the Depository Distribution and Information System (DDIS), the on-line system that manages all item and classification number assignments to libraries.

The Depository Services Staff (DSS) is the unit within the Library Division that is best known to depository librarians. The DSS is responsible for the actual functioning of the Depository Library Program. It handles all designations, terminations, and changes in the status of depository libraries. It monitors the health and effectiveness of the depository program by regular inspections and its Biennial Survey of depository libraries, collections, and staff.[13]

The Depository Services Staff has for several years also acted as an unofficial complaints department for depositories. It is to this office that most regional and selective librarians first turn when they have a question or problem. Certainly the most meaningful contact that depositories have with the DSS staff is the inspection process. An inspection of each depository library should occur about every three years. In reality, because of budget cuts and hiring freezes, this process may only happen every five to eight years. Generally inspectors will cover a whole state or region on an inspection, in order to visit as many libraries as possible on a trip. A depository inspection is a very intense encounter between the GPO inspector and the depository library staff. The purpose of the inspection is to see that the depository library is following both the letter and spirit of the laws concerning the Depository Library Program. The inspectors are particularly concerned that the materials made available through tax dollars for the program are being used to best advantage and that the public has full and free access to this information.

To achieve as much equity and consistency as possible, the inspectors use a standardized form called "The Inspection Report," based primarily on the *Instructions to Depository Libraries*.[14] The inspection report is divided into seven different segments, with one more reserved for regional libraries:

I. Collection Development
II. Bibliographic Control
III. Maintenance
IV. Human Resources
V. Physical Facilities
VI. Public Service
VII. Cooperative Efforts
VIII. Regional Services

Using these categories, the inspectors examine the organization and operation of each depository library in great detail. Each of these seven categories is subdivided further into two sections. Section I covers the basic requirements that all depositories are expected to meet. A library is rated either satisfactory or unsatisfactory in this section. If a library is rated as satisfactory, Section II then provides the inspector the opportunity to assign a ranking of "good" or "excellent" in that category.

The entire inspection visit normally takes about four or five hours. The inspectors arrive at the library and usually begin with a tour of the facilities. They are looking for evidence of good management and compliance with the *Instructions for Depository Libraries*. They will chat with the librarians and staff, make notes, examine their findings, and then present an oral report to the Documents Librarian and the director of the library on the results of the inspection. The library will receive an official notice and the completed "Inspection Report" in about six to eight weeks.

If a library is found deficient and receives an "unsatisfactory" in three or more categories, it fails the inspection process and is put on probation for six months. The probationary period gives the library time to correct its problems and improve its services and technical deficiencies. Any time after the probationary period, the library may be inspected again, at the convenience of the DSS. If the library corrects its problems and passes the second inspection, its probationary status is removed. If problems still remain, the library will be asked to send a written progress report to the Chief Inspector in about six months. If the library does not pass the second inspection, and if the inspector does not see any progress or signs of improvement, then the library can be eliminated from the depository program. In such a case, the Superintendent of Documents sends a letter informing the library that it has been dropped from the program and is no longer a depository library.

The inspection process is a very useful and productive tool for both the GPO and depository libraries. It fosters good communication between the library and GPO officials; it enables both parties to learn more about the Depository Library Program; and it helps libraries to improve and better their depository services. The process also allows librarians to provide input to the GPO about the system and the procedures that govern it. A section of the Inspection Report, called the "inspection comment sheet," allows the librarian to make comments about the inspection process and the inspector, the librarian's own regional library, and the Government Printing Office and its services and publications. These comments are taken very seriously by the GPO, and any comments made are passed on to the proper office for consideration. The GPO also has GPO Form 3794, the "Depository Library Inquiry Form," which librarians can use to ask questions and seek information about various problems that affect them. The Library Programs Service encourages use of this form and, in fact, one of the questions in the "Inspection Report" asks the library if the Inquiry Form is used to communicate with the GPO.

The DSS has prepared an excellent pamphlet, entitled *Preparing for a Depository Inspection*,[15] which explains in some detail how an inspection works and how to prepare for one. The inspection staff frequently give workshops in states that are about to be inspected. The Regional Depository Librarian is usually the host of these workshops and can support selectives by explaining the process and helping to prepare for the experience.

Besides these duties, the Depository Services Staff is responsible for all federal Depository Library Program publications, including *Administrative Notes*, the official newsletter of the Federal Depository Library Program. This very informative newsletter not only has the latest news about the system, but also contains notices of meetings, such as the Depository Library Council, and information about cataloging, processing, and other technical matters. It is an invaluable source of news and should be read immediately when it is received. The DSS also sponsors workshops for depository staff in Washington. These workshops enable librarians and their staffs to visit with members of the GPO, tour the facilities, and see how the system operates.

Another important service the DSS provides is hosting the Interagency Depository Seminar each May. This valuable, week-long seminar is an excellent introduction to major government information dissemination activities, with presentations given by agencies such as the Census Bureau, the Office of the Federal Register, and the Library of Congress. Starting in April 1992, the Depository Services Staff will hold the first Federal Depository Conference. This conference, open to all depository librarians and their staffs, will enable librarians to meet with each other and GPO officials to talk about common problems and issues facing the depository system.

Another important function that the DSS performs is publication and revision of the *Instructions to Depository Libraries*. This publication is the closest thing to an owner's manual that a depository librarian can possess. Its chapters deal with shipping lists, claiming, microfiche, termination of depository status, biennial surveys, and everything else that is necessary to help a depository library carry out its proper function. A useful supplement to the *Instructions* is the *Federal Depository Library Manual*,[16] a Depository Library Council publication, which adds helpful information gathered from practicing documents librarians.

The Depository Distribution Division

The Depository Distribution Division (DDD) is the second division in the organizational structure of the Library Programs Service. Its major responsibility is the distribution of government publications to depository libraries, including all electronic formats. This includes preparing them for shipment, storing the publications, packaging them, and mailing the publications. The bulk of this work is handled by the Depository Mailing Branch, which operates the "lighted bin system." This system helps to sort publications for distribution to the appropriate depository library. The Mailing Branch also handles all claims from depository libraries for both paper and microfiche items missing from depository shipments.

The Information Technology Program

The Information Technology Program, reporting to the Director of LPS, until recently had the responsibility of acquiring electronic products for distribution. This program now has responsibility for monitoring and managing all electronic pilot projects conducted by the GPO. One of the most visible of these projects is the GPO Electronic Bulletin Board. On June 3, 1991, the Government Printing Office instituted an electronic bulletin board, called "The Federal Depository Library Program Bulletin Board" (FDLP/BB), as part of the Library Division. It is still in the experimental phase, but it was a major policy decision by the GPO to begin this project, and it is likely that the FDLP/BB will be made a part of Depository Services. The bulletin board has information from *Administrative Notes*, alerts and news items about the LPS, current shipping lists, and other information concerning the system. This bulletin board will become more important in the future as both librarians and the GPO learn how to use and manipulate this exciting new medium.[17]

CONGRESSIONAL OVERSIGHT OF THE GPO

The congressional body that exercises oversight authority over the Government Printing Office is the Joint Committee on Printing (JCP). The United States Code explicitly states that "[t]he Joint Committee on Printing may use any measures it considers necessary to remedy neglect, delay, duplication, or waste in the public printing and binding and the distribution of Government publications."[18]

The JCP is, in reality, an oversight committee for the Government Printing Office, reviewing major decisions, actions, and all purchases made by the GPO. It is chiefly responsible for all the printing and binding for the United States government, and periodically issues its *Government Printing and Binding Regulations*[19] for this purpose. Ultimately, it is responsible for the Depository Library Program and the dissemination of government information.

The Joint Committee on Printing is composed of the Chair and four members of the House Administration Committee, and the Chair and four members of the Senate Rules and Administration Committee. The House and Senate share control of the JCP. Every two years, with the beginning of a new Congress, the chair of the JCP rotates between the House and the Senate. In the 102d Congress, the chair belonged to the House, so in the 103d Congress it transfers to the Senate. Traditionally, the Chairs of the House Administration and Senate Rules Committee act as the Chairs of the Joint Committee during their respective terms.

In the past, JCP staff members reported at the semiannual Depository Library Council meetings. These reports kept both the Depository Library Council and depository librarians who attended DLC meetings informed about JCP activities and legislative and statutory matters of importance to the Depository Library Program. Council members and the audience had several chances to ask questions of the JCP staff and to mingle with them during breaks and after hours. Since the format of the Council meetings was changed to exclude congressional and agency updates, starting with the Fall 1991 meeting, JCP staff no longer report. However, JCP staff still attend the "Federal Update" meetings of the ALA/Government Documents Round Table's Federal Documents Task Force (FDTF), held at the Association's annual and midwinter meetings. The FDTF has expanded its update meeting to two separate sessions (one for GPO/JCP and another for federal agencies) to facilitate this information exchange.

Although the Joint Committee on Printing has oversight responsibility over the Government Printing Office, it is not a legislative committee, and therefore cannot introduce or consider legislation. That authority is vested in several other committees that play a large role in the operations of the JCP. The two most important committees are the House Administration Committee and the Senate Rules and Administration Committee. Because the chairs and members of the JCP come from these two committees, any activities that require legislative action generally come from one or both of these committees.

At budget time, both the House and Senate Appropriations Committees also assume some authority over the GPO. The annual budget request, or the "Budget Estimate Justification" document for the Government Printing Office, is published in the December/January time frame. Later, actual hearings are held by both the House and Senate Appropriations Committees, with testimony from the Public Printer and the staff as they defend the budget. Witnesses from organizations such as the ALA and other interested groups and individuals are often invited to testify at these later hearings. These published transcripts provide excellent information about the GPO program and its operation. They often reveal new policies and procedures affecting the Depository Library Program and public access issues.

Any public hearings about the Government Printing Office or matters affecting the Depository Library Program are important for librarians to follow. Librarians are often invited to testify at these hearings, and their testimony can help shape public policy and inform congresspersons and their staffs of library issues.

ROLE OF FEDERAL AGENCIES IN INFORMATION DISTRIBUTION

Government agencies gather, write, and publish most of the information that is sent through the Depository Library Program. It is important to remember that many of the people involved in decision making for government information dissemination and policy development are not elected officials and are not connected with the GPO. Most government agencies have printing officers who help design and produce information. These printing officers are familiar with the standards and regulations of the Joint Committee on Printing and are knowledgeable about the printing process. They also work closely with the Government Printing Office. They can be a valuable resource for documents librarians, in helping track down publications or finding out why information is not in the system. The GPO has produced an excellent document on the publishing process that contains information about printing officers and the printing process, entitled *Guide to Federal Publishing*.[20]

In government agencies, one can often identify units that work with the public, providing information of varying types. Frequently these offices will have "information" in their title, or they may be called "public affairs," "user services," "consumer advisor," etc. They too can be very helpful in locating publications or in understanding relationships with Congress and the GPO. Many agencies also have libraries, reading rooms, or reference centers. The librarians who run these collections are often happy to help fellow librarians find information or locate fugitive publications.

There are several useful services for locating various federal publications and information offices. One of the best sources that depository librarians have is *The United States Government Manual*. The *Manual* includes organizational information for agencies and provides addresses, telephone numbers, and names. Another useful feature is its inclusion of regional offices for various agencies. Regional offices are often easier for librarians to contact and nearer to a particular depository library. These offices can sometimes direct the librarian to the exact person or office holding the information. Many agencies also produce telephone directories that are available on deposit and can help in locating information offices.

REGIONAL LIBRARIES

Currently there are 53 regional depository libraries in the United States. These libraries play an important role in helping the depository program be effective. To be designated as a regional, a library must be a depository library, must have the prior approval of its state library authority, and must be named by a United States Senator. No more than two libraries in each state may be designated as a regional depository library.

Regional depository libraries must be willing and able to assume more responsibilities than selective libraries. Their major duty is to ensure that state or regional depository resources are as complete and comprehensive as possible, guaranteeing that the public of the region has equitable and comprehensive access to federal government information. The law requires that all regionals accept and retain permanently all government publications designated as depository items by the GPO. The only exceptions are publications that are superseded or that have been authorized for discard by the Superintendent of Documents. To aid the regional in building the most complete collection possible, the law requires selective depositories within the region to keep all publications that they receive for at least five years. Before a selective depository library can discard a publication, it must have the permission of the regional librarian. This enables the regional to monitor the collections of the selectives within the state and ensures that the regional library has first access to any discarded item. Other selectives within the region also can add discarded items to their collections through this process.

Additionally, regional libraries provide other services. They serve as reference centers for both selectives and non-depository libraries. Because their collections are more complete, they usually have the best collections of federal documents. Many regionals have begun to set up electronic mail reference systems, which have great potential for improving public access. Regionals also must provide interlibrary loan service to their selective depositories, and most offer this service to the non-depository libraries in their districts as well.

Regional libraries often take an active part in organizing workshops and meetings for the selectives in their region and acting as a consultant for all depository matters. Selectives should feel free to call or visit their regional. Regionals can build good communication and trust by frequent visits to selective depositories in their state. Unfortunately, many regionals also suffer from budget problems and lack of travel funds. This can be overcome by active participation in any state or regional documents organization, by effective use of electronic mail and telephone, and by inviting all selective librarians to visit the regional often.

Personal visits are the best method for a regional librarian to get to know the problems and capabilities of individual selective libraries. It is especially important that regionals try to accompany the GPO inspectors during the inspection process. The regional can help selectives prepare for an inspection, answer questions, and alleviate any fears. They also can help the inspector to better understand the selective being visited, and can often clear up problems or misunderstandings that occur on the inspection site. However, it is important for a regional to be a cooperative member of a visit and not interfere or hamper the inspector or the inspection process. Criticism or advice to the inspector should be handled privately and in confidence.

Regionals can assist their selectives with many of the technical processing problems that occur regularly. Most regionals are happy to make copies of shipping lists, check for receipt of a document, aid in identifying classifications numbers, lend documents for photocopy, and do other necessary housekeeping details for selectives. Most regionals will also make contact with the GPO for selectives and help clear up claims or procedural questions. It is a good idea for selective librarians to contact their regional first with any problems.

DEPOSITORY LIBRARY COUNCIL

The Depository Library Council (DLC) to the Public Printer of the United States is a unique and valuable body in the depository system. Created in 1972, the current DLC is composed of 15 members who act as advisors to the Public Printer. Five new Council members are appointed every year by the Public Printer to serve a three-year term. The Council is headed by a chair who is chosen by the Council members and confirmed by the Public Printer. The chair selects a secretary to serve the Council. The Bylaws require that the Council meet twice a year. In the past, the spring meeting was held in different places throughout the United States, while the fall meeting was always in Washington. In 1991, as the result of reorganization under the orders of Public Printer Robert Houk, all meetings now take place in Washington. In the past, the Council dealt with both policy discussions and operational matters of concern to depository librarians, such as classification, distribution problems, claims, indexing, and cataloging of government publications. Under the new organization, the Council concentrates on broader policy issues concerning the Government Printing Office, the depository library program, and public access issues.

Summaries of Council meetings are published in *Administrative Notes*. Verbatim transcripts of Council meetings are no longer published. The Council chair gives a report at the GODORT Federal Documents Task Force Update held at each ALA meeting. Council activities are also included regularly in *Documents to the People*, the newsletter of GODORT.

AWARENESS OF THE INFORMATION ISSUES

The issues that government information librarians must deal with are varied and complex. They often overlap and intermingle in ways that can be very confusing. Maintaining awareness through professional reading is crucial for the documents librarian who wishes to be well informed. There are numerous monographs available that discuss the politics of government information. Monitoring current journals and on-line discussion lists, such as GovDoc-L, are also important activities. Among the best of these journals are *Government Publications Review*, *Documents to the People* (DttP), *Government Information Quarterly*, and the GPO's *Administrative Notes*.

An outline for thought will help one arrive at a basic understanding of the critical issues and put them in perspective. Five general "areas of awareness" can be used as a framework for classifying the information issues that are of the greatest concern in the 1990s. They are:

- information policy development and reform

- electronic publishing and information handling

- access to and dissemination of government information

- high-performance computing and high-capacity telecommunications networking

- the future of the GPO and the Depository Library Program.

Information Policy Development and Reform

During the 1980s, it became apparent that the government information policy that had served the nation for over 132 years was obsolete. The technology available to produce and disseminate information bore little resemblance to that used when the original federal information laws were formulated. By the end of the decade, as government agencies produced more information in electronic forms, even the Depository Library Act of 1963 (78 Stat. 3542), and the Paperwork Reduction Act of 1980 (44 U.S.C. 3501 *et seq.*) no longer described policy adequate for the new "Information Age."

Government agencies at all levels are now gathering, storing, and disseminating their information in electronic form, not only because it is faster to collate, cheaper to store and revise, and easier to disseminate, but also because the sheer volume of information that must be handled demands it. This is a simple fact with profound implications for our libraries, our society, and the history of our democracy. The issue is best summarized in an announcement for a conference on government information policy sponsored by the Chief Officers of State Library Agencies in October 1988: "Technology has directed a powerful confluence of diverse interests and responsibilities into the complex world of ... government information and dissemination. This phenomenon is occurring without the advantage of comprehensive policy work preceding at any level of government to channel the direction of its force."[21]

The fundamental question is how the principles guaranteeing free and equitable access to government information prescribed in Title 44 will be preserved and enhanced in the age of machine-readable information and supertelecommunications. Librarians must work to ensure that public access to government information is maintained through libraries and educational institutions at acceptable costs and in a form useful and understandable to all who need it. Working through their professional associations, government information librarians are lobbying the federal government to formulate a new information policy that will extend the original intentions of Title 44 into the age of electronic information. Federal information policy reform and development will come through new and revised statutes from Congress and new and revised regulations from the agencies of the executive branch.

Several specific policy issues are presently under development. These include:

1. Privatization of government information and information services, i.e., whether the private information industry should have a greater hand in publishing and distributing for profit information gathered by the government at public expense.

2. Reconfirmation of the Depository Library Program as the means of ensuring that there will be no geographic or economic barriers to public access to government information.

3. Cost recovery for government agencies, through cost sharing with libraries and user fees for other users of government information, to support financially the development of electronic information systems in the agencies.

4. Elimination or consolidation of printed publications into electronic form only, or their complete discontinuation.

5. Multiple-format distribution (e.g., paper, fiche, and electronic) to depository libraries for high-profile government publications, such as the *Federal Register* and the *Congressional Record*.

6. Fugitive publications that exist, but are never cataloged or distributed, so that their access by the public is severely limited.

To date, Congress's main legislative focus has been on revisions to Title 44 and the Freedom of Information Act (FOIA).[22] Currently there are several bills in Congress that would change the various publishing sections of Title 44 and amend FOIA to account for advances in information technology.

Over the last five years, the primary action by Congress has been to revise the sections of Title 44 known as the "Paperwork Reduction Act" (PRA).[23] Formulated during the Carter administration, the 1980 Paperwork Reduction Act authorized the creation of the Office of Information and Regulatory Affairs (OIRA) within the Office of Management and Budget. The twofold purpose of the act, and the OIRA, was to reduce the paperwork burden of U.S. government agencies on industry and individuals and to control the overextensive collection of information by government agencies. However, as the need for a federal government information policy became evident by the mid-1980s, and because of the lack of statutory reform in Congress, the OMB/OIRA began to develop its own legal structure for managing federal information, using the PRA as authorization for their actions. In 1985, it introduced *OMB Circular A-130*, a groundbreaking document that attempted to deal comprehensively with executive branch information production and dissemination. The original *Circular A-130* stressed "maximum feasible reliance on the private sector for the dissemination of products and services" to support government publishing, and ignored the fundamental principles of Title 44 regarding free access to public information.[24] Unfortunately, from the perspective of librarians and many in Congress, the OIRA was motivated more by the Reagan administration's budget-cutting programs and the incentive to recover costs of publishing government information than by a desire to manage federal information efficiently.

By the time the PRA was up for reauthorization in 1990, the OIRA's rule-making had been marked by a history of implementing Reagan administration ideology, which sought to restrict the flow of federal information rather than to develop paperwork efficiency. Its reauthorization presented Congress with a major opportunity to update federal information policy and restrain the politically driven OIRA. However, information-handling technology was well advanced into a new age. The question of reauthorizing and redefining the authority and mission of the OIRA and federal agencies was complicated by the need to develop a new policy reflecting technology's impact on the "life cycle" of information—that is, the creation, management, dissemination, and preservation of electronic information—and to define the roles of the government, public and private sector publishers, and libraries.

In mid-1992, the OMB/OIRA made a further attempt to establish broad federal electronic information policy, through revisions to *Circular A-130*. However, the current proposed changes leave major gaps in a sound electronic information policy. Even in its revised form, *A-130* represents a major change in government information philosophy, in that it allows agencies to exclude electronic products and services from distribution to federal depository libraries. Nor does the present revision of *A-130* address the need to control restrictions on government information by private government contractors, the need for public notice regarding incremental information management decisions in the agencies that have a cumulative impact on access to and availability of information, or the need for electronic information standards in the agencies.

Given the complexity of these issues, Congress has chosen to formulate new information policy with many different legislative proposals, rather than by using an omnibus-like piece of legislation to revise the PRA. In the 102d Congress, Senators Glenn and Nunn both introduced bills reviving action on the PRA by amending only certain sections of the law (S. 1044 and S. 1139, respectively). The Glenn bill emphasized broader information management functions. The Nunn bill, on the other hand, sought to give the OIRA regulatory authority and focused on the PRA's charge to reduce paperwork in the interests of small business. Two other bills introduced in the 102d Congress were written to develop new pieces of information policy through revisions to the Freedom of Information Act. The Improvement of Information Access Act (IIA) (H.R. 3459), introduced by Rep. Major Owens, aimed at revising Title 5 of the U.S. Code by reaffirming the public's right to government information and directing federal agencies to improve the scope and effectiveness of their information products and services, especially in the indexing and access of electronic records. Senator Leahy also introduced the Electronic Freedom of Information Act of 1991 (S. 1940). This bill would strengthen the public's right of access to government electronic records subject to FOIA requests.

In the coming years, more specific information guidelines and regulations will continue to be debated and promulgated by the chief rule-making agencies of the executive branch, such as the Office of Management and Budget. Government information librarians must carefully watch the activity in Congress and closely monitor the OMB's actions in the future to protect the principle of free access to federal information.

Electronic Publishing and Information Handling

The transition of government information from print to electronic forms is a driving force behind policy reform. This simple fact creates a melange of issues concerning the structure and form of electronic information. These issues will have an impact upon access and dissemination of government information. One problem involves the standards that must be developed, both for telecommunications and the structure of electronic files, to ensure their accessibility and utility. Standards for computer programming, format of data files, and communications are required to assure that government information is accessible and widely disseminated in a usable form. Without electronic standards and coordination among government agencies, electronic federal information will become a complex jumble of uncontrolled, inaccessible data. At best, it is probable that each agency developing electronic databases will go its own way, creating a milieu of benign neglect for the needs or rights of the public. At worst, it could allow an ideologically driven administration to use the new technology for evasion and secrecy.

Just as important are questions of privacy, confidentiality, and the preservation of electronic data held by government agencies. It will be necessary to formulate statutes and regulations to ensure that the rights of citizens to information about their government and their own personal privacy are guaranteed in the Information Age. An Electronic Freedom of Information Act and an Electronic Confidentiality Law are needed for the 21st century.

Not discounting political ideology, as government agencies fight to control tight budgets, they will continue to develop a proprietary view of their information resources, seeing them as a means to augment lean budgets through cost recovery, if not as an outright profitable commodity. *Commodification* is the word generally used to characterize this trend, within government agencies, to view electronic information resources as something of economic value to the government and private licensers. In other words, government information has become a commodity and has the potential for changing public agencies into the proprietors of an information bank, rather than distributors of information about their activities and their public missions.

Access to and Dissemination of Government Information

The third major area for awareness covers issues related to controlling the actual acquisition of information and its distribution. The management of government publishing is now in a transitional period, with an ill-defined future. There currently is no concise or comprehensive government information policy stating how electronic data should be collected, managed, preserved, and disseminated. The statutory framework of government publishing established in Title 44 of the U.S. Code is not viable in an age when ink need never touch paper to distribute information and ideas.

The expansion of the executive branch in size and authority has further debilitated the historically loose control held by Congress over the ebb and flow of government publishing. The latter half of the 1980s witnessed the OMB's attempts to establish federal information policy through administrative regulation. The inability of Congress to revise information statutory law has left the public in a policy vacuum.

Although the buzzword of the 1980s was *privatization*, it has a companion of equal concern: *centralization*. The heart of this issue is the danger of centralizing information policy and regulatory control within an agency that is primarily concerned with federal fiscal management. In the cases of privatization and centralization, the results of government information management can be much the same: less government information is available and less is accessible, because it is considered too expensive for tax-based budgets to collect and disseminate, or because it is considered too esoteric to be profitable by private sector publishers. In either case, it is the authority of the budget officer that drives an agency's information program, not its public mission or the decisions of its information professionals.

This has led to an information policy conflict in the federal government over the inconsistencies between the legislative intent and regulatory implementation of information policies. It can be seen in the conflict that developed when the OMB attempted to use the Paperwork Reduction Act to create a specific information policy that many believed was not within the scope of the legislative intent of the PRA's language. Librarians must be aware of this typical form of political conflict that develops between the policy outlined by Congress and the administrative platform implemented by the executive branch through regulatory law.

High-Performance Computing and High-Capacity Telecommunications Networking

On December 9, 1991, the High-Performance Computing Act became law. It established the National Research and Education Network (NREN)[25] and mandated the creation of a computer link among federal and industrial laboratories, educational institutions, libraries, and other public and private research facilities by 1996. The last advance in networking had been in 1986, when the National Science Foundation began funding multipurpose regional networks of computing facilities. This had created the NSFNET, which is the backbone of today's Internet computer network. Estimates are that over 727,000 computers, or "hosts," are attached to the Internet. These computers, ranging in size from microcomputers to mainframes, reside at academic and research institutions, military and government laboratories, and commercial firms in the United States and around the world.[26] The NSFNET/Internet is seen as the central component for development of the NREN.

As it is envisioned, the NREN will be built as a "superhighway" system for computers, adding high-performance computing and high-capacity/high-speed telecommunications to the Internet structure through the use of fiber optic cables. The goal of the NREN is to be able to move information between computers at the rate of about 100,000 typed pages each second. Notwithstanding the immensity of this technological leap, the political and social impact of NREN is critical to depository librarians.

The vision of the NREN that is most appealing to librarians is that of a network serving the public through traditional intermediary institutions, such as schools, universities, libraries, public service organizations, government agencies, and local free-nets, along with commercial information services. However, the vision of a public NREN remains to be realized in the formulation of the federal rules and policy. Because a comprehensive and consistent electronic information policy has not yet been developed, librarians must continue to play a significant role. Their effectiveness will depend upon their ability to define a new structure for libraries in a network environment and to articulate in Washington a vision for the NREN that provides open access to public electronic information. There is a need to form new coalitions with information specialists and users to develop programs for network use, and to shift lobbying efforts in Washington from amending library laws to creating new legislation that will provide federal support for developing libraries in an electronic environment.

Development of the NREN has inspired a very broad base of interest in government information policy issues. The issues that government information librarians have been debating for many years now have a commonality outside the government information environment. Many of the key policy issues surrounding the NREN fall into the same major areas of federal information management policy outlined earlier.

It has been the creed of depository librarians that government information is a public good, and that libraries are the natural centers for distribution and provision of public access to it. The growing debate over what the NREN will be, and how it will be used, is highlighting the concept of information as a public good and raising it beyond the narrow scope of federal depository libraries and a few associations of government information users. Consequently, development of NREN policy will result in policy changes far beyond the network itself. If the NREN is to meet public information needs, Title 44 must be revised to include electronic government information products and services and to mandate that federal agencies provide access on the NREN to their databases. Discussions of the future of the NREN should also focus the attention of depository librarians on the development of regulations, such as *Circular A-130*. Policy must be developed that will reaffirm the government's obligation to provide its citizens with open access to public information, provide standards for government electronic information, develop electronic information locator systems, and connect federal agencies to the NREN. Development of the NREN, and the need to define its vision, demand the development of a consistent and modern federal information policy.

Depository libraries have a great potential for offering the best range of government information services on the NREN. They can ensure free access to the NREN to a great number and diversity of users, and the Depository Library Program has the foundation to operate in an NREN environment. A primary feature that makes the distribution of electronic information through the DLP attractive is the program's geographic and social distribution. Although it is argued that the development of home computer technology and more widely available telecommunication access to on-line government information will obviate the need for depository libraries, for the foreseeable future, as the NREN develops, the problem of a growing gap between information "haves" and "have-nots" will continue to exist. By the nature of their geographic distribution and commitment to free access to government information, a network of depository libraries would ensure equitable access to the NREN for all citizens, regardless of location or access to information technology. Federal depositories in both academic and public libraries would play an important role as intermediaries to individuals and small businesses who cannot afford home computers or access to the research, educational, and commercial services that will ultimately form the NREN. Linking depository libraries and federal agencies to the NREN could create a "virtual" depository library, reaching far beyond the physical collections of even the largest depository libraries and linking decentralized government resources into a useful collection of information.

Future of the GPO and the Depository Library Program

Today the authority, role, and economic viability of the Government Printing Office and the Federal Depository Library Program are in question. The technology of information resources management is only a part of the dilemma faced by the GPO and its depository libraries. Economic and political barriers also must be overcome if the GPO and the DLP are to fulfill their missions.

Federal agencies can now bypass the GPO and do their own "desktop" publishing, or disseminate machine-readable formats such as CD-ROMs or magnetic tapes. They can provide direct dial-up or network access to their on-line data files. Privatization also plays a major role, as many agencies distribute their electronic data files through private vendors, making them available only on a fee basis from a profit-making organization. In these situations, technology hinders equitable public access to public information. By bypassing the GPO and the DLP, agencies diminish the bibliographic control of government information. Additionally, government information kept outside the GPO Sales Program undermines the revenue base of the GPO and the DLP. Ultimately, the individual citizens suffer, because they cannot afford to pay fees for access to government information, or simply cannot find it because it is not cataloged or indexed anywhere.

However, it is the economic and political issues that will have the greatest impact on the future role and development of the GPO and the DLP, not the technological problems. The primary economic issue is, of course, whether the GPO and depository libraries can find the money to buy the hardware and pay for trained staff to run the systems and make the information useable. Although the GPO has much of the basic technology it will need in place, it will still require significant appropriations before it becomes a gateway to other government databases and disseminates information in useable electronic formats. Similarly, libraries must face budget problems of their own. Depositories in large public libraries and at larger academic institutions have a distinct advantage. Most of them have the computers and enough trained staff to deal with electronic information. However, the severity of current fiscal conditions will require even these institutions to shift finances from collection development to electronic transfer of information. For smaller depositories without federal support, the question will be whether they can continue to participate in the Depository Library Program.

For the GPO and the DLP, political, economic, and policy development issues go hand in hand. The GPO either must be appropriated more money to modernize, or must be allowed to transfer these costs on to libraries or users. GPO counsel has opined that, under current Title 44, depository libraries cannot charge user fees for government information and the GPO is obligated to pay all its costs of disseminating electronic information. Therefore, the GPO must fight for better appropriations from Congress. Depository libraries must assist the GPO in pursuing higher appropriations, or shift precious budgetary resources from supporting collections of printed materials toward providing access to electronic services.

The future of the GPO and the DLP rests in modernizing the legislative intentions of the public printing and documents sections of Title 44 and in protecting depository libraries from access and user fees. Currently, there are bills before Congress that, if passed into law, would be the first step in reconfirming the mission of the GPO and the DLP and in developing modern information policy. The GPO Wide Information Network Data Online (WINDO) Act (H.R. 2772), introduced on June 26, 1991, by Rep. Charles Rose, Chairman of the JCP, and its companion bill, the GPO Gateway to Government Act (S. 2813), introduced by Senators Gore, Ford, Sarbanes, and Simon, would establish on-line access to electronic databases of the federal government through a computer "gateway" service in the GPO. The gateway would be a single-account, single-point-of-access method of searching numerous federal databases and retrieving information from them. The WINDO/Gateway Act would give the GPO authority to develop user-friendly interfaces, menus, indexes, on-line help, and other aids to improve the facility for depository libraries and general users. It also would provide on-line access to depositories without charge.

In addition, the GPO is planning for its own future. In January 1992, the GPO released its outline for building a strategic plan, entitled *GPO/2001: Vision for a New Millennium*. The report delineates goals for developing human resources, staff training, products and services, technology, organizational structure, financial resources, and new facilities. Perhaps most importantly, the report calls for a legislative program for modernizing Title 44 that would:

- promote the execution of laws relating to the production, procurement, and dissemination of government information products and services;

- eliminate duplication of effort, reducing expenditures and promoting economy to the fullest extent consistent with the efficient and effective operation of the government's information functions; and

- provide for the utilization of electronic information technologies in the dissemination of government information products and services.[27]

These are three fundamental areas in which new policy development is needed. It will require specific statutory language amending Title 44 to implement these goals and establish a comprehensive federal information policy suitable for the new age of government information, in which the GPO and the DLP can play their traditional roles in a modern fashion.

CONCLUSION

Every government information librarian should have a working knowledge of the executive and legislative branches of government and the key decision makers in federal information policy. With this information and an understanding of the issues, they can begin to lobby for specific information policies.

But how does one go about lobbying? First, librarians must be in contact with government officials in the agencies, as well as in Congress, to provide them with information they may not have about the impact of any decision affecting the depository program. Second, depository librarians need to inform public officials about the ramifications to the public when government information ceases to be available, is unreliable, or is inadequate. Third, librarians must identify who the decision makers are and understand their personal goals and biases. Our government is populated with many dedicated civil servants at all levels, but it is essential to know the professional background of persons entering government, and to which jobs they go when they leave government service. It is often the only way of understanding the political motivations of the information policy makers and federal information managers.

Library and professional organizations, such as the American Library Association, Special Libraries Association, and others profiled in appendix 12.1, perform two very important functions for documents librarians. They offer the means for staying informed about the activities of government agencies and they provide a forum for exchanging and testing ideas. Through their publications and conferences, professional associations and interest groups help librarians understand and keep abreast of the issues. They are important methods of networking and getting to know the information professionals outside, as well as within, the field of librarianship. They provide the profession with the structure and lobbying force in Washington, D.C., necessary to sustain a consistently prominent platform in the interests of library users. Finally, they offer individual librarians opportunities, through testifying and lobbying, to be involved with public policy activities and to have an impact on the organization and politics of government information.

NOTES

[1] Joint Resolution 25, 12 Statutes at Large 117.

[2] U.S. Government Printing Office, *GPO/2001: Vision for a New Millennium* (Washington, DC: U.S. Government Printing Office, 1991), 8.

[3] U.S. Government Printing Office, *GPO Annual Report 1990* (Washington, DC: U.S. Government Printing Office, 1991), 4-7.

[4] 3 Statutes at Large 140.

[5] 28 Statutes at Large 601.

[6] *GPO Annual Report 1990*, 21-22.

[7] Ibid. 30, 39.

[8] Ibid. 30.

[9] U.S. Congress. House Committee on House Administration, *Oversight on the U.S. Government Printing Office General Sales Program* (Washington, DC: U.S. Government Printing Office, 1990), 41-43.

[10] U.S. Government Printing Office, *An Explanation of the Superintendent of Documents Classification System* (Washington, DC: U.S. Government Printing Office, 1990).

[11] U.S. Government Printing Office, *GPO Classification Manual: A Practical Guide to the Superintendent of Documents Classification System* (Washington, DC: U.S. Government Printing Office, 1986).

[12] U.S. Government Printing Office, *List of Classes of United States Government Publications Available for Selection by Depository Libraries* (Washington, DC: U.S. Government Printing Office).

[13] The Biennial Survey is mailed to all depositories every two years. The data gathered have varied from year to year, but the GPO is trying to standardize data and definitions in order to develop time series data.

[14] U.S. Government Printing Office, *Instructions to Depository Libraries* (Washington, DC: U.S. Government Printing Office, 1988).

[15] U.S. Government Printing Office, *Preparing for a Depository Inspection* (Washington, DC: U.S. Government Printing Office, 1991).

[16] Depository Library Council to the Public Printer, *Federal Depository Library Manual* (Washington, DC: U.S. Government Printing Office, 1985).

[17] There is an excellent introduction to the FDLP/BB in *Administrative Notes* 12 (August 1991): 12. This issue tells documents librarians how to sign in, set up a password, and move around in the system. There is also an LPS systems operator that can be contacted by telephone at 202-512-1126.

[18] 44 U.S. Code sec. 103.

[19] U.S. Congress. Joint Committee on Printing, *Government Printing and Binding Regulations* (Washington, DC: U.S. Government Printing Office, 1990).

[20] U.S. Government Printing Office, *Guide to Federal Publishing* (Washington, DC: U.S. Government Printing Office, 1991).

[21] Chief Officers of State Library Agencies, 1988 Conference Announcement.

[22] 5 U.S. Code sec. 501 *et seq.*

[23] 44 U.S. Code sec. 3501 *et seq.*

[24] OMB *Circular A-130*, 50 *Federal Register* 52,730, (December 24, 1985).

[25] High-Performance Computing Act of 1991, Public Law No. 102-194 (December 9, 1991).

[26] L. Russell Herman, Jr., "The Internet is Humongous, Dominated by the U.S., and Growing Rapidly," *Connect* (June 1992): 12-13.

[27] U.S. Government Printing Office, *GPO/2001: Vision for a New Millennium* (Washington, DC: U.S. Government Printing Office, 1991), 34.

APPENDIX 12.1
KEY ORGANIZATIONS IN GOVERNMENT INFORMATION

This section is an annotated list of the key organizations that are involved in government information issues and provide the means for librarians to stay informed, become involved, and contribute directly to the development of information policy and a new structure of government information dissemination.

Library Organizations

American Association of Law Libraries (AALL)

AALL is an organization of approximately 4,800 librarians working in courts, bar associations, law societies, law schools, private law firms, and federal, state, and county governments. Its headquarters is 53 West Jack Boulevard, Suite 940, Chicago, IL 60604. Phone: 312-939-4764.

Publications:

American Association of Law Libraries Newsletter is the association's monthly publication containing association, chapter, and committee news and the schedule of association meetings. AALL has a subgroup that covers government information. The Government Documents Special Interest Section (GD/SIS) publishes a quarterly newsletter, *Jurisdocs*, containing news and articles about government information at all levels of government. The current *Jurisdocs* editor is David Batista, Rutgers State University-Camden, School of Law Library, 5th and Penn Streets, Camden, NJ 08102. Phone: 609-757-6469. Fax: 609-757-6488. GD/SIS also runs a federal legislation hotline called Gov-Line, updated weekly, on the status of legislation dealing with federal information issues when Congress is in session. The Gov-Line number is 312-939-7774. Gov-Line information is also published on several on-line discussion lists, including GovDoc-L.

The American Library Association (ALA)

Founded in 1876, the American Library Association is the largest library association in the world, with over 50,000 individual and organizational members. As such, it is the primary professional organization for librarians in the United States. Its mission spans the concerns of all types of libraries, including state, public, academic, and special libraries in business, government, commerce, the arts, armed services, hospitals, prisons, and other institutions. ALA is comprised of numerous subject-based committees appointed by the president; 11 divisions organized according to library type; 17 round tables covering special fields of librarianship not within the scope of a division; 57 chapters; and 22 affiliated organizations. Some of the committees that often deal with government information issues or have interest in that area are the ALA Committees on Freedom and Equality of Access to Information; Intellectual Freedom; Legislation; and Public Information. Two other divisions have also been active in the government information forum: the Association of College and Research Libraries (ACRL), and the Library Information Technology Association (LITA). Besides the Government Documents Round Table, round tables such as the Federal Librarians, Intellectual Freedom, and Maps and Geography Round Tables are also active on government information issues. ALA Headquarters is 50 East Huron Street, Chicago, IL 60611. Phone: 312-944-6780; toll-free: 800-545-2433. Fax: 312-440-9374. ALA also maintains an office in Washington, DC (address given below under ALA/GODORT) to support its extensive government relations efforts.

Publications

ALA Handbook of Organization (annual). A guide to the structure of the ALA, including names of officials, committee members, etc. *ALA Washington Newsletter*, published periodically, covers federal actions in Washington that affect libraries and ALA programs, and also contains an "ALA Action Alert" on pending federal legislation or regulations. Numerous other periodicals and monographs are produced by the various units of the ALA. All publications are available to members, depending upon membership in the ALA's individual units, and most are available through subscription. Another occasional publication of special interest is *Less Access to Less Information by and about the U.S. Government: A Chronology*, prepared by the ALA Washington Office. This series of chronologies, which document the federal government's efforts to restrict and privatize government information, is available upon request from the ALA Washington Office.

American Library Association/Government Documents Round Table (ALA/GODORT)

The Government Documents Round Table (GODORT) of the American Library Association is the primary professional association for government information librarians. The purposes of GODORT, according to the Bylaws, are:

- to provide a forum for discussion of problems and concerns, and for the exchange of ideas by librarians working with government documents;

- to provide a force for initiating and supporting programs to increase availability, use, and bibliographic control of documents;

- to increase communication between documents librarians and other librarians; and

- to contribute to the extension and improvement of education and training of documents librarians.

GODORT is organized into three main task forces: the Federal Documents Task Force, the State and Local Documents Task Force, and the International Documents Task Force. GODORT supports a very active Legislation Committee that takes a direct role, through the ALA, in dealing with the lawmaking initiatives of both the executive and legislative branches of the federal government. GODORT's primary functions and activities are: writing resolutions for the ALA; developing position papers by its membership; maintaining varied correspondence addressing government information issues; providing a pool of experts on government information in libraries to act as congressional witnesses and speakers; providing educational outreach programs; sponsoring annual programs at the ALA Conferences; and, generally, educating and informing government information policy makers. GODORT sponsors a National Action Alert Network (NAAN) to communicate with its membership and respond quickly to federal and/or state legislative or regulatory proposals. GODORT also runs the Agency Liaison Program, through which its members develop personal contacts with specific individuals on the publishing and information staffs of federal agencies. Additionally, the Round Table maintains a database of discontinued federal documents titles. A list of GODORT officers and committee chairs, with their addresses and telephone numbers, is published in each March issue of *Documents to the People*. Information on current GODORT officers and on becoming a member can be obtained from the GODORT/ALA Staff Liaison, ALA Washington Office, 110 Maryland Avenue, NE, Washington, DC 20002. Phone: 202-547-4440. Fax: 202-547-7363.

Publications:

Documents to the People (*DttP*) is the official publication of ALA/GODORT. *DttP* provides current information on government publications, technical reports, and maps at local, state, national, foreign, and international levels; related government activities; and government information librarianship. It is published in March, June, September, and December. The bylaws of GODORT are published annually in the December issue of *DttP*. *DttP* is free to members of ALA/GODORT and is $20.00 per year ($25.00 outside the U.S.) to nonmembers. The current editor is Mary Redmond, New York State Library, Cultural Education Center, Albany, NY 12230. Phone: 518-474-3940. Fax: 518-474-5163.

Association of Research Libraries (ARL)

The Association of Research Libraries (ARL) is an organization of more than 100 university, public, private, and national research libraries. Individuals cannot be members of the ARL directly, as it is an organization of libraries. Library directors of the member libraries meet to discuss issues of common concern. The ARL concentrates mainly on research library management, technology, automation, and interlibrary cooperation, but it has a very active government relations office and takes a very close interest in federal legislative issues, particularly those on government information. Many ARL member libraries are federal depository libraries. The ARL's headquarters is Euram Building, 21 Dupont Circle NW, Washington DC 20036. Phone: 202-323-2466. Fax: 202-462-7849.

Publications

The *ARL Newsletter* is issued monthly. The ARL also publishes occasional monographs, special reports, SPEC kits, and various statistical surveys. All publications are available for purchase from the association.

Federal Library and Information Center Committee (FLICC), U.S. Library of Congress

FLICC is an organization of government agency libraries and government information centers. This is essentially the library association of federal government librarians. As such, its interests center on policies and problems relevant to federal libraries. FLICC also provides federal libraries with computerized services through its Federal Library and Information Network (FEDLINK), including on-line cataloging, interlibrary loan services, acquisitions, and serials control, as well as on-line access to federal research databases. Its headquarters is located at U.S. Library of Congress, Federal Library and Information Center Committee, Washington, DC 20540. Phone: 202-707-6055. Fax: 202-707-2171.

Publications:
FLICC Newsletter is published quarterly and is available from FLICC headquarters.

Special Libraries Association (ALA)
The Special Libraries Association (ALA) is made up of over 12,000 librarians who work in libraries attached to businesses, research centers, government, universities, newspapers, museums, and other specialized institutions. Because many special libraries are also federal government depository libraries, the SLA also has taken a strong and active role in government information issues in recent years, and has become one of the primary organizations representing the interests of government information librarians in Washington. Its headquarters is located at 1700 18th Street, NW, Washington, DC 20009. Phone: 202-234-4700. Fax: 202-265-9317.

Publications:
Besides monographs and brochures, the SLA publishes *Special Libraries*, a quarterly focusing on the professional interests of the association and professional policies and activities. The subscription cost is included in the membership dues. The price for nonmembers is $48 per year in the United States and Canada ($53 for other foreign subscribers).

Nonlibrary Organizations

American Society for Information Science (ASIS)
The ASIS is a nonprofit organization of information science professionals with an emphasis on information technology. The organization's interests encompass the creation, transformation, storage, retrieval, and dissemination of information, particularly through the application of modern technology. The ASIS is organized into 21 Special Interest Groups, or SIGs, which are concerned with the various aspects of information management and communication. The address of the society is: American Society for Information Science, 1424 16th Street, NW, Suite 404, Washington, DC 20036. Phone: 202-462-1000. Fax: 202-462-7494.

Publications:
The *Journal of the American Society for Information Science—JASIS* is published six times a year; subscription cost is included in the membership dues. The *Bulletin of the American Society for Information Science* is published six times a year, and its cost is included in membership dues, but it is also available by subscription. The ASIS also publishes the *Annual Review of Information Science*, and various SIGs publish their own newsletters.

Association of Public Data Users (APDU)

The Association of Public Data Users is comprised of organizations and individuals concerned with use of machine-readable and hard-copy public statistical data. It is a nonprofit organization and works to improve public access to and use of government statistics and statistical software issued by government agencies. The APDU holds annual conferences, promotes cooperation and exchange of data among its members, and serves as a representative of the interests of its members with federal and state governments and other public information producers. Information about APDU can be obtained from the Association of Public Data Users, Princeton University Computing Center, 87 Prospect Avenue, Princeton, NJ 08544-1002. Phone: 609-258-6025. Fax: 609-258-3943.

Publications:
APDU Newsletter (monthly) and an annual membership directory. Publications are distributed to members only.

Coalition for Networked Information (CNI)

The Coalition for Networked Information is a cooperative project of the Association of Research Libraries, CAUSE, and EDUCOM. CAUSE is an association of administrators of colleges and universities; its main purpose is to enhance the effectiveness of higher education administration through the use of computer technology. EDUCOM also is an organization of colleges and universities, formed to promote resource sharing in higher education through the application of information technology.

Founded in March 1990, CNI was created to "promote the creation of and access to information resources in networked environments in order to enrich scholarship and to enhance intellectual productivity." The purpose of CNI is to develop coalitions of shared interests in computer networks and to "discover" and encourage joint projects for network development, particularly where the NREN is concerned. The organization "sunsets" on June 30, 1993, with the possibility of another three-year term. At the end of that period, all resources will revert to the three founding associations. More than 150 organizations and institutions belong to the Coalition Task Force, a subgroup of CNI organized to perform special projects within CNI's range of activities. Along with associations such as the ALA, the Coalition Task Force includes institutions of higher education, publishers, network service providers, computer hardware and system companies, library networks, and public and state libraries. Periodically CNI issues "Calls for Statements of Interest and Experience" on specific projects. In this way, individuals, institutions, and organizations willing and capable of contributing to CNI initiatives are identified. Each "Call" describes a proposed project or study and information on how to submit a "Statement of Interest." Depending upon the project, funding for expenses is sometimes granted. Respondents do not have to be affiliated with the CNI or the Coalition Task Force to submit a proposal in answer to a "Call." The address for the Coalition is 21 Dupont Circle, NW, Washington, DC 20036. Phone: 202-296-5098. Fax: 202-872-0884.

Council of Professional Associations on Federal Statistics (COPAFS)

The interests of COPAFS center on U.S. federal government statistical policy and programs. It is active on issues concerning government statistical policies, priorities, quality and compatibility of data, data collection, access to information, and equitable dissemination practices. COPAFS represents 17 professional associations and claims a membership of over 250,000. It includes such organizations as the American Sociological Association, Association of Public Data Users, and the American Public Health Association. Contact with the Council can be made at: Council of Professional Associations on Federal Statistics, 1429 Duke Street, Suite 402, Alexandria, VA 22314. Phone: 703-836-0404. Fax: 703-684-2037.

Publications:
News from COPAFS is published monthly.

Computer Professionals for Social Responsibility (CPSR)

The CPSR is an organization of approximately 2,700 individuals in the computer science field. It is dedicated to educating policy makers, the public, and those in the computer industry about the social implications of computer use. Particular interests are in areas such as computers and nuclear weapons, computers in the workplace, and computers and issues of privacy and civil liberties. Advocating public responsibility in the use of computer systems, the CPSR has been active on issues regarding the development of the National Research and Education Network and government electronic information policies. The CPSR's headquarters is located in Palo Alto, California. Its address is P.O. Box 717, Palo Alto, CA 94301. Phone: 415-322-3778. Fax: 415-322-3798.

Publications:
The *CPSR Newsletter* is published quarterly; its cost is included in membership dues.

Council of State Governments (CSG) and Chief Officers of State Library Agencies (COSLA)

The Council of State Governments operates as an information center and clearinghouse for state government executives and their staffs. The CSG maintains a library of over 20,000 volumes consisting primarily of state government administrative and research publications, planning documents, and machine-readable bibliographic and nonbibliographic data. The CSG Division of Information Services is developing a National State Information System (NSIS) that will provide on-line access to the CSG library catalog and other electronic information. The CSG follows most state government information policy and management issues. The COSLA is an arm of the CSG and its mission is to provide an organization for dealing with the problems of state libraries and issues of library development. The COSLA has been particularly active on issues of electronic information and computer networking. It is located at the Council of State Governments, P.O. Box 11910, Iron Works Pike, Lexington, KY 40578. CSG phone: 606-252-2291; COSLA phone: 606-231-1878. Fax: 606-231-1928.

Publications
State Government News is a monthly publication providing current news and information on state government developments. Many articles cover information policy and information resource management issues at the state and local levels. The *Journal of State Government* presents an in-depth, bimonthly look at state government issues. The *State Government Research Checklist* is a bimonthly tabloid providing news of current acquisitions by the CSG State Information Center and of current developments in state information policy and management. The *COSLA Directory* is published annually for $12.50.

Information Industry Association (IIA)
The IIA is a trade association representing publishers and companies that produce and distribute information products and services, including reformatting and value-added government information. It is keenly interested in the privatization of government information services and the unrestricted availability of government information, particularly in electronic form. The IIA works at all levels of government to influence information resource management and policy development, and provides a very effective lobbying force for private sector views in the information policy debate. Its headquarters is Information Industry Association, 555 New Jersey Avenue, NW, Suite 800, Washington, DC 20001. Phone: 202-639-8262. Fax: 202-639-4403.

Publications:
The *Friday Memo* is the IIA biweekly newsletter that carries news about the association and events in Washington. It supplements the quarterly *Information Times*. The IIA also publishes *Information Sources*, an annual membership directory that includes information on industry products, services, and systems. The *Friday Memo* and *Information Times* are generally available to members only.

Public Citizen
Public Citizen is a nonprofit consumer group formed by Ralph Nader to support citizen advocates in lobbying, litigation, and protection of consumer rights. Public education is also one of the goals of the organization, for which it lobbies, presents expert testimony in Congress, and arranges media coverage. Public Citizen also sponsors Congress Watch, a subdivision. In recent years, Public Citizen has taken an interest in government information activities and policy development and has become a leading advocate of open and equitable access to federal government statistical and economic data. Public Citizen, P.O. Box 19404, Washington, DC 20036. Phone: 202-293-9142.

Publications:
Public Citizen, a monthly magazine, covers consumer issues and includes an activists' alert section. The subscription cost is included in membership dues and is $20 per year for nonmembers.

OMB Watch (OMBW)
OMBW is a representative organization of individuals, libraries, community groups, and government agencies that advocates greater public awareness of government administrative regulation, particularly regarding the activities of the Office of Management and Budget. It was formed in 1983 in reaction to the

growth in power of the OMB, and it works to increase the public accountability of that office. Its address is OMB Watch, 1731 Connecticut Avenue, NW, 4th Floor, Washington, DC 20009. Phone: 202-234-8494. Fax: 202-234-8584.

Publications:

The *Government Information Insider*, a bimonthly magazine, focuses on government information policy. It is $75 a year for individuals, community groups, libraries, and government agencies; $175 per year for businesses and professional organizations. *OMB Watch* is a bimonthly newsletter covering OMB initiatives and activities. Subscriptions are $35 per year and $100 per year, respectively, for subscribers as previously listed.

Taxpayer Assets Project (TAP)

The Taxpayer Assets Project was formed in 1989 by Ralph Nader to investigate issues related to the management of publicly owned assets such as public lands, patents, government intellectual property, and government information resources. TAP has been active on government information issues, particularly the dissemination of federal economic and census data and the quality of government information services. TAP has been a strong supporter of the American Library Association and the interests of libraries. Contact with TAP can be made at the Taxpayer Assets Project, P.O. Box 19367, Washington, DC, or 7-Z Magie, Faculty Road, Princeton, NJ 08540. Phone: 609-683-0534. Fax: 609-258-2809.

Publications:

TAP has no regular publication. However, various TAP documents on government information issues are available by contacting that project.

13

Costs and Benefits of Running a Documents Collection

Carol Turner
Assistant Director for Public Services,
University of Florida Libraries
University of Florida

This chapter focuses on the costs and benefits of a documents collection—what expenditures are required to provide documents service, in terms of dollars and staff effort, and what benefits are derived by the library and the community it serves. Described in this chapter are methods for defining costs and gathering cost data; some approaches to analyzing, interpreting, and using cost data; and suggestions on comparing costs with benefits. Possibilities for cost recovery also are briefly examined. In approaching this topic, the author assumes a library with a separate and comprehensive documents unit. This library is a U.S. federal depository with a collection of documents from its own state and local area. It acquires documents from major international agencies and selects a limited number of documents from foreign countries. Processing of most documents is done by the documents unit staff, but about 15 percent of the documents received are fully cataloged and housed in other library locations.

WHO NEEDS COST INFORMATION AND WHY?

Because most documents are free or inexpensive, little effort has been devoted in the profession to determining the costs of maintaining and providing access to a documents collection. However, it is increasingly apparent that services often have hidden costs that raise their price tag, and that maintaining a large documents collection is generally an expensive operation. As librarians become more economically savvy, and as libraries and other institutions strive to meet demands for accountability, both the documents librarian and the library administrator must seek solid data on the cost of document service.

Knowing the cost of an operation is an essential part of sound management. Furthermore, accurate cost information is needed in specific cases requiring analysis or decision making. Examples of the types of decisions that can be made with such data are:

- determining whether to institute a service;

- assessing various options for providing service;

214 □ Costs and Benefits of Running a Documents Collection

- analyzing the efficiency and cost-effectiveness of an existing service;

- evaluating the opportunity cost of a service (i.e., what alternative services could be provided with the dollars dedicated to supporting this service); and

- balancing the cost of a service against the benefit it provides (e.g., costs borne by a depository library to meet its obligation versus the value obtained from depository status).

To understand and use cost data effectively, further analysis may be essential to answer critical questions, such as:

- What is the cost per physical unit?

- What is the cost per service transaction?

- What changes in costs occur when there are changes in the library's document service?

- How do the costs of depository obligations compare with the cost of selecting and acquiring individual documents that fit the library's collection profile?

- How does the cost of processing documents using a document classification scheme compare with the cost of using the cataloging and classification scheme used in other parts of the library?

- Is it more cost-effective to centralize or decentralize document processing, housing of documents, and reference service?

Although these questions are difficult to answer, dealing with them will strengthen both documents librarians' understanding and their ability to manage collections effectively.

COST DEFINITIONS

There are several ways to define costs. *Total costs* are made up of direct costs and indirect costs. "The direct costs are all the costs that can be specifically identified with a project or activity.... The indirect costs are those that are not readily assignable to a specific project or activity."[1] Salaries of documents librarians, commercially published indexes to documents, and microform reader/printers purchased for the documents collection represent direct costs for documents services. Indirect costs include such items as salaries of staff in the personnel, accounting, and administrative offices; janitorial service; utilities and rent; and the cost of supporting services such as acquisitions, cataloging, and preservation. Generally, analysis of direct costs is particularly useful for internal purposes, such as determining the costs of specific operations or services and then comparing them with the costs of comparable tasks within the library. Another example of direct cost analysis would be to do a longitudinal study, examining changes in these costs over time.

The addition of indirect costs provides data needed to determine the total cost of documents service. These data are particularly useful in describing costs of services to an external audience. Reporting externally is important for libraries generally and for documents collections specifically. There is widespread belief that library service (particularly providing access to government information) should be free. Having clear data available on the nature and volume of services provided, the activities required to provide them, and their individual and aggregate costs highlights the true cost of library service, while underlining its value.

Another way of defining costs is to divide them into fixed and variable costs. A *fixed cost* does not change over a given time or range of activity, while a *variable cost* is stable for a given unit of activity, but changes with activity volume. For example, the cost of a microfilm reader/printer is fixed, while the cost of paper and toner is variable and dependent on volume of activity. In calculating the cost of providing service, it is necessary to understand the concept of fixed and variable costs and to ensure that the variable costs included accurately reflect activity level.

A further way to list costs is according to the budget categories used by a specific library or its parent institution. Individual libraries divide cost categories in a variety of ways, but the following general categories (under various names or groupings) usually appear in the annual operating budget:

- personnel, salaried;
- personnel, hourly;
- books and other library materials;
- equipment;
- expendable supplies, materials, and services;
- automation; and
- facilities.

Capital improvements, such as a new building or major renovation, are generally not treated as part of the annual operating budget.

IDENTIFYING AND GATHERING COSTS

The process of identifying library costs sometimes seems daunting to the uninitiated. Upon reflection, however, specific costs become readily apparent and can be verbalized and pinpointed. This section discusses the major components of any library's costs: salaries, books and materials, equipment, supplies, automation, and facility expenses. Each component's total cost in the overall expenditures of a particular library will depend on the library's size and environment.

Personnel, Salaried and Hourly

Personnel costs are generally the largest component in the budget. Direct personnel costs include salaries and wages paid to all staff working with documents (librarians; paraprofessional, technical, and clerical staff; student assistants; and other hourly employees). Benefits (health insurance, retirement contributions, etc.) contributed by the employer are also part of this cost, and should not be overlooked, as they may add 25 percent or more to personnel costs.

The full cost of documents service also must reflect indirect personnel costs, that is, personnel in other parts of the library that support documents service. To compute and assign these costs, one must assess all the support units in terms of the percentage of their personnel costs that reasonably can be attributed to documents. It may be difficult to divide these costs with precision, but it is important to have confidence in their general validity, and it is a necessary component of the total cost of documents service. If some documents are ordered by acquisitions staff rather than by documents collection staff, part of one or more staff members' salaries and benefits should be counted. Or, if documents-related work is sporadic and divided among several staff members, a more accurate cost estimate would be the cost of a percentage of acquisitions personnel equal to the percentage of the total documents-related acquisitions workload. This kind of calculation should be made for cataloging, for binding and preservation, and for all other library units that provide any service for the documents collection. The cost of administrative functions, such as personnel, purchasing, accounting, systems, and general administration supporting documents services, also must be tabulated as part of the indirect cost of that service. These costs should be prorated by the size of the documents collection staff relative to the size of other service units' staff. For example, if personnel office salaries and benefits total $50,000, and documents staff represent 10 percent of the total library staff, $5,000 for personnel services should be added to the cost of documents operations.

Books and Other Library Materials

Library materials are a major cost item in library operations. In many depository library programs, however, materials are provided free of charge. Nevertheless, to respond to the needs of most users, most documents collection development plans require the acquisition of materials not deposited for free, and most libraries do incur substantial costs for material purchases. Depository libraries may order second copies of popular documents, purchase materials that are not available on deposit, and acquire commercially produced reference materials that enhance access to the collections. Many documents, especially those not issued by the U.S. federal government, are not available on deposit and must be purchased. The cost of these (e.g., a census from a foreign country; a scholarly monograph from an international agency; a journal from a state economic agency; or a local planning document produced under contract by a consultant) can be substantial. Often libraries also choose to purchase commercial indexes and their accompanying microform sets to expand the documents collections. These sets are easy to use, provide ready physical access to materials, and serve to back up and preserve the original copy, which may be in poor physical condition, missing from the collection, or never acquired. Research libraries might purchase primary source material that served as the basis for published government reports. For example, printed reports from the U.S. decennial census are distributed to depository libraries. However, some researchers also require additional resources, such as the census schedules in microform that provide detailed information reported in the census from 1790 to 1920; printed census maps; or computer tapes of a recent census that permit data correlation and manipulation not possible with the printed sets. These materials are government documents and their costs contribute to the cost of maintaining the documents collection and providing an appropriate level of service. Sometimes the only way certain documents, such as those issued in foreign countries, can be acquired is through an exchange. If materials must be purchased for an exchange, the cost of these purchases must also be included in a comprehensive review of documents costs.

Equipment

Equipment costs are an increasingly important and visible part of documents service. Twenty years ago, a document unit's equipment needs did not go far beyond providing an adequate number of typewriters for staff and, perhaps, a microform reader for library users. Today staff require terminals and computer workstations for both processing and collection access. There are also substantial equipment requirements for users of the collection. Although large research libraries have always acquired some documents in microformat, and thus needed some appropriate readers and storage cabinets, the inclusion of microfiche in the U.S. depository program in the late 1970s has made this equipment essential. Today access to documents collections requires a variety of microform reading equipment, some of which must provide printing capability. Storage cabinets are as necessary to house and preserve microforms as shelving is for printed documents. It is essential to project growth in this format and include funds for cabinet purchase in a budget. This is a continuing and substantial commitment. Another piece of equipment ubiquitous in libraries is the photocopy machine, essential for both users and staff. A documents unit should have its own machine(s) or have ready access to suitable library equipment.

With the inclusion of documents in on-line catalogs, and particularly with the growing development of information in electronic format, the equipment need that generates the most discussion and concern today is computer equipment (see chapter 7). Terminals are needed to provide basic access to the documents collection. Furthermore, without appropriate computer workstations, the information contained in many of the collection's documents is inaccessible. The initial cost of necessary equipment is substantial, and there are ongoing and quite high costs because of its short life and rapid obsolescence. The cost of equipment should be divided by its estimated years of useful life to provide figures for inclusion in the annual costs of service.

Expendable Supplies and Services

The expendable supplies and services category covers a myriad of items required for ongoing operations, including small equipment items written off as expense, supplies, and contracted services. Specific costs may include:

- office supplies (paper, pens, pencils, tape, ribbons, etc.);

- book supplies (labels, barcodes, security targets, etc.);

- telephone service;

- postage;

- printing expenses;

- travel expenses;

- maintenance contracts (for photocopiers, microform equipment, computer equipment, etc.);

- building repairs and maintenance; and

- software for office applications.

Some of these costs can be attributed to the documents collection directly. Others must be computed using an estimate of the documents service's share of these expenditures on a library-wide basis.

Automation

Automation is a substantial cost in many libraries. Are documents ordered or cataloged electronically? Are they included in the on-line catalog? As appropriate, the documents collection's portion of costs for automated processing and for access to the on-line catalog should be computed and counted in the total cost of documents service. Do library staff use electronic mail for communication? Are on-line services used to support the reference and information program? These automation costs also must be included in the costs of providing service.

Facilities

Facility costs are part of the total costs of operation, too. Mortgage or debt payment, rent, and upkeep of facilities are a significant part of some library budgets, and these costs should be calculated for the documents collection. In many institutions, facility costs are handled centrally and are not readily available. It is important, however, to estimate facilities costs if one is attempting to calculate full service costs. In that case, the going cost rate per square foot for the area in which the library is located can be used.

Non-Dollar Costs

Although all costs can eventually be discussed in terms of money, the dollar costs might not be immediately apparent. Maintaining a documents collection represents a choice, and that choice has an opportunity cost. Staff effort and dollars not devoted to maintaining a documents collection could be diverted to other areas. Without a documents collection, perhaps the library could build and maintain other special collections, strengthen its reference and instruction program, or catalog new receipts more quickly than it does presently. Furthermore, if a library chooses to have a documents collection, it may be diverting user assistance from its primary clientele to the public, perhaps increasing general levels of traffic and security concerns. Any service that requires or creates specialization of staff can bring additional costs, as in the case of patent depository status.

COST ANALYSIS

Useful library cost analysis requires defining functions and then identifying costs directly attributable to those functions. The documents librarian should know how much it costs, in terms of both full-time employees (FTE) and dollars, to carry out the various functions of the collection. To obtain these data, one has to determine the amount and level of staff assigned to each function. This information may be available in job assignments or personnel evaluations, but a specific study is likely to require staff time logs. A standard list of functions or activities, with definitions for each, should be developed. The list should then be discussed with all staff so that data are comparable. It will be particularly helpful if such a list has been developed for the library as a whole, so that cross-departmental comparisons can be made. The level of specificity will depend on the purpose for which data are being gathered. The librarian might, for example, want to know the staff effort and cost in terms of dollars of major library functions, and so would divide all activities into the following major categories:

- selection;
- acquisition;
- cataloging/classification;
- physical processing;
- collection management, including weeding;
- preservation;
- reference;
- circulation;

- shelving/stack management; and

- facilities management.

Within the documents collection, it is useful to know the cost of processing versus the cost of reference service. Another typical cost analysis of value is the cost of the U.S. federal documents operation compared to the cost of the international documents operation. Beyond total cost, it is informative to look at the cost per document or cost per title for specific operations. For example, what is the cost of selecting, ordering, and processing 100 individual state document titles versus the cost of handling 100 comparable U.S. federal documents received on deposit? What is the cost of checking in 100 serial issues manually compared to checking them on-line? What is the cost per reference question answered or per circulation transaction completed? These kinds of efficiency measurements are very useful for understanding costs, and they can be particularly helpful when time series data are available or when one desires to measure the cost impact of a change in procedure. These data can contribute substantially when difficult choices are to be made. If resources are augmented or reduced, what will the impact be? With sound data on the cost in staff effort and dollars of various operations, more informed choices can be made.

Having such data available also makes it possible to analyze the opportunity cost of a given decision. An exchange system of sorts comes into play. For example, it is known that .5 FTE is needed to accomplish x, .3 FTE is required to accomplish y, and .2 FTE can accomplish z. If only .5 FTE is available, and .5 FTE is assigned to x, then y and z represent the opportunity cost of choosing x. Setting priorities and making choices when resources are scarce is a constant task of management. If cost data are available throughout the library, very rational decisions can be made about which functions can be carried out most efficiently.

BENEFITS

Though they may be difficult to locate, determine, and evaluate, costs are still much more solid and easy to define than benefits. Costs can be computed in dollars, but benefits are much more subjective and less easily quantified. However, efforts have been made to define the benefits of depository library status.[2] A library can calculate the value of priced documents and estimate the value of those received free on deposit. By then multiplying the collection size by the value of documents, one can arrive at the overall monetary value of the collection.

In such analysis, the intellectual value is secondary to the dollar value. One of the major benefits of government information for the researcher and the citizen is that it is primary source material. A document is official, it comes from a single authorized source, and it may not be available elsewhere. As electronic information is increasingly made available by government agencies, the benefits of access to government information—voluminous and manipulable—continues to grow. Furthermore, such data very likely are available nowhere else. Finally, providing access to government information greatly enhances the stature of the library, both as a resource and service center within the community and as a major participant in the information society generally. These are all intellectual or societal benefits to which monetary value cannot be assigned.

COST RECOVERY

Fees for service and the potential for cost recovery are very controversial topics in librarianship, particularly in documents librarianship. Access to government information is critical to an informed electorate, and libraries have an opportunity to provide this needed service. However, the cost of providing access to this information can be substantial, and it is increasing as new electronic products necessitate large expenditures for hardware, software, and communication. Although libraries are not permitted to charge for access to federal documents received on deposit, can libraries pass along the costs of electronic access if that access is not supplied by government? This is a difficult issue that raises basic philosophical questions. It has been argued that, as costly new technology makes possible faster access to more information, the user increasingly will have to pay a share of the costs and libraries will be justified in charging users for value added. But how does one define *value added*? Which costs should be absorbed by the library and which should be recovered from users? Is it preferable to offer enhanced access on a fee-for-service basis than not to offer it at all? Do fees for service unfairly restrict access to those who can pay? These and other questions relating to how these costs are borne are likely to be debated for some time. Their resolution will, no doubt, have a significant impact on the future of documents collections.

CONCLUSION

Identifying and understanding costs are essential to sound management of any document collection, particularly in an environment of increasing costs and rising demands for performance measures and accountability. Defining direct and indirect costs, including both fixed and variable costs, and having the capacity to determine the cost of specific functions are parts of this process. Although it is more difficult to quantify benefits than costs for library services, it is essential that this type of analysis be undertaken as costs grow in providing access to government information.

NOTES

[1] Julie A. C. Virgo, "Costing and Pricing Information Services," *Drexel Library Quarterly* 21 (Summer 1985): 80.

[2] See Ridley Kessler, "White Paper on Depository Program Expenses for Libraries and Users," *Documents to the People* 20 (March 1992): 27-30; Sandra K. Faull, "Costs and Benefits of Federal Depository Status for Academic Research Libraries," *Documents to the People* 8 (January 1980): 33-39.

14

Government Documents: Assets or Liabilities? A Management Perspective

Nancy M. Cline
Dean of the University Libraries
The Pennsylvania State University

In light of the extensive array of concerns facing library administrators, one must honestly assess the importance of maintaining a government documents collection. This question takes on considerable significance if the collection is large and comprehensive. There was a time when libraries could consider a documents collection to be a source of free materials, and the status of being a depository library and managing the related collection required only a modest level of funding. This is no longer the case. The contemporary library situation requires a thorough comprehension of costs and a clear understanding of how well such a collection meets the needs of a specific library's clientele.

Typically, the range of administrative concerns relating to inclusion of a documents collection in the library includes planning and budget, collection development and management, bibliographic control, circulation, reference services, library instruction, and facilities. The commitment to acquire, maintain, and service a government documents collection cuts across nearly every area of library administration and management. How, then, does one determine the value of such a collection and determine its placement within administrative priorities? Is such a collection a luxury for a given library? Has the library been carrying a liability? Has the collection been underutilized? If the library is considering starting such a collection, how should it embark on such a program? How does one determine the scope and level of commitment?

Although the perspective that I know best is that of a large academic research library, I believe this chapter will encourage directors and librarians of many types of libraries to review their options and reach an understanding appropriate for their libraries. I focus most of my attention on U.S. federal government publications, because they represent the largest collection of government publications and are the ones available to the largest number of libraries.

COSTS AND BENEFITS OF GOVERNMENT DOCUMENTS COLLECTIONS

Government documents are a critical information resource for the typical research library in the United States. The U.S. government remains the world's largest publisher, and, for better or worse, these publications are frequently cited in a variety of other sources. Sheer volume alone predicts that many libraries either must develop systematic methods of acquiring U.S. documents or must deal with specific requests for these titles over time. Statistics such as census data, vital and health data, agricultural commodities, import/export data, and budgets require that users identify, retrieve, and consult U.S. government documents.

In developing collections to serve one's clientele, for any large academic or public library, government documents are likely to be a part of the general collection strategy. These government publications can range from laws and codes to finely edited books to pamphlets of limited temporal value. They include patents, technical reports, statistical compendia, policy issuances, records of Congress, papers of presidents, maps, microfiche, and electronic databases. They collectively provide an opportunity to study the successes and failures of federal policies over the years, to study the styles of rhetoric, debate, and bombast as evidenced in the *Congressional Record* and congressional hearings, and to study how the nation is described in data, maps, photographs, or text.

There are multiple methods of acquisition. Developing collections of government documents is not as straightforward as ordering and paying for trade books or journals. Acquisitions programs may include the use of depository programs, departmental distribution channels, appeals to offices or legislators, deposit accounts, or occasionally outright purchases. Government documents work requires that librarians develop an understanding of the printing and publishing processes, be familiar with a broad array of different distribution methods, and become knowledgeable about the purposes and practices of different agencies and how they differ from those of legislative bodies. In sum, working with government documents forces one to deal with government procedures, policies, and practices in their splendid diversity and occasional disarray.

The library must decide on the extent to which it wishes to support a separate department for government documents. Usually, this choice is closely tied to options available in the physical facility, as well as to the level of staffing that can be directed to a separate unit. Many libraries provide excellent reference service for government information resources regardless of whether they have a separate department or have integrated the government documents into other departments. It is perhaps more important to address the availability of bibliographic access. If the library has implemented an on-line public access catalog, it needs to consider entering records for government documents into that catalog. This will enable users readily to locate government publications in the natural course of their work with the main collections of the library. The administrator should recognize that "free" collections require considerable investment if they are to be really useful. The costs of processing and making them accessible and of providing reference service are of consequence. As value is added, costs are increased. At the same time, there are many instances in which one can exploit these special resources, offsetting constrained acquisitions budgets, and increase the library's capability to respond to its users' needs.

From the administrative perspective, what is the significance of having documents in the academic research library? Where do these resources fit in the array of collections and services, which range from microfiche to rare manuscripts? Government documents can prove to be a significant resource, particularly if the collections have historical strength. There is often a general tendency to regard documents collections as being of lesser importance—after all, they did not cost the library much money to acquire. Viewed from the upper administrative levels, documents collections tend to have neither high appeal nor a particularly high value, certainly not when compared to rare and special collections or costly scientific journal collections. In balancing what may seem conflicting perceptions, the administrator needs to weigh the *purpose* of government publications, especially U.S. government publications, in determining their value to the library as an organization.

Maintaining a government documents collection in an academic library is one more way in which the relevance of the academic institution is tied to the surrounding social context. Having documents collections in our libraries offers librarians a chance to serve, in a visible way, the "public good"; to establish and earn the trust of the public; and to develop political skills, such as lobbying and working with legislators and their staff. Some libraries see their stature in the local community, region, or state enhanced through their designation as a depository library, assuming they are effectively meeting their responsibilities in providing the public with access to documents.

It is also important to develop a capability within a library for finding information about federal, or even state, programs. In the increasingly litigious and regulatory environment that affects education as well as information policies, librarians have to be attentive to the laws, regulations, and agency policies that affect their ability to meet their clients' information needs. The presence of a documents collection with trained librarians and staff may provide the library with an edge in the monitoring of regulations, in the pursuit of information for funding opportunities, in the tracking of health and safety regulations, or in remaining current on any number of federal issues.

In assessing the role of government documents in the library, the administrator is faced with the question of where and how to invest limited budget resources to meet the major needs of the institution. If it is important to develop the capability to work with government information resources, is that best accomplished with a documents department or in other ways? Does the library need to develop special expertise with government information resources to respond to institutional needs? The role and responsibility of depository libraries may have to be separated from the local issues of deciding how much government information is needed for the collections and services. If the institutional needs are modest, perhaps the depository status would be a needless burden. If the needs are significant, the depository status might enable the library to be a part of a larger national program that would result in shared expertise in working with documents.

With a documents unit and staff, the library can develop expertise and specialized knowledge about the government, its processes, and its information resources. One can develop the expertise needed to participate in the shaping of information policy issues; certainly one will understand that there are different ways in which to influence the outcomes (via Congress, agencies, the GPO, the ALA, or other professional organizations). One advantage of supporting a good-sized documents collection is often evident in the document librarians. This is one group within the library profession that works across the traditional "borders" that typically define academic libraries, public libraries, and special libraries. The issues relating to government information resources transcend any single type of library and enable documents librarians to benefit more readily from collaborative efforts that build upon one another's experiences. Issues of collection development and management, of service to the public, and of interaction with the government agencies that produce the information are faced by all librarians and staff in all types of libraries. The flow of information and the sharing of techniques and strategies among various types of libraries enables channels of support and even trust to be developed that can subsequently be tapped to help solve other types of problems. This network can be beneficial to the library in many unanticipated ways.

"Documents," as a department or in distributed units, can afford an exceptional training ground. Work in government documents often includes a combination of public service and technical service, and exposes individuals to career options leading to reference, cataloging, collection development, and library administration. It may even lead some into public careers (if they can cope with the arcane bureaucracies for distributing and publishing government information, they can probably handle the hustings). Documents librarians also may become expert in the teaching of government organization, or contribute to the teaching programs in subjects such as politics, law, government, and public policy.

The knowledge and the breadth of library experiences to which a documents librarian is exposed can result in the development of a very versatile information professional. Certainly, in a large separate documents collection, the librarian is expected to develop a portfolio that includes collection development, access services, resource sharing, reference services, acquisitions, and bibliographic processing. The career directions that can evolve from this broad base of library experiences are limitless. As a measure of those opportunities, one can look over the position titles of the authors of the chapters in this book, or look over the names of those who have been in leadership roles in GODORT over past years to see the types of positions those individuals hold today. The exposure to political and legal issues, information policy, and the complex bureaucracies that comprise our governments proves to be an excellent education for other responsibilities in the library and information professions.

Whether the venue is federal, state, international, or foreign national, the documents librarian needs to be attentive to matters falling under the rubric of "information policy." If documents librarians interact with other sections of the library, their knowledge of information policy issues may be quite useful in developing a broader understanding of the risks and benefits that stand to affect libraries and their host institutions in the current governmental context. Government documents librarians were among the first to express concern over the potential for copyright of government databases such as ERIC. They were among the first to express concern over possible fees for services relating to the delivery of information that had been in the public domain as "government publications." My intent here is not to take a position on copyright nor on fees for services, but to make the point that the early signs of change were noticed by those working most closely with government information, namely, the documents librarians and staff. If administrators wait until issues become clearly formed and the lines of demarcation are drawn, information policy issues may have reached the point where there remain few ways to alter their direction. Shaping policy issues is often most effective when done at the early stages, before all the political figures and agencies have defined their positions. In this regard, most libraries have made only marginal use of the expertise of documents librarians.

FUTURE OF GOVERNMENT INFORMATION IN LIBRARIES

As libraries face the prospect of diminishing budgets and spiraling costs, there will be many opportunities for library administrators to evaluate the advantages and disadvantages of maintaining a documents collection. The factors that influence today's decisions will continue to change, as libraries meet the challenges of managing an increasing amount of information in computer-based formats and as our clientele change their expectations. Perhaps the major issues facing administrators in the next decade will be to determine the number of access ports to provide for users to be connected to government databases, files, and on-line texts. How will we accommodate the user's need to walk away from the library with a printed copy of the electronic text housed in or accessed through our libraries? The needs of scholarship are changing, and the public's information needs will also change as computers and networks become more ubiquitous in everyday life. In all likelihood, the U.S. depository library system will undergo major modifications in the coming decade to take advantage of the new information context.

Although the specific nature of the management decisions will change, the need will remain to look at government information in terms of the local collection needs, the manner in which we provide reference and research services relating to government information, and the interaction among libraries, whether it is for hard-copy resource sharing or for referral of specialized reference inquiries. The library will still have to address the level of commitment it will make to government information. What is today a manual to guide the work of those handling document collections will also serve to frame the decisions of the future.

It is important that we develop and maintain a strong network of librarians who understand the special nature of government documents, who will work to ensure that the agencies and other governmental offices carry out their defined responsibilities for the publication and distribution of government information, and who will participate in the changes that the computer and related technologies are bringing. Whether these librarians and related staff are located in a separate department or are integrated into other library units; whether the printed materials circulate outside the building or must be consulted on-site; whether the instruction is done by documents librarians or by a large cadre of librarians who have learned how to teach users about government information—these particulars do not matter. These issues can be resolved by local preferences. But in every library of size, the administrator must develop in the staff the special expertise for handling government information resources and services. In the coming years, this special emphasis will move to reference services, accessing "documents" in any publication format, and assisting users with the significant amounts of data in electronic formats.

Although this text serves as a guide to those now administering documents collections, I close with a challenge for the future: Direct your efforts to building a staff with the versatility to address the changes that are coming. Any library faced with scaling back collections and services should be mindful of the need to retain a base of knowledge within its professional staff, to work with government information in its changing formats. As libraries realign responsibilities in the face of budget constraints, it will be important to build that expertise, to develop skilled librarians who can work with the increasing array of government databases and extract the maximum value from them for the institution's clientele. It is necessary to develop within the library a knowledge of the broad range of information policy issues affecting the production and distribution of government information sources. There is no reason to expect the federal government to go out of the information business, but in the future it may take a very different investment from libraries to provide access to its many information products.

Selected Bibliography

The following selected bibliography reflects literature that appeared primarily during the 1980s and 1990s. The emphasis is on publications that discuss management issues facing government information librarians. For an update to and expansion on these sources, the reader is encouraged to review the "Recent Literature on Government Information" column that appears regularly in *Government Publications Review.*

GENERAL ADMINISTRATION

Canadian Government Publishing Centre. *The Depository Services Program.* Ottawa: Supply and Service, 1986.

Carriger, L. "Administering Documents Collections." *Texas Libraries* 38 (Summer 1976): 75-81.

Cherns, Jack J. *Availability and Use of Official Publications in Libraries.* Paris: United Nations Educational, Scientific and Cultural Organization, 1983.

Cunningham, Willis L. F. "IGO Depository Collections in U.S. Libraries: A Directory and Analysis." *Government Publications Review* 18 (July/August 1991): 371-97.

Depository Library Council to the Public Printer. *Federal Depository Library Manual.* Washington, DC: U.S. Government Printing Office, 1985.

Faull, Sandra K. "Costs and Benefits of Federal Depository Status for Academic Research Libraries." *Documents to the People* 8 (January 1980): 33-39.

Gordon, C. C. "Administrative Reorganization: An Attempt to Control Government Documents in the Library." *Government Publications Review* 6 (1979): 241-348.

Hale, Barbara, and Sandra McAninch. "The Plight of the U.S. Government Regional Depository Libraries in the 1980s: Life in a Pressure Cooker." *Government Publications Review* 16 (July/August 1989): 387-95.

Hardie, Lelane. "Depository Versus Nondepository Status: A Look at the Costs." *RQ* 28 (Summer 1989): 455-58.

Harleston, Rebekah M., and Carla J. Stoffle. *Administration of Government Documents Collections.* Littleton, CO: Libraries Unlimited, 1974.

Hernon, Peter. *GPO's Depository Library Program: A Descriptive Analysis.* Norwood, NJ: Ablex, 1985.

Jackson, Ellen Pauline. *Manual for the Administration of the Federal Documents Collection in Libraries.* Chicago: American Library Association, 1955.

Kerze, Naomi V. "Separate vs. Integrated: The Disappearing Debate Over the Organization of United States Government Publications in Depository Libraries." *Government Publications Review* 16 (September/October 1989): 439-45.

Kessler, Ridley R., Jr. "White Paper on the Depository Program for Libraries and Users." *Documents to the People* 20 (March 1992): 27-30.

Lane, Margaret T. *Selecting and Organizing State Government Publications.* Chicago: American Library Association, 1987.

———. *State Publications and Depository Libraries.* Westport, CT: Greenwood Press, 1981.

Larson, Kathleen T. "Establishing a New GPO Depository Documents Department in an Academic Law Library." *Law Library Journal* 72 (Summer 1979): 484-96.

Merritt, LeRoy Charles. *The United States Government as Publisher.* Chicago: University of Chicago Press, 1943.

Morton, Bruce. "Random Thoughts on Numbers: The Need for Minimum Uniform Statistical Reporting Standards for United States Depository Libraries." *Government Publications Review* 11 (May/June 1984): 195-202.

Nakata, Yuri. *From Press to People: Collecting and Using United States Government Publications.* Chicago: American Library Association, 1979.

Nakata, Yuri, Susan J. Smith, and William B. Ernst. *Organizing a Local Government Documents Collection.* Chicago: American Library Association, 1979.

Nollen, Sheila H. "Practical Aspects of Managing a Government Publications Collection: An Annotated Bibliography." *Illinois Libraries* 68 (May 1986): 333-41.

Pokorny, Elizabeth J. *U.S. Government Documents: A Practical Guide for Non-Professionals in Academic and Public Libraries.* Englewood, CO: Libraries Unlimited, 1989.

Reynolds, Catherine J. *Planning Space for the Government Documents Collection in Research Libraries.* Boulder, CO: University of Colorado Library, 1977.

Roberts, Nancy L. "Setting Up a Depository Library." *Illinois Libraries* 68 (May 1986): 341-45.

Ryoo, Heija B. "Managing an Integrated Depository Documents Collection." *Government Information Quarterly* 2 (1985): 299-313.

Schaaf, Robert W. "International Organizations Documentation: Resources and Services of the Library of Congress and Other Washington Based Agencies." *Government Information Quarterly* 1 (1984): 59-73.

Schauer, Bruce P. *The Economics of Managing Library Service.* Chicago: American Library Association, 1986.

Smith, G. Stevenson. *Managerial Accounting for Libraries and Other Not-for-Profit Organizations.* Chicago: American Library Association, 1991.

Stephenson, Mary Sue, and Gary R. Purcell. "Application of Systems Analysis to Depository Library Decision Making Regarding the Use of Technology." *Government Information Quarterly* 1 (1984): 285-307.

Trumpeter, Margo C., and Richard S. Rounds. *Basic Budgeting Practices for Librarians.* Chicago: American Library Association, 1985.

U.S. Government Printing Office. *Instructions to Depository Libraries.* Washington, DC: U.S. Government Printing Office, 1988.

Vinson, Michael. "Cost Finding: A Step-by-Step Guide." *The Bottom Line* 2, no. 3 (1988): 15-19.

Virgo, Julie A. C. "Costing and Pricing Information Services." *Drexel Library Quarterly* 21 (Summer 1985): 75-98.

Waldo, Michael. "Historical Look at the Debate Over How to Organize Federal Government Documents in Depository Libraries." *Government Publications Review* 4 (1977): 319-29.

Watson, Paula D. "Documents Reorganization at the University of Illinois at Urbana-Champaign." *Illinois Libraries* 64 (October 1982): 1023-26.

Watts, Carol. "The Depository Library Inspection Program." *Reference Services Review* 10 (September 1982): 55-62.

ACQUISITIONS/COLLECTION DEVELOPMENT

Berkiares, Susan E. "Obtaining Free United States Government Publications." *Illinois Libraries* 69 (September 1987): 455-58.

Dow, Susan. "A Selective Directory of Government Document Dealers, Jobbers and Subscription Agents." *Serials Librarian* 14 (1988): 157-85.

Durrance, Joan C. "Providing Access to Local Government Information: The Nature of Public Library Activity." *Government Information Quarterly* 5 (1988): 155-67.

Eisenbeis, Kathleen. "Special Documents as Sources for Maps." *Special Libraries Association Geography and Map Division Bulletin* 128 (June 1982): 32-35.

Gehringer, M., T. Peterson, and J. A. Williamson. "Getting the Ungettable: Hard to Locate Federal Documents." *Law Library Journal* 72 (Fall 1979): 659-73.

Hajnal, Peter I. "Collection Development: United Nations Material." *Government Publications Review* 8A (1981): 89-101.

Hernon, Peter. *Collection Development and Public Access of Government Documents: Proceedings of the First Annual Library Government Documents and Information Conference.* Westport, CT: Meckler, 1982.

Hernon, Peter, and Gary R. Purcell. *Developing Collections of United States Government Publications.* Greenwich, CT: JAI, 1982.

Hodge, Stanley P., et al. "Formulating an Integrated Library Government Documents Collection Policy." *Government Information Quarterly* 6 (1989): 199-213.

Holterhoff, Sarah. "Depository Document Selection in Academic Libraries: A Core List of Items Selected." *Government Information Quarterly* 2 (1985): 275-89.

Larsgaard, Mary. "United States Publishers and Distributors of Globes and Plastic Relief Maps." In *Map Librarianship*, 238. Littleton, CO: Libraries Unlimited, 1978.

Magrill, Rose Mary, and Doralyn J. Hickey. "Government Publications." In *Acquisitions Management and Collection Development in Libraries*, 123-31. Chicago: American Library Association, 1984.

McClure, Charles R. "An Integrated Approach to Government Publication Collection Development." *Government Publications Review* 8A (1981): 5-15.

Moody, Marilyn K. "Selecting Documents: Using Core Lists of Item Selection." *RQ* 26 (Spring 1987): 305-9.

_____. "United States Documents: Basic Selection Sources." *Collection Building* 6 (Spring 1984): 38-40.

Morton, Bruce. "Implementing an Automated Shelflist for a Selective Depository Collection: Implications for Collection Management and Public Access." *Government Publications Review* 9 (July/August 1982): 323-44.

_____. "Items Record Management System: First Step in the Automation of Collection Development in Selective GPO Depository Libraries." *Government Publications Review* 8 (1981): 185-96.

_____. "Toward a Comprehensive Collection Development Policy for Partial United States Depository Libraries." *Government Publications Review* 7 (1980): 41-46.

Morton, Bruce, and J. Randolph Cox. "Cooperative Collection Development between Selective United States Depository Libraries." *Government Publications Review* 9 (May/June 1982): 221-29.

Rawan, Atifa R., and Robert Mitchell. "Building State and Local Publications Collections: The Arizona Experience." *Government Publications Review* 18 (January/February 1991): 71-82.

Wade, D. M. "Acquisitions Guide: United States Government Audiovisuals." *Government Publications Review* 7 (1980): 15-21.

Wilson, John S. "Weeding the Partial Depository: The Cornerstone of Collection Development." *Documents to the People* 16 (June 1988): 91-94.

Zink, Steven D. "Analysis of Non-Depository Documents in the Government Publications Collection." *Collection Building* 4 (1982): 39-43.

_____. "For Collection Development Officers: An Introduction to Government Publications." *Collection Building* 6 (Fall 1984): 4-8.

CATALOGING/PROCESSING

Bahr, Alice Harrison. "Cataloging U.S. Depository Materials: A Reevaluation." *College and Research Libraries* 47 (November 1986): 587-95.

Becker, Karen A. "Using FINDER Information Storage and Software for Government Documents." *Library Software Review* 9 (January/February 1990): 14-17.

234 □ Selected Bibliography

Bolner, Myrtle Smith, and Barbara Kile. "Documents to the People: Access Through the Automated Catalog." *Government Publications Review* 18 (January/February 1991): 51-64.

Bower, Cynthia E. "OCLC Records for Federal Depository Documents: A Preliminary Investigation." *Government Information Quarterly* 1 (1984): 379-400.

Bowerman, Roseanne, and Susan A. Cady. "Government Publications in an Online Catalog: A Feasibility Study." *Information Technology and Libraries* 3 (December 1984): 331-42.

Castonguay, Russell. *A Comparative Guide to Classification Schemes for Local Government Documents Collections.* Westport, CT: Greenwood Press, 1984.

DiCarlo, Michael A. "U.S. Government Document Collections and the IOLS." In *Proceedings of the Conference on Integrated Online Library Systems*, 195-200. Canfield, OH: Genaway & Associates, 1984.

Gilliam, Virginia. "CODOC in the 1980s: Keeping Pace with Modern Technology." In *New Technology and Documents Librarianship*, edited by Peter Hernon, 89-98. Westport, CT: Meckler, 1983.

──────. "The CODOC System: An Update for the Mid 1980s." *Government Publications Review* 14 (1987): 465-69.

Higdon, Anne. "Federal Documents Processing with OCLC: The Texas Tech Experience—Planning, Utilization, Future." In *Government Documents and Microforms*, 89-97. Westport, CT: Meckler, 1984.

Jamison, Carolyn C. [Sherayko]. "Automating Documents Processing Activities: Variations on a Theme at Penn State." *Documents to the People* 15 (December 1987): 226-28.

──────. "Loading the GPO Tapes: What Does It Really Mean?" *Government Publications Review* 13 (September/October 1986): 549-59.

Kirby, Diana Gonzalez. "Using a Bibliographic Database Management System to Improve Access to State Government Posters." *Library Software Review* 9 (January/February 1990): 10-13.

Kiser, Chris, and Clyde Grotophorst. "GOVDOX: A Government Documents Check-in System." *Library Software Review* 7 (January/February 1988): 42-43.

Mooney, Margaret T. "GPO Cataloging: Is It a Viable Current Access Tool for U.S. Documents?" *Government Publications Review* 16 (May/June 1989): 259-70.

_____. "Matching Library Holdings Against GPO Tapes: Issues, Concerns, and Solutions." *Government Publications Review* 17 (September/October 1990): 421-28.

Myers, Judy E. "The Government Printing Office Cataloging Records: Opportunities and Problems." *Government Information Quarterly* 2 (1985): 27-56.

Obringer, Dave. "Beyond Technical Services: Using a PC-based Database to Create a Government Documents Holding List." *Library Software Review* 11 (January/February 1992): 9-10.

Oliva, Victor T., and Michael K. Reiner. *Using INNOVACQ to Process G.P.O. Titles.* Garden City, NY: Adelphi University, 1989.

Pemberton, J. E. *Bibliographic Control of Official Publications.* New York: Pergamon, 1982.

Poole, Mary Elizabeth. *Documents Office Classification.* 5th ed. Arlington, VA: U.S. Historical Documents Institute, 1976.

Powell, Margaret S., Deborah Smith Johnston, and Ellen P. Conrad. "The Use of OCLC for Cataloging U.S. Government Publications: A Feasibility Study." *Government Publications Review* 14 (1987): 61-76.

Simmons, R. M. "Handling Changes in Superintendent of Documents Classifications." *Library Resources and Technical Services* 15 (Spring 1971): 241-44.

Stephenson, Mary Sue, and Gary R. Purcell. "The Automation of Government Publications: Functional Requirements and Selected Software Systems for Serials Control." *Government Information Quarterly* 2 (1985): 57-76.

Stwalley, Louise. "A Microcomputer Catalog for Municipal Documents." *Government Publications Review* 16 (January/February 1989): 63-72.

Swanbeck, Jan. "Federal Documents in the Online Catalog: Problems, Options, and the Future." *Government Information Quarterly* 2 (1985): 187-92.

Thompson, Ronelle H. H. "Managing a Selective Government Documents Depository Using Microcomputer Technology." *CRL News* 50 (April 1989): 260-62.

Turner, Carol, and Ann Latta. *Current Approaches to Improving Access to Government Documents.* Washington, DC: Association of Research Libraries, 1987.

United Nations Documents Series Symbols, 1946-1977; Cumulative List with Indexes. New York: United Nations, Dag Hammarskjöld Library, 1978.

United Nations Document Series Symbols, 1978-1984. New York: United Nations, Dag Hammarskjöld Library, 1986.

U.S. Government Printing Office. *GPO Classification Manual: A Practical Guide to the Superintendent of Documents Classification System.* Washington, DC: U.S. Government Printing Office, 1986.

Walbridge, Sharon. "OCLC and Government Documents Collections." *Government Publications Review* 9 (1982): 277-87.

Wise, Suzanne. "Automating Government Documents Check-in Using PC File:db." *Library Software Review* 10 (July/August 1991): 258-61.

COLLECTION MAINTENANCE AND USE

Baber, Carolyn D., and Stephen D. Zink. "Mainstreaming Microforms: The Physical Integration of U.S. Government Printing Office Microforms into the Documents Stacks." *Microform Review* 16 (Fall 1987): 291-95.

Cook, Kevin L. "Gathering Useful Circulation Data in the Documents Department." *RQ* 25 (Winter 1985): 223-27.

Eddy, Julie Jones, and Ann H. Zwinger. "In-house Preservation of Early U.S. Government Maps." *Government Publications Review* 15 (January/February 1988): 41-47.

Horton, Carolyn. *Cleaning and Preserving Binding and Related Materials.* 2d ed. Chicago: American Library Association, 1969.

Kirby, Diana Gonzalez. "Managing Government Sponsored Posters in the Academic Library." *Government Information Quarterly* 6 (1989): 283-94.

McClure, Charles, Vicki W. Phillips, and John B. Phillips. "Microformatted Government Publications." *Government Publications Review* 8A (1981): 127-33.

Morton, Bruce. "New Management Problems for the Documents Librarian: Government Microfiche Publications." *Microform Review* 11 (Fall 1982): 254-58.

Quinlan, Nora. "Strategies for Coping with Government Documents as Rare Books." *Documents to the People* 16 (December 1988): 178-79.

Reynolds, Catharine J. "How Many Government Publications in a Linear Foot?" *Documents to the People* 7 (May 1979): 96-99.

Sinkule, Karen. "Problems with Promoting Use of Microform Documents." *RQ* 26 (Fall 1986): 21-29.

Stewart, James. "But What Do I Do With All These Maps?" *Illinois Libraries* 68 (May 1986): 347-49.

Stratford, Juri. "Public Access to Government Document Microforms." *Microform Review* 17 (December 1988): 292-94.

Watson, Paula D., and Kathleen M. Heim. "Patterns of Access and Circulation in a Depository Document Collection under Full Bibliographic Control." *Government Publications Review* 11 (July/August 1984): 269-92.

Yannarella, Philip A., and Rao Aluri. "Circulation of Federal Documents in Academic Depository Libraries." *Government Publications Review* 3 (Spring 1976): 44-49.

Zink, Steven D. "Impending Crisis in Government Publications Reference Service." *Microform Review* 11 (Spring 1982): 106-11.

TECHNOLOGY

Hernon, Peter. "Depository Library Collections and Services in an Electronic Age: A Review of the Literature." *Government Information Quarterly* 4 (1987): 383-97.

Jacobs, Jim. "U.S. Government Computer Bulletin Boards: A Modest Proposal for Reform." *Government Publications Review* 17 (September/October 1990): 394-96.

Kovacs, Diane K. "GovDoc-L: An Online Intellectual Community of Documents Librarians and Other Individuals Concerned with Access to Government Information." *Government Publications Review* 17 (September/October 1990): 411-20.

McGrane, James. "The Edgar Challenge, Automating the U.S. Security and Exchange Commission's Internal Review Processes, Filing, and Information Dissemination Systems: A Development Note." *Government Publications Review* 18 (March/April 1991): 163-69.

Myers, Judy. "Effects of Technology on Access to Federal Government Information." In *New Technology and Documents Librarianship*, 27-42. Westport, CT: Meckler, 1983.

Schaubman, Debbi. "Electronic Data for GPO: Its Financial Impact on Depository Libraries." *Bottom Line* 5 (Spring 1991): 25-29.

Smith, Diane H. "Depository Libraries in the 1990s: Whither, or Wither, Depositories?" *Government Publications Review* 17 (July/August 1990): 301-24.

―――. "Online Government Databases: Into the Maelstrom." *Database* 11 (June 1988): 56-62.

Staninger, Steven W. "Using the U.S. Bureau of the Cenus CD-ROM Test Disk 2: A Note." *Government Publications Review* 18 (March/April 1991): 171-74.

Stephenson, Elizabeth. "Data Archivists: The Intermediaries the Census Bureau Forgot, A Review Essay of the 'Role of Intermediaries in the Interpretation and Dissemination of Census Data Now and in the Future.'" *Government Publications Review* 17 (September 1990): 441-47.

STAFFING AND REFERENCE SERVICE

Boyd, Anne Morris, and Rae Elizabeth Rips. *United States Government Publications.* 3d ed. New York: H. W. Wilson, 1949.

Brimmer, Brenda, et al. *Guide to the Use of United Nations Documents.* Dobbs Ferry, NY: Oceana, 1962.

Directory of Government Collections and Librarians. 6th ed. Washington, DC: Congressional Information Service, 1991.

Fisher, Mary L. *Guide to State Legislative and Administrative Materials.* 4th ed. Littleton, CO: F. B. Rothman, 1988.

Guide to Official Publications of Foreign Countries. Bethesda, MD: Congressional Information Service, 1990.

Hajnal, Peter. *Guide to United Nations Organization Documentation & Publishing for Students, Researchers, Librarians.* Dobbs Ferry, NY: Oceana, 1978.

Hajnal, Peter, ed. *International Information: Documents, Publications, and Information Systems of International Governmental Organizations.* Englewood, CO: Libraries Unlimited, 1988.

Harley, Bruce L., and Patricia J. Knobloch. "Government Documents Reference Aid: An Expert System Development Project." *Government Publications Review* 18 (January/February 1991): 15-33.

Harrington, Michael. *The Guide to Government Publications in Australia.* Canberra, Australia: Australia Government Publishing Service, 1990.

Herman, Edward. *Locating United States Government Information: A Guide to Sources.* Buffalo, NY: H. W. Wilson, 1983.

Hernon, Peter, and Charles R. McClure. "The Quality of Academic and Public Library Reference Service Provided for NTIS Products and Service." *Government Information Quarterly* 3 (1986): 117-32.

Selected Bibliography □ 239

Jeffries, John. *A Guide to the Official Publications of the European Communities.* 2d ed. London: Mansell, 1981.

Kinder, Robin, ed. *Government Documents and Reference Services.* New York: Haworth, 1991.

McClure, Charles R. *Improving the Quality of Reference Service of Government Publications.* Chicago: American Library Association, 1983.

Moody, Marilyn. "Critical Issues in Government Information Reference Service." *RQ* 27 (Summer 1988): 479-83.

Morehead, Joe, and Mary Fetzer. *Introduction to United States Government Information Sources.* 4th ed. Littleton, CO: Libraries Unlimited, 1992.

O'Hara, Frederic J. *Informing the Nation: A Handbook of Government Information for Librarians.* New York: Greenwood Press, 1990.

Reference Service for Publications of Intergovernmental Organizations, Papers from the IFLA Workshop, Paris, August 24, 1989, edited by Alfred Kagan. Munich; New York: K. G. Saur, 1991.

Richard, Stephen. *Directory of British Publications: A Guide to Sources.* 2d ed. London; New York: Mansell, 1984.

Robinson, Judith Schiek. *Tapping the Government Grapevine.* Phoenix: Oryx Press, 1988.

Rodgers, Frank. *A Guide to British Government Publications.* New York: H. W. Wilson, 1980.

Schmeckebier, Laurence Frederick. *Government Publications and Their Use.* 2d rev. ed. Washington, DC: Brookings Institution, 1969.

Sears, Jean L., and Marilyn Moody. *Using Government Publications.* Phoenix: Oryx Press, 1986.

Smith, Karen F. "Robot at the Reference Desk?" *College and Research Libraries* 47 (September 1986): 486-90.

Sulzer, Jack, and Roberta Palen. *Guide to the Publications of Interstate Agencies and Authorities.* Chicago: American Library Association, 1986.

Williams, Saundra, and Eric Wedig. "Improving Government Information and Documents Reference Skills Through a Staff Development Program." *RQ* 24 (Winter 1984): 143-46.

EDUCATION

Fink, Debora. *Process and Politics in Library Research: A Model for Course Design.* Chicago: American Library Association, 1989.

Goehlert, Robert U. "Promoting the Use of Federal Documents: An Experimental Current Awareness Service." *Government Publications Review* 7A (1980): 27-32.

Kuhlthau, Carol Collier. "Developing a Model of the Library Search Process: Cognitive and Affective Aspects." *RQ* 28 (Winter 1988): 232-42.

McClure, Charles R. *Users of Academic and Public GPO Depository Libraries.* Washington, DC: U.S. Government Printing Office, 1989.

Reeling, Patricia, Mary Fetzer, and Daniel O'Connor. "Use of Government Publications in an Academic Setting." *Government Publications Review* 18 (September/October 1991): 489-515.

Watson, Paula D., and Kathleen M. Heim. *Federal Documents Use in the Research Library Setting.* Urbana-Champaign, IL: University of Illinois Libraries, 1984.

White, H. S. "Library Education and Government Documents Work." *Government Publications Review* 13 (January/February 1986): 135-45.

INFORMATION POLICY

Association of Research Libraries. Task Force on Government Information in Electronic Format. *Technology and U.S. Government Information Policies: Catalysts for New Partnerships.* Washington, DC: Association of Research Libraries, 1987.

Bass, Gary, and David Plocher. *Strengthening Federal Information Policy: Opportunities and Realities at OMB.* Washington, DC: Benton Foundation, 1989.

Caudle, Sharon L., and Donald A. Marchand. *Managing Information Resources: New Directions in State Government: A National Study of State Government Information Resources Management.* Syracuse, NY: School of Information Studies, Syracuse University, 1989.

Freides, Thelma. "The Federal Information Controversy from an Economic Perspective." *College and Research Libraries* 47 (September 1986): 425-37.

Hernon, Peter, and Charles R. McClure. *Federal Information Policies in the 1980s: Conflicts and Issues.* Norwood, NJ: Ablex, 1987.

———. *Public Access to Government Information: Issues, Trends, and Strategies.* Norwood, NJ: Ablex, 1989.

Hernon, Peter, and Harold C. Relyea, eds. *United States Government Information Policies: Views and Perspectives.* Norwood, NJ: Ablex, 1989.

Hoduski, Bernadine Abbott. "Political Activism for Documents Librarians." In *Communicating Public Access to Government Information*, 1-11. Westport, CT: Meckler, 1982.

Kahin, Brian. "Information Policy and the Internet: Toward a Public Information Infrastructure in the United States." *Government Publications Review* 18 (September/October 1991): 451-72.

McClure, Charles R. *Federal Government Provision of Public Information, Issues Related to Public Access, Technology, and Laws/Regulations.* Washington, DC: U.S. Government Printing Office, 1984.

McClure, Charles R. "Information Policy Issues and Access to U.S. Government Information." *The Reference Librarian* 32 (1991): 25-42.

Morehead, Joe. *Essays on Public Documents and Government Policies.* New York: Haworth Press, 1986.

Perritt, Henry H. "Determining the Content and Identifying Suppliers of Public Information in Electronic Form." *Government Publications Review* 17 (July/August 1990): 325-32.

Schaaf, Robert W. "Information Policies of International Organizations." *Government Publications Review* 17 (January/February 1990): 49-61.

Smith, Diane H. "The Commercialization and Privatization of Government Information." *Government Publications Review* 12 (January/February 1985): 45-63.

Snowhill, Louise. "Privatization and the Availability of Federal Information in Microform: The Reagan Years." *Microform Review* 18 (Fall 1989): 203-9.

Sorokin, Leo T. "The Computerization of Government Information: Does it Circumvent Public Access Under the Freedom of Information Act and the Depository Library Program?" *Columbia Journal of Law and Social Problems* 24 (1991): 267-98.

U.S. Congress. House of Representatives. Committee on Government Operations, Government Information, Justice, and Agriculture Subcommittee. *Federal Information Dissemination Policies and Practices* April 18; May 23; and July 11, 1989. Washington, DC: U.S. Government Printing Office, 1990.

U.S. Congress. Office of Technology Assessment. *Defending Secrets, Sharing Data: New Locks and Keys for Electronic Information.* Washington, DC: U.S. Government Printing Office, 1987.

———. *Informing the Nation: Federal Information Dissemination in the Electronic Age.* Washington, DC: U.S. Government Printing Office, 1988.

U.S. Government Printing Office. *GPO/2001: Vision for a New Millennium.* Washington, DC: U.S. Government Printing Office, 1991.

Wilkinson, Patrick. "Political, Technological, and Institutional Barriers to U.S. Government Information." *RQ* 24 (Summer 1987): 425-33.

Notes About Contributors

Susan Anthes

Susan Anthes is currently Associate Director for Public Services at the University of Colorado, Boulder Libraries. From 1971 to 1981, she was the international documents librarian at The Pennsylvania State University Libraries and was heavily involved with bibliographic instruction. At the University of Colorado, she has taught several credit courses on library research and served as Coordinator for Library Instruction. Her publications include "Teaching Library Literacy" in *College Teaching: The Collaborative Course*; "Innovative Teaching and Learning" in *Community/Junior College*; and "Government Publications," a chapter in *Process and Politics in Library Research*. She has co-authored the "New Publications" column in *Documents to the People* since 1986.

Debora Cheney

Debora Cheney is Head of the Documents/Maps section at The Pennsylvania State University Libraries. From 1990 to 1992, she was the state/local documents librarian and a social science cataloger at Penn State. Prior to that she worked as a reference librarian at Bucknell University. Throughout her professional career, her areas of emphasis have been in reference and the use of technology to meet user needs. She has authored several articles on the use of software and on-line systems and is a frequent speaker on these issues. She has been an active member of ALA/RASD's Machine Assisted Reference Section.

Nancy Cline

Nancy Cline is Dean of the University Libraries at The Pennsylvania State University. She has also held positions as Assistant Dean of Bibliographic Resources and Services; Chief, Bibliographic Resources; and Head of the Government Documents section. She has been an active member of the American Library Association, the Association of Research Libraries, the Research Libraries Group, and EDUCOM. She has frequently been invited to present papers and serve on panels addressing issues relating to research libraries and academic computing, telecommunications, and information policies. Her publications include the topics of strategic planning, management issues, computing services, and information policy. Ms. Cline's service to other organizations and government agencies includes work with the Library of Congress, U.S. Government Printing Office and Public Printer, Office of Technology Assessment, National Endowment for the Humanities, and The Pennsylvania State Library.

Diane Garner

Diane Garner is Head of the Documents and Non-Book Formats Department at Harvard College Library. She was formerly Head of the Documents/Maps section at The Pennsylvania State University Libraries. She has worked with documents for the past 17 years. She is active in ALA/GODORT and has served as editor of its official publication, *Documents to the People.* She was Book Review Editor of *Government Publications Review* and now serves on its editorial board. She was the recipient of a Catharine Reynolds Grant Award from Readex/ALA/GODORT and the winner of the Bernard L. Fry Award for the best article in *Government Publications Review* in 1988. She is co-author of *The Complete Guide to Citing Government Documents.* She has also served as an exchange librarian in Lima, Peru, and Bujumbura, Burundi.

Ridley Kessler

Ridley Kessler is currently Regional Librarian of North Carolina, working at the University of North Carolina, Chapel Hill. He has also held positions at UNC-Chapel Hill as the federal and international documents librarian and has taught document librarianship in the University's library school for over 15 years. He has been active within the profession at both the state and federal levels. He has been a member and chair of the Depository Library Council. He has lobbied effectively for government information policies on Capitol Hill. In 1990 he was awarded the Distinguished Service Award from the Public Printer and in 1992 he was the recipient of the CIS/GODORT/ALA Documents to the People Award.

Barbara Kile

Barbara Kile has over 20 years of experience working with documents at Connecticut College, Purdue University, and Rice University. Her present position at Fondren Library is Assistant to the University Librarian for Public Relations and Development. Before that she was Director of the Division of Government Publications & Special Resources. She has been very active in ALA/GODORT, serving as Chair in 1982-1983. Her honors and awards include Beta Phi Mu, CIS/GODORT/ALA Documents to the People Award, and ALA Library Fellow. Ms. Kile spent the first half of 1990 as a Library Fellow at the National Central Library in Taipei, Republic of China, working with the staff of the Government Documents Department and lecturing at various libraries and library schools in Taiwan. She coordinated the cleanup project of GPO records by Louisiana State University, Texas A&M, and MARCIVE, Inc. She also edited the fifth and sixth editions of the *Directory of Government Document Collections and Librarians.*

Bruce Morton

Bruce Morton is currently Assistant Dean of Libraries for Public Services at Montana State University. Prior to that he served for four years as Head of the Reference Department at Montana State and eight years as Government Information Librarian at Carleton College. He has held numerous offices within ALA/GODORT and served on the Depository Library Council to the Public Printer. He received his M.L.S. from the State University of New York College at Geneseo, and a B.A. and M.A. from The Pennsylvania State University. Since

1985 he has been Associate Editor of the journal *Government Publications Review*. He has published and spoken widely on government information librarianship and government information policy issues.

Sandra K. Peterson

Sandra K. Peterson has been Documents Librarian at the Government Documents Center, Seeley G. Mudd Library, Yale University, New Haven, Connecticut, since 1984. Her career as a government documents librarian spans 25 years, including positions at the College of William and Mary, the University of Northern Iowa, and Oberlin College. She has served as member and chair of the Depository Library Council to the Public Printer; as Chair of ALA/ GODORT; and as a councilor-at-large in the American Library Association. In 1989-1990 she worked as Association of Research Libraries Visiting Program Officer on the reauthorization of the Paperwork Reduction Act. She has served as a speaker, book reviewer, and author on government information issues and has been the Federal Documents Editor for *Government Publications Review* since 1985.

Carolyn C. Sherayko

Carolyn C. Sherayko has been Head of Original Cataloging at Indiana University since 1989. Prior to that she held the positions of Social Sciences Cataloger/Documents Librarian at The Pennsylvania State University and Documents Librarian at Appalachian State University. At Penn State, she directed the automation of circulation, processing, and serials control of federal, state, and international documents. She holds an M.L.S. from the University of North Carolina and an M.A. from Appalachian State University. She has been an active member of the GODORT cataloging committee and has written and spoken on mainstreaming documents into library processing.

Diane H. Smith

Diane H. Smith is currently Chief of Reference and Instructional Services at the Pennsylvania State University. Before that she served as the United States librarian and Head of Documents/Maps at Penn State. She has held several offices in ALA/GODORT, including Chair in 1985-1986. She also has been a member and chair of the Depository Library Council to the Public Printer. She has written and spoken widely on the issues of technology in documents collection and on United States information policy. With Diane Garner, Ms. Smith co-authored *The Complete Guide to Citing Government Documents.*

Jack Sulzer

Jack Sulzer has been Head of General Reference at The Pennsylvania State University Libraries since 1990. Before that he had over 10 years' experience as the state/local documents librarian at Penn State. He has been extremely active in documents organization at the state and federal levels. He served as Chair of ALA/GODORT in 1990-1991 and was recently appointed to the Depository Library Council to the Public Printer. In 1993, he was awarded the Distinguished Service Award by the Public Printer.

Susan Tulis

Susan Tulis is currently Head of the Documents Department, Arthur J. Morris Law Library, University of Virginia. Previously she was a documents librarian at Alderman Library at the University of Virginia. She has been an active member of both the American Library Association and the American Association of Law Librarians. She has served as Chair of ALA/GODORT and has twice been appointed to the Depository Library Council to the Public Printer. Ms. Tulis is the executive editor for legal information for *Government Publications Review*, editor of the Virginia Library Association's *Shipping List*, regional editor of *ALA's Guide to United States Map Resources*, and co-editor of the sixth edition of the *Directory of Government Document Collections and Librarians*.

Carol Turner

Carol Turner is currently Assistant Director for Public Services at the University of Florida Libraries, University of Florida. She was formerly Assistant Director for Administrative Services at Florida, and for 10 years prior to that she served as Chief Librarian of the Jonsson Library of Government Documents, Stanford University. She has held numerous offices, including Chair of ALA/GODORT, and she served as a member of the Depository Library Council to the Public Printer. Her interests include management, statistical analysis, accountability, and performance measures. She holds an M.B.A. from Santa Clara University and an M.L.S. from Rutgers.

Index

AALL. *See* American Association of Law Libraries
AB Bookman Directory, 7
Access
 and commodification, 198
 and dissemination, 7, 60, 111, 116-20, 124, 130, 170
 electronic, 13, 14, 17, 77, 111-13, 116-24, 193-99
 freedom of, 111, 116, 119, 120, 130, 173, 195-98
 integrated, 44, 80
 microformats and, 113, 116
 of monographic series, 76
 separate, 43, 80
 signage and, 81, 176, 178
 and stacks planning, 81
 for state documents, 161
 technical guidelines for, 120
 tools for documents collections, 168-69
Accession-order-based schemes: selected bibliography of, 56
Acid-free folders, 82, 87
Administrative Notes, 36, 119, 170, 189, 190, 194
Advance data sheets, 83
Africa, 39
Agriculture Canada, 52
ALA Handbook of Organization, 206
ALA Washington Newsletter, 206
Alaska Statewide Collection Development Steering Committee, 20
Alexander Library (Rutgers University), 113
"Amendments of Selections" card, 32, 90
American Association of Law Libraries, 205
American Association of Law Libraries Newsletter, 205

American Book Trade Directory, 92
American Historical Association, 89
American Library Association, 3, 16, 194, 202, 205, 212, 224. *See also* GODORT
American National Standards Institute
 government document defined, 2
American Public Health Association, 210
American Society for Information Science, 208
American Sociological Association, 210
American Statistics Index (ASI), 16, 160, 162, 180
Amtrak, 36
Anglo-American Cataloging Rules, 18, 187
Anglo-American Cataloging Rules, 2d ed. (AACR2R), 68
Annual Review of Information Science, 208
Antiquarian book dealers' catalogs, 89, 90
APDU Newsletter, 209
Archival classification
 selected bibliography of, 54, 55
Archival Products, 110
Archival supplies, 87, 88
 and suppliers, 110
Archivist of the United States, 87
ARL Newsletter, 207
ARL Statistics, 62
ASIS. *See* American Society for Information Science
Association of College and Research Libraries, 22, 205
Association of Public Data Users (APDU), 209, 210
Association of Research Libraries, 20, 207, 209
Auction records, 90

247

248 □ Index

Australia
  government publications, 162
Automated circulation systems, 132

Barcoding, 6, 132
  smart, 71, 72
Batista, David, 205
Bernan Associates, 16, 61
Bibliographic control
  and access, 43, 44, 60, 77
Bibliographic instruction, 170, 173, 174, 178-82
Bibliographic records
  databases of, 44
  for electronic publications, 77
  one-by-one record creation, 69, 70
  tape loads, 70
Bibliographic utilities, 12, 18, 21, 44, 49, 69, 70. *See also* OCLC; RLIN; WLN
Biennial Survey (U.S. GPO), 34, 63
Binding
  preparation and records for, 88
Bookends, 82, 87
Books in Print, 14
Boolean operators, 14, 179
Brochures
  Social Security, 4
BRS, 45
Brussels Convention of 1886, 2, 6
"Budget Estimate Justification" document (GPO), 191
Bulletin boards. *See* Electronic bulletin boards
Bulletin of the American Society for Information Science, 208
Bureau of American Ethnology, 89

Canada
  acquiring federal documents of, 38, 39
  depository program in, 6, 38, 39, 91, 162
  parliamentary publications, 91
  Supply and Service Catalogue Numbers within, 51
Canadian Communications Group Publishing, 11, 13, 80
Canadian Government Publications: Consolidated Annual Catalogue, 51
Carter administration: and Paperwork Reduction Act, 7, 196

Cassette tapes: special handling of, 84
Castonguay, Russell: *A Comparative Guide to Classification Schemes for Local Government Documents Collections*, 54
Cataloging, 6, 12, 63-75, 120
Cataloging Branch - Library Programs Service, 187
Cataloging journals, 76
CAUSE, 209
CD-ROMs, 11, 16, 20, 23, 77, 111, 116, 118-21, 201
  archival nature of, 116
  circulation of, 116
  labeling, 61, 62
  manual updating on, 84
  Monthly Catalog versions on, 73
  patron advantages of, 45
  U.S. Bureau of Census, 121
Census Test Disk no. 2, 119
Central Printing Plant (GPO), 184
Chadwyck Healey, 39
Checklist of United States Public Documents 1789-1970: A Dual Media Edition of the U.S. Superintendent of Documents Public Documents Library Shelf Lists, 72
Chief Officers of State Library Agencies (COSLA), 210
Circulation
  automation systems of, 132
  of documents, 129-33
  of electronic media, 131
  and noncirculating materials, 131
  preparation for, 62
  and staffing costs, 132
CIS
  indexes and abstracts of, 13
  ordering government information, 16, 35
  microformat collections, 112
  user guides of, 168
Classification schemes, 17, 18, 20, 61, 72. *See also* Library of Congress; SuDoc
  and reclassification, 73, 75
  selected bibliography, 54, 55, 56
Cleaning and Preserving Binding and Related Materials (Horton), 87
Closed stacks, 81. *See also* Access
CLSI, 132
Coalition for Networked Information, 209

Index □ 249

Coast and Geodetic Survey, 89
Coastal charts: storage of, 86
CODOC, 54
Collection development
   automation implications for, 12, 13
   classification and, 17
   and government information formats/genres, 10, 11
   integration in, 21, 22, 80
   literature of, 9
   policy design for, 18, 19
   and statistics, 22, 23
   tools for, 14
Collection level indicators: codes for, 28-30
Collection maintenance, 80-92
   automation of, 92
   costs for staff and, 132-33
   and preservation, 87-88
   and staff training, 135
   and weeding, 90-92
Commerce Business Daily, 174
Committee on Statistical Measurement (ALA/GODORT), 62
Commodification: of government information, 198
Compact disc
   manual updating on, 84
   storage units, 87
Comparative Guide to Classification Schemes for Local Government Documents Collections, (Castonguay), 54
Computer-assisted instruction (CAI), 177
Computer Professionals for Social Responsibility (CPSR), 210
Congress Watch, 211
Congressional Directory, 179
Congressional Information Service. *See* CIS
Congressional Record, 3, 117, 131, 196, 223
   on CD-ROM, 117, 119, 120
Connecticut: state publications, 2
Conspectus, 20, 21
Consumer Information Catalog (GPO), 186
Consumer Information Center (GPO), 186
Controlled vocabulary: vs. free text, 179
COSLA Directory, 211
Cost management
   and analysis, 219-20
   for automation, 218

benefits and, 220, 222-25
documents collection, 213-22
for equipment, 217
facility, 218
identifying costs and, 215, 221
for library materials, 216
for personnel, 216
for supplies and services, 218
Cost recovery: in documents librarianship, 221
Council of Professional Associations on Federal Statistics (COPAFS), 210
Council of State Governments, 210
CPSR Newsletter, 210
Cumulations, 82
   indexes of, 83
Cunningham, Willis F.: "IGO Depository Collections in U.S. Libraries: A Directory and Analysis," 38
Current awareness publications, 180
Current Industrial Reports, 82
Current Population Reports series, 76
Customer Services (GPO), 184

Daily List of Documents Issued at Headquarters, 37
Database management software, 75
dBASE, 92, 122
DDC. *See* Dewey Decimal Classification system
DECK service (Bernan Associates), 61
Department of State Bulletin (U.S.), 117
Department of State Dispatch (U.S.), 117
Department of Supply and Service Catalogue Numbers (Canada), 51, 53
Depository Administration Branch - Library Programs Service, 187
Depository Distribution and Information System (DDIS), 187
Depository Distribution Division - Library Programs Services, 187
   electronic formats distribution, 190
Depository laws: and citizen access issues, 173
Depository libraries (U.S.), 15, 33, 34, 39, 84, 222, 224
   benefits of, 220, 222
   in Canada, 38, 39, 53
   collection evaluation for, 90
   costs for, 117-18
   electronic formats in, 111, 116-18
   future of, 194, 200, 201, 226

250 □ Index

Depository libraries (U.S.)—*cont.*
  historical maps collections in, 86
  and IGO documents, 38
  inspections of, 187-89, 193
  for local documents, 40
  maps, charts, and atlases available for, 96-104
  and publications languages, 37
  reconfirmation of, 195
  regional, 34, 192
  responsibilities of, 80, 183
  selective, 192-93
  state government documents, 40
  status termination of, 189
  types of, 4, 5
  of United Nations, 36, 37
  "virtual," 200
Depository Library Act of 1963, 195
Depository Library Council, 119, 189, 191
  mission of, 183, 194
"Depository Library Inquiry Form," 189
Depository Library Program (DLP), 116, 118, 124, 185, 191, 201
  inspection program of, 188
Depository Mailing Branch, 190
Depository Services Staff (DSS), 187, 189
Deputy Public Printer, 184
Dewey Decimal Classification (DDC) system, 18, 20, 53
DIALOG, 14, 16, 45
DIALORDER, 14
Diazo microfiche, 85, 114
Direct costs
  for document collections, 214, 221
  for personnel, 216
Directory of Government Document Collections and Librarians, 4, 162
Directory of U.N. Serial Publications, 38
Discard list, 91, 92
Diskettes, 10, 19, 77
  filing units for, 87
  labeling, 61, 62
  special handling, 84, 86
DocEx: services, 15, 35
Docket and Digest (SEC), 113
Documentation Section of the Canadian Government Publishing Centre, 51, 52
"Documents Assistant," 92
Documents Catalog, 184
Documents Control Section (U.N.), 50

Documents Expediting Project (Library of Congress). *See* DocEx
Documents Index, 184
Documents/Maps Section Training Manual (The Pennsylvania State University Libraries)
  adaptation Table of Contents, 151, 152, 153
  training procedure outline of, 154, 155, 156
Documents reference
  access tools for, 168-69
  desk reference collection, 167
  managing, 157-70
  nature of, 157-58
  and nonbook media, 166
  public affairs file for, 170
  "ready reference," 164
  scheduling for, 164-65
  staffing, 158, 162, 164, 167
  statistics for, 165
  taxonomy of, 160-62
  and user needs, 158, 163
Documents to the People, 194, 207
DOS: courses on, 122

Ebsco, 75
EC. *See* European Community
Economic Bulletin Board, 116, 118, 119, 120
EDGAR system (SEC), 117
EDUCOM, 209
"Electronic Acquisition and Dissemination Survey." *See* "Technology Tea"
Electronic bulletin boards, 77, 111, 120, 175
  archival nature of, 116
  participation in, 177, 178
Electronic Confidentiality Law, 198
"Electronic Corner" (*Administrative Notes*), 119, 170
Electronic discussion lists, 35
Electronic Freedom of Information Act of 1991, 198
Electronic information, 17
  commodification of, 198
  cost recovery for, 195
  dynamic nature of, 166
  growth of, 76, 166
  policy standards for, 195-99
  and privacy issues, 198
  seriality of, 69

Electronic journals, 77
Electronic mail reference systems, 193
Electronic media: users' cheat sheet, 170
Electronic reference sources, 175
Employees
  interviewing, 136, 137
  references for, 137, 139
  selection of, 135, 138, 139
  training, 134, 135, 139-41, 144-50
Endust, 87
Energy Resource Abstracts, 169
Environmental Protection Agency: technical reports of, 3
EPA Journal, 130
EPA Publications Bibliography, 83
Equipment costs: for document collections, 217, 218
Equipment maintenance: and staff training, 135
ERIC database, 35, 180, 225
Erie Basin Commission, 3
Errata, 83
Europa Yearbook, 38
European Communities Office for the Official Publications, 80
European Community, 11, 13, 83, 92
European Documentation Centers, 5
European Economic Commission, 5
Explanation of the Superintendent of Documents Classification System, 187
EXTRACT software, 121

FAO. *See* Food and Agricultural Organization
Faxon, 75
Federal Acquisitions Regulation, 84
Federal Depository Library Manual, 190
Federal Depository Library Program Bulletin Board (FDLP/BB), 116, 190
Federal Documents Task Force (ALA), 191, 194
Federal Librarians (ALA), 205
Federal Library and Information Center Committee (Library of Congress), 207, 208
Federal Library and Information Network, 208
Federal Register, 89, 131, 196
FEDLINK. *See* Federal Library and Information Network
Fee-for-service, 45, 221

Fertility of American Women, 76
Fetzer, Mary, 163
Fiber optic cables: and super-telecommunications, 199
Fixed costs: for document collections, 215, 221
Fixed fields, 64
Floppy diskettes, 10, 19, 77, 111
  filing units, 87
  labeling, 61, 62
  special handling, 84, 86
Food and Agricultural Organization, 5
Ford, Wendell H. (U.S. senator), 201
Foreign documents, 2, 6
  acquisition of, 39, 40
  exchange, 6
Foreign Relations of the United States, 87
Freedom of Information Act, 196, 197
Free-text searching, 14
  vs. controlled vocabulary, 179
Freeware, 46
Friday Memo, 211
Fugitive publications, 36, 118

General Services Administration, 186
General Wage Determinations Issued Under the Davis-Bacon and Related Acts, 84
Geological Survey, 85
Girl Scouts of America, 89
Glenn, John (U.S. senator), 197
GODORT (ALA), 2, 16, 62, 162, 176, 205, 225
  Education Committee, 147, 170
  government document defined by, 3
  purposes of, 206, 207
  state training meetings, 121
Gore, Albert, Jr. (U.S. senator), 201
GovDoc-L, 35, 92, 119, 159, 166, 194
Government documents
  barcoding, 62
  bibliographic control of, 43-56
  bibliographic instruction for, 170, 173, 174, 178-80
  circulation policy for, 129-31
  classification schemes for, 46-56, 72
  CD-ROM accessing of, 45, 46
  and collection costs and benefits, 213-24
  and collection development, 9-17
  collection maintenance, 80-92
  definition, 1-3

Government documents—*cont.*
  and electronic formats, 77, 111, 116, 181
  "fee vs. free," 7
  international, 2, 6
  labeling, 61-62
  notation system for, 47
  on-line cataloging of, 6, 63-71
  outreach programs for, 173-80
  oversized, 81
  preservation of, 87, 88
  processing, 60-69, 75
  provincial, 2
  rare, 89
  reference desk management for, 157-70, 182
  retrospective conversion of, 71, 72
  serials control for, 75, 76
  special handling of, 84-87
  special publishing patterns of, 82
  staff training for, 134-50
  state, 2
  statistics, 62
  and technological access issues, 111, 117-19
  types of, 3, 4
  weeding, 90-92
Government Documents Round Table of the American Library Association. *See* GODORT (ALA)
Government Documents Special Interest Section (AALL), 205
Government information
  accessing by CD-ROM, 45, 46, 120
  acquisition of, 31-40
  bibliographic control of, 43-56, 201
  Canadian, 38, 39, 50-54
  cataloging, 63-75
  centralization of, 198
  circulation of, 129-33
  classification schemes for, 46-56
  collection development for, 9-18, 23, 24
  collection integration, 21, 22
  conspectus method, 20, 21
  commodification of, 198
  in electronic formats, 23, 76, 77, 119-22, 181, 195
  exchange lists for, 34
  federal agency distribution role, 192
  "fee vs. free," 7
  foreign, 39, 40
  fugitive publications, 36
  future of, 226
  generic range of, 10
  IGO documents, 38
  key organizations in, 205-12
  nature of, 181
  non-depository items, 35-38
  out-of-print, 17
  and outreach goals, 174-81
  policy issues and reform, 7, 195-202
  politics of, 183-95
  preservation of, 87, 88
  printing and production of, 184
  privatization of, 195, 198, 201
  and public access, 3, 7, 13, 60, 111, 116-20, 124, 130, 170, 173, 176-77, 184, 194-201
  purchase of, 15-17
  sources of, 11
  special handling, 84-87
  special publishing patterns, 82
  statistics, 62
  subject/format matrix, 19
  types of, 3, 4
  and U.N. documents, 36-38, 50, 51
  weeding, 90-92
Government Information Insider, 212
Government Information Quarterly, 194
Government Printing and Binding Regulations, 190
Government Publications and Their Use (Schmeckebier), 162
Government Publications Review
  collection development issue, 10
  political discussions within, 194
Government Reports Announcements (GRA), 16, 35
Government Reports Index (GRI), 16, 35
GPO. *See* U.S. Government Printing Office
GPO Classification Manual: A Practical Guide to the Superintendent of Documents Classification System, 187
GPO Electronic Bulletin Board, 190
GPO Gateway to Government Act, 201, 202
GPO Library Program Service, 15
GPO-OCLC cataloging: archive tapes of, 45
GPO Publications Reference File (DIALOG), 14
GPO/2001: A Vision for a New Millennium, 124, 202

Index □ 253

GPO Wide Information Network Data Online, 201, 202
Great Britain, 39
Guide to Federal Publishing (GPO), 192
Guide to Microforms in Print, 89
Guide to Official Publications of Foreign Countries, 39, 162
Guidelines for the Depository Library System for U.S. Government Publications, 60, 71, 88, 130

Hajnal, Peter: *International Information: Documents, Publications and Information Systems of International Governmental Organizations*, 38
Harleston, Rebekah, 182
Hasse, Adelaide R., 47, 89
Her Majesty's Stationery Office (HMSO), 39
Hermes Project, 116, 119
Hernon, Peter
   Developing Collections of U.S. Government Publications, 9, 10
   outreach goals outlined, 174
High-Performance Computing Act, 199
Hogarth Representatives, 39
Hollinger Corporation, 110
Horton, Carolyn: *Cleaning and Preserving Binding and Related* Materials, 87
Houk, Robert, 194
House of Representatives, U.S., 4, 82, 191
   documents and reports, cumulations of, 83
   LEGIS system, 124
   rare documents of, 89
Hydrography/Transportation CD-ROM, 120
Hypermedia, 177

IASSIST. *See* International Association for Social Science Information Services and Technology
ICPSR. *See* InterUniversity Consortium on Political and Social Research
IGO depositories, 38
"IGO Depository Collections in U.S. Libraries: A Directory and Analysis" (Cunningham), 38

IGO documents
   acquisition of, 38
   reference work and, 163
Improvement of Information Access Act, 197
Index to Congressional Publications (CIS), 16, 160, 162, 180
Index to Current Urban Documents, 161
Index to International Statistics, 163
Indexes: of cumulations, 83
Indirect costs
   for document collections, 214, 215, 221
   for personnel, 216
"Information Age": policy reforms for, 195, 198
Information Industry Association, 211
Information Sources, 211
Information Technology Program (GPO), 190
Information Times, 211
Innovative Interfaces Inc., 132
"Inspection Report," 188
inspection comment sheet, 189
Instructions for Depository Libraries Receiving United Nations Materials, 36, 37
Instructions to Depository Libraries (GPO), 80, 83, 189, 190
   disposition principles, 90
   free access defined in, 130
   and inspections, 188
   superseded publications, 91
Intellectual Freedom (ALA), 205
Interagency Depository Seminar (GPO), 189
Intergovernmental depositories, 5
International Association for Social Science Information Services and Technology (IASSIST), 121
International Court of Justice, 37
International Governmental Organizations. *See* IGOs
International Information: Documents, Publications and Information Systems of International Governmental Organizations (Hajnal), 38, 163
Internet, 21, 159, 199
Interstate compacts, 2
InterUniversity Consortium on Political and Social Research (ICPSR), 122
Interviewing: potential employees, 139
Int-Law, 92

254 □ Index

Introduction to United States Public Documents (Morehead), 162
Item numbers, 32, 33, 34, 70, 92, 112
  deselection of, 90, 91
  for electronic sources, 120
  SuDoc file of, 187
Item records file, 13
  and circulation policy, 132
ITIS database project (U.S. DOE), 119

Jackson, Ellen, 182
Japan: government publications, 162
Jennerich, Edward J.: *The Reference Interview as a Creative Art*, 145
Jewel cases: for compact disks, 87
Job descriptions: for documents collections staff, 136
Joint Committee on Printing, 36, 119, 184, 190, 191, 201
Jones-Eddy, Julie, 86
Journal of State Government, 211
Journal of the American Society for Information Science, 208
JURIS system (U.S. Department of Justice), 124
Jurisdocs, 205

Keywork-out-of-context (KWOC), 54

Labels
  computer-scannable, 62
  for special formats, 61, 62
Lane, Margaret
  State Publications and Depository Libraries, 5, 130
  Selecting and Organizing State Government Publications, 40
  State Publications and Depository Libraries, 40
Leahy, Patrick (U.S. senator), 197
LEGIS system (U.S. House of Representatives), 124
Legislative documents, 3
Legislative Indexing Vocabulary of the Congressional Research Service of the Library of Congress: and PRF subject access, 14

Leishman and Taussig, 39
Less Access to Less Information by and about the U.S. Government: A Chronology, 206
LEXIS, 161
Librarian of Congress, 87
Library Government Documents and Information Conference, 9
Library Information Technology Association (LITA), 205
Library Journal, 16
Library of Congress, 6, 63, 68, 189
  SCORPIO system, 124
Library of Congress Cataloging Distribution Service, 69
Library of Congress classification, 18, 20, 53
Library of Congress Rule Interpretations (LCRIs), 68
Library Programs Services (LPS), 84, 119, 186, 187, 190
Library Resources and Technical Services, 75
"Lighted bin" system, 33, 190
Linen tape, 87
List of Classes of the United States Government Publications Available for Selection by Depository Libraries, 14, 15, 187
  appendix to, 14
Listservs, 35, 92
LITA. *See* Library Information Technology Association
Literary Market Place, 92
Local area networks, 46
Local documents: acquisition of, 40
Local government information, 161
Lotus 1-2-3: courses on, 122
Louisiana State University, 70
LS 2000, 132

Machine indexing, 46
Machine-readable cataloging. *See* MARC format
Machine-readable magnetic tape services, 70
Magnetic tape, 77
Major Studies and Issue Briefs of the Congressional Research Service Cumulative Index, 169
Manhattan: IGO publications, 38

Map curators, 90
Maps, 1, 10
  format integration, 68
  in historical collections, 85
  labeling, 61
  preserving, 86
  seriality of, 69
  special handling of, 84, 85
  storage of, 86
Maps and Geography Round Tables (ALA), 205
MARC format (Library of Congress), 18, 63, 64, 68
MARCIVE, Inc., 70
MARC II format, 18
McClure, Charles R., 10, 21
Meckler Publishing, 9
Merritt, LeRoy Charles: *The United States Government as Publisher*, 3
Microfiche, 10, 19, 111-13, 189
  collection maintenance for, 85
  equipment for, 217
  growth of, 112
  headers for, 85
  key-word listing in, 14
  labeling, 61
  seriality of, 69
  special handling of, 84
  types, 85
Microfilm, 10
Microforms, 1, 6, 89, 122
  circulation of, 131
  in depository libraries, 111
  in government document collections, 112
  housing requirements for, 114
  providing access to, 113, 114
  reading equipment for, 217
  user dissatisfaction with, 113
Miller, Suzanne: *U.S. Public Documents, A Practical Guide for Non-Professionals in Academic and Public Libraries*, 140, 142
Modem: and information access, 14, 120
Monographs: and serials, 68, 69
Monthly Catalog CD-ROM, 168, 179
Monthly Catalog of U.S. Government Publications, 13, 15, 16, 18, 35, 44, 73, 112, 147, 160, 162, 168, 179, 180, 184, 187
Monthly Checklist of State Publications, 83, 161

Mooney, Margaret T., "GPO Cataloging: Is It a Viable Current Access Tool for U.S. Documents?", 44, 92
Morehead, Joe: *Introduction to United States Public Documents*, 162
Morton, Bruce, 9, 12, 92
Multiple Versions Forum, 68
Municipal depositories, 5

Nader, Ralph, 211, 212
Nakata, Yuri, 182
NASA. *See* National Aeronautics and Space Administration
National Academy of Sciences, 36
National Action Alert Network (GODORT), 207
National Aeronautics and Space Administration (NASA), 3, 31, 36, 113
  technical reports of, 3
National Museum (U.S.), 89
National Research and Education Network (NREN): political and social impact of, 199, 200
National Science Foundation, 199
National Technical Information Center, 16, 35, 180
National Trade Data Bank, 20
National Trade Data Bank (NTDB) CD-ROM, 120
NATO. *See* North Atlantic Treaty Organization
Needs and Offers List (GPO), 34, 92
New Zealand: government publications, 162
News from COPAFS, 210
1990 GPO Annual Report, 184, 186
Nonbibliographic databases, 181
Nonbook materials: special handling of, 84, 86
Non-depository libraries, 49, 193
  acquiring U.N. publications, 40
  Canadian, 53
  state government publications, 40
Non-depository titles, 31, 35, 37
Non-U.S. national documents, 162
North American Collections Inventory Project, 20
North Atlantic Treaty Organization (NATO), 11
Notation system, 47, 48. *See also* SuDoc classification

NOTIS, 132, 147
NSFNET, 199. *See also* Internet
NTIS. *See* National Technical Information Center
Nunn, Sam (U.S. senator), 197

OAS. *See* Organization of American States
Occupational Safety and Health manuals, 84
OCLC, 18, 44, 45, 49, 64, 69, 70, 161
Offers list, 34
Office Gazette of the Patent Office: patent numbers, 88
Office of Information and Regulatory Affairs, 196, 197
Office of Management and Budget (OMB), 196, 197
Office of the Federal Register, 189
Official publications
  defined, 2
  of U.N., 36, 38
Official Records (U.N.), 36, 38, 83, 89, 131
OMB Circular A-130, 196, 197, 200
OMB Watch (OMBW), 211, 212
102d Congress, 191, 197
103d Congress, 191
"One Minute Librarian," 148
1:1,000,000-Scale DLG Data, 120
One-wipe dust cloths, 87
On-line database vendors, 45
On-line public access catalogs. *See* OPACs
OPACs, 6, 21, 49, 64
  advent of, 13
  and bibliographic policy issues, 68
  and circulation policy, 132
  and collection development, 13, 21
  research strategizing with, 179
  statistics-gathering standards, 63
OPEC, 38
Open stacks, 81. *See also* Access
Organization for Economic Cooperation and Development, 11
Organization of American States (OAS), 2, 3, 11
Outline of Classification (Canadian), 51, 53
Outreach: development of, 174, 175, 176. *See also* Bibliographic instruction
  program goals for, 174, 178, 182
  types of, 176, 177, 178
Owens, Major, 197
Ownership stamps, 60

Pacific Northwest Conspectus Project, 20
PAIS, 180
Pamphlet holders, 81, 87
Paperwork Reduction Act of 1980, 7, 195
  revisions to, 196
Parliamentary Debates (British), 3
Patent depository status, 219
Patent research, 4
Pathfinders, 170
PAU, 38
The Pennsylvania State University, 44
Performance appraisal, 149
Performance evaluation, 148, 149, 150
Pokorny, Elizabeth: *U.S. Public Documents, A Practical Guide for Non-Professionals in Academic and Public Libraries*, 140, 142
Post, William Leander, 47
Posters
  item numbers of, 105-9
  special handling of, 84
  storage of, 86
Preparing for a Depository Inspection, 189
Preservation techniques, 80, 87, 88
  for maps, 86
  and supplies, 87
PRF. See Publications Reference File
Primary materials: vs. secondary, 181
Printing Act of 1895, 4, 184
Privatization, 195, 198, 201
Procurement Services (GPO), 184
Production Services (GPO), 184
Profile
  costs of, 71
  of collections, 70
Promotion
  of documents collections, 174-78, 182
  types of, 176, 177, 178
Provenance, 17, 18, 46, 51, 53, 72, 81
Public Affairs Information Service Bulletin. *See PAIS*
Public Citizen, 211
Public Citizen, 211
Public domain software, 121
Public Law 101-423, 87
Public Printer of the Government Printing Office, 4, 87, 184, 185, 194

Public printing, 184. *See also* Title 44
Public relations, 176, 177, 178
Public service
 desk etiquette, 145
 staff training for, 135, 142, 147-48
Publications Reference File (PRF), 14, 15, 18, 35, 166
Purcell, Gary R., 5
 Developing Collections of U.S. Government Publications, 9, 10

Queen's Printer number, 85

Rain check, 34
Rare Books and Manuscripts Section of the American Library Association, 90
Rare books librarians, 90
Rare documents, 89, 90
 characteristics of, 89
 special handling for, 90
Readex Corporation, 16, 35, 38, 112
Readex International Documents Catalogue, 38
Reagan administration
 cost-cutting measures of, 7, 196
 privatizing of government information goals, 116, 196
Reclassification, 73, 75
"Recommended Minimum Technical Guidelines" (GPO), 120
Reference desk
 managing, 163-70
 nonbook media, 166
 practical aids for, 169, 170
 and service priorities, 143, 145, 158, 164
 statistics for, 165
 training for, 142, 143, 145, 147, 148, 159, 170
Reference Interview as a Creative Art (Zaremba and Jennerich), 145
Regional depository libraries, 192, 193
Reportorial documents, 3
Research Libraries Group, 20
Research Library Information Network, 18, 49, 64, 69, 163
Research Publications, 39
Research strategies: and bibliographic instruction, 179-181
Resources in Education, 83
 accession numbers in, 88

Retrospective conversion, 71, 72
Reynolds, Catharine, 82
Rice University, 70
Richardson Bill, 184
RLG. *See* Research Libraries Group
RLIN. *See* Research Library Information Network
Robinson, Judith Schiek: *Tapping the Government Grapevine*, 162
Rose, Charles (U.S. representative), 201
Rutgers University, 113

Sales publications reference. *See Publications Reference File*
Sarbanes, Paul S. (U.S. senator), 201
Satellite transmission: of government information, 23
Schmeckebier, L. F., 89
 Government Publications and Their Use, 162
Scholarly Resources, 112
SCORPIO system (LC), 124
Seavey, Charles A., 89
Secondary copies: disposal of, 91
Secondary sources: vs. primary, 181
Security Exchange Commission: EDGAR system, 117
Selecting and Organizing State Government Publications, (Lane), 40
Selective libraries, 192, 193
SE-LIN labels, 61
Senate, U.S., 4, 191
 documents maintenance of, 82
 rare documents of, 89
 reports and documents, cumulations of, 83
Separate shipments, 33
Serials
 cataloging of, 75, 76
 control for government publications, 75
 and monographs, 60, 69
 within series, 76
Service documents, 3
Shareware, 46, 121
Shelflists, 12, 13, 43
 access tool, 12, 43
 automated, 12, 13
 in card catalog, 12, 43
Shipping List Service (MARCIVE), 61
Shipping lists, 18, 33, 34, 60, 61, 120, 187, 189, 190
 corrections, 73

Signs: for access promotion, 81, 176, 178, 181
Silver halide microfiche, 85, 114
Simon, Paul (U.S. senator), 201
Slip laws, 83
Slip opinions, 83
Slip treaties, 83
Smithsonian Institution, 72
Social Security: brochures, 4
SOD-13 guidelines, 112
Software
 for database management, 75
 locating, 121
 public domain, 121
 training staff with, 121, 122
 types of, 120
Space planning, 80, 82
 for mixed formats, 81
 and weeding, 91
Special Libraries, 208
Special Libraries Association, 202, 208
Special List of Canadian Government Publications, 38
Split runs, 75
Stack maintenance, 80-82
Staff training
 and development, 134, 135, 139, 140-50
 manual for, 139-41, 144-45
State depositories, 5
State government classification schemes: selected bibliography, 56
State government documents (U.S.), 40
State government information, 161
State Government News, 211
State Government Research Checklist, 211
State Publications and Depository Libraries (Lane), 5, 40, 130
Statistical Package for the Social Sciences (SPSS), 122
Statistical Reference Guide, 161
Statistics Canada Serials: disposition criteria, 91
Statistics in Brief, 82
Statutory and Agency Distribution Program (GPO), 185, 186
Stephenson, Mary Sue, 75
Stewart, James A., 86
Storage: of government information, 11
Subject-based classification schemes: selected bibliography of, 55, 56

Subject Bibliography Series (GPO), 14, 15
Subscription agents: serials, 75
SuDoc classification, 13, 14, 17, 18, 32, 47-52, 61, 71-73, 75, 80, 81, 187
 and automated circulation systems, 132
 explanation of, 140
 for microfiche, 85
 provenance base of, 17, 18, 46
 reclassification and, 73
 segregation, 18
 for serials, 76
Superintendent of Documents Classification. *See* SuDoc
Superintendent of Public Documents, 184, 186, 193
 responsibilities of, 185, 189
Superseded editions, 82, 83, 193
 categories of, 91
Super-telecommunications, 195, 199
Supplements, 82, 83, 84
Supply and Services Canada, 38, 39

Talas-Division of Technical Library Services, 110
Tapping the Government Grapevine (Robinson), 162
Taxpayer Assets Project (TAP), 212
Technical processing: staff training for, 135
Technology, 6, 12, 13
 and commodification, 198
 and costs of information delivery, 7, 124
 in document collections, 111-24, 181
 and freedom of access issues, 111-18, 122, 181, 195-98
 and information policy reform, 195-99
 interactive, 177
"Technology Tea," 118, 119
Telecommunications
 high-capacity/high-speed, 199
 networking, 194
 policy standards for, 197
Texas A&M University, 70
Texas: state publications, 2
Third World countries: official publications of, 162
Thirteenth Congress, 184
Tiger CD-ROMS, 120
Title 5 (U.S. Code), 197

Index □ 259

Title 44 (U.S. Code), 36, 129, 184, 195, 196, 200, 201
   need to modernize, 118, 124, 196, 202
Toxic Release Inventory (EPA), 119
Trademark research, 4
Transmittals, 82-84
Tree Identification Handbook, 48

U.N. *See* United Nations
UN (listserv), 92
U.N. Catalogue of Documentation in Microfiche, 38
U.N. Index, 168
U.N. Sales Office, 38
UNDOC: Current Index, 13, 16, 37, 83
UNESCO: depository libraries of, 5
UNIPUB, 16, 38
UNIPUB Standing Order Catalog, 38
United Nations, 2, 3, 11, 13, 38
   acquiring publications of, 36
   depository program of, 5, 36, 38, 83
   Documents Control Section, 50
   publications of, 36, 50
   Series Symbol System of, 50
United Nations Children's Fund, 37
United Nations Conference on Trade and Development: publications of, 36
United Nations Development Programme: publications of, 36
United Nations Documentation News, 37
United Nations Industrial Development Organization: publications of, 36
United Nations New Publications, 37, 38
United Nations Publications Catalogue, 37, 38
United Nations Sales Publications Numbers, 51
United Nations Secretariat, 80
United Nations Series Symbol Classification System, 50, 51, 85
United Nations Treaty series, 37
   treaty numbers in, 88
The United States Government as Publisher (Merritt), 3
United States Government Manual, 179, 192
University of Colorado, 82
University of Guelph (Canada), 54
University of Kentucky, 72
University Products, 110
University Publications of America, 112

U.S. Census Bureau: depository program, 4, 36, 189
U.S. Congress, 4, 183, 184, 191, 201, 224
   information policy reforms and, 195-97, 199
   role in information distribution, 192, 198
U.S. Defense Mapping Agency, 85
U.S. Department of Agriculture, 72
U.S. Department of Commerce: *Economic Bulletin Board*, 116
U.S. Department of Education Integrated Postsecondary Education Data System (IPEDS), 62, 63
U.S. Department of Energy, 31, 36, 113
   ITIS database project of, 119
U.S. Department of Justice: JURIS system, 124
U.S. Department of the Interior, 72
U.S. Federal Depository Program
   established, 4
   regional, 11
   selective, 11, 12
   state programs, 5
U.S. Government Manual, 36
U.S. Government Printing Office, 2, 11, 12, 14, 18, 22, 31, 33-35, 44, 47-49, 68-71, 76, 80, 84, 116, 119, 170, 178, 183, 193, 224
   and access modernization, 201, 202
   Biennial Survey, 34
   and classification errors, 73
   and collection development resources, 14
   congressional oversight of, 190
   direct deposits, 34
   document dissemination activities, 184
   exchange lists, 34
   and fugitive documents, 36
   future of, 194, 200-201
   guidelines for electronic formats, 120
   history of, 184
   inspection program of, 187-89, 193
   Library Division of, 187-90
   "lighted bin" system, 33
   microfiche publications of, 85, 112, 113
   mission of, 184, 201
   pilot projects of, 119
   sale of electronic products from, 185
   surveys from, 22, 32
USMARC, 64

USMARC format: for electronic publications, 77
USMARC Formats for Bibliographic Data, 64
U.S. Patent and Trademark Office: depository program, 4, 5, 36
U.S. Public Documents, A Practical Guide for Non-Professionals in Academic and Public Libraries (Pokorny and Miller), 140, 142
U.S. Supreme Court opinions, 116
User guides, 168

Variable costs: for document collections, 215, 221
Variable fields, 64
Vesicular microfiche, 85
Videotape, 10
  special handling of, 84
Vital Statistics of the United States, 83
VTLS, 132

Weeding, 11, 21
  criteria for, 80, 90
  and permission to withdraw, 91
Weekly Checklist of Canadian Government Publications, 6, 38, 39
Weekly Compilation of Presidential Documents, 83
Western Europe: government publications, 162
Western Library Network, 18, 49
WESTLAW, 161
WHO. *See* World Health Organization
Wilson, John S., 91
WINDO. *See* GPO Wide Information Network Data Online
WLN. *See* Western Library Network
Work-study programs, 137
World Health Organization: depository library program, 5

Zaremba, Elaine: *The Reference Interview as a Creative Art*, 145
Zwinger, Ann H., 86

361653

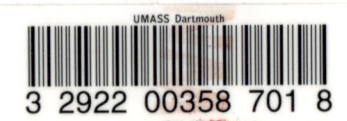